PUBLISHED ANNUALLY SINCE 1905

··· LLEWELLYN'S 2019 ···

# MOON SIGN BOOK

Plan Your Life by th

D1450413

# Llewellyn's 2019 Moon Sign Book®

ISBN 978-0-7387-4610-4

Cover design by Kevin R. Brown
Editing by Aaron Lawrence
Stock photography models used for illustrative purposes only and may not
    endorse or represent the book's subject.
Copyright 2018 Llewellyn Worldwide Ltd. All rights reserved.
Typography owned by Llewellyn Worldwide Ltd.

Weekly tips by Penny Kelly, Mireille Blacke, and Charlie Rainbow Wolf.

Any Internet references contained in this work are current at publication time, but the publisher cannot guarantee that a specific location will continue to be maintained.

Astrological data compiled and programmed by Rique Pottenger. Based on the earlier work of Neil F. Michelsen.

You can order Llewellyn annuals and books from *New Worlds*, Llewellyn's catalog. To request a free copy of the catalog, call toll-free 1-877-NEW-WRLD, or visit our website at www.llewellyn.com.

Llewellyn Publications
A Division of Llewellyn Worldwide Ltd.
2143 Wooddale Drive
Woodbury, MN 55125-3989
www.llewellyn.com

Printed in the United States of America

# Table of Contents

# What's Different About the Moon Sign Book?

Readers have asked why *Llewellyn's Moon Sign Book* says that the Moon is in Taurus when some almanacs indicate that the Moon is in the previous sign of Aries on the same date. It's because there are two different zodiac systems in use today: the tropical and the sidereal. *Llewellyn's Moon Sign Book* is based on the tropical zodiac.

The tropical zodiac takes 0 degrees of Aries to be the Spring Equinox in the Northern Hemisphere. This is the time and date when the Sun is directly overhead at noon along the equator, usually about March 20–21. The rest of the signs are positioned at 30-degree intervals from this point.

The sidereal zodiac, which is based on the location of fixed stars, uses the positions of the fixed stars to determine the starting point of 0 degrees of Aries. In the sidereal system, 0 degrees of Aries always begins at the same point. This does create a problem though, because the positions of the fixed stars, as seen from Earth, have changed since the constellations were named. The term "precession of the equinoxes" is used to describe the change.

Precession of the equinoxes describes an astronomical phenomenon brought about by Earth's wobble as it rotates and orbits the Sun. Earth's axis is inclined toward the Sun at an angle of about 23½ degrees, which creates our seasonal weather changes. Although the change is slight, because one complete circle of Earth's axis takes 25,800 years to complete, we can actually see that the positions of the fixed stars seem to shift. The result is that each year, in the tropical system, the Spring Equinox occurs at a slightly different time.

## Does Precession Matter?

There is an accumulative difference of about 23 degrees between the Spring Equinox (0 degrees Aries in the tropical zodiac and 0 degrees Aries in the sidereal zodiac) so that 0 degrees Aries at Spring Equinox in the tropical zodiac actually occurs at about 7 degrees Pisces in the sidereal zodiac system. You can readily see that those who use the other almanacs may be planting seeds (in the garden and in their individual lives) based on the belief that it is occurring in a fruitful sign, such as Taurus, when in fact it would be occurring in Gemini, one of the most barren signs of the zodiac. So, if you wish to plant and plan activities by the Moon, it is helpful to follow *Llewellyn's Moon Sign Book*. Before we go on, there are important things to understand about the Moon, her cycles, and their correlation with everyday living. For more information about gardening by the Moon, see page 61.

# Weekly Almanac

### Your Guide to
### Lunar Gardening
### & Good Timing for Activities

# ♑ January

## December 30–January 5

*'Tain't worthwhile to wear a day all out before it comes.*

~SARAH ORNE JEWETT

| Date | Qtr. | Sign | Activity |
|------|------|------|----------|
| Jan. 5, 8:28 pm–<br>Jan. 7, 1:46 am | 1st | Capricorn | Graft or bud plants. Trim to increase growth. |

If you want something different in your life, get a camera and start taking photos of people, plants, animals, places, bugs, birds, sunsets, trees, foods, and anything else that catches your eye. As you learn how to frame various shots, capture stunning colors, play with effects, or even discover the unexpected UFO or unexplained ghost, you will learn to see the world differently!

⬤

*January 5*
*8:28 pm EST*

JANUARY

| S | M | T | W | T | F | S |
|---|---|---|---|---|---|---|
|   |   | 1 | 2 | 3 | 4 | 5 |
| 6 | 7 | 8 | 9 | 10 | 11 | 12 |
| 13 | 14 | 15 | 16 | 17 | 18 | 19 |
| 20 | 21 | 22 | 23 | 24 | 25 | 26 |
| 27 | 28 | 29 | 30 | 31 |   |   |

# January 6–12

*Alone we can do so little; together we can do so much.*

~Helen Keller

| Date | Qtr. | Sign | Activity |
|---|---|---|---|
| Jan 9, 2:44 pm–<br>Jan 12, 3:18 am | 1st | Pisces | Plant grains, leafy annuals. Fertilize (chemical). Graft or bud plants. Irrigate. Trim to increase growth. |

There are always a million reasons to put off exercise. One of those reasons is clothing. Sometimes what you wear every day is a huge obstacle to exercise and freedom of movement. Assess your wardrobe with an eye toward making it much more movement-friendly, and then buy a few items that have been made for movement. You'll be surprised at how conscious you become of your body and the way you use it, and you'll feel younger, too.

_____

_____

_____

_____

2018 © Rido81 Image from BigStockPhoto.com

### January

| S | M | T | W | T | F | S |
|---|---|---|---|---|---|---|
|  |  | 1 | 2 | 3 | 4 | 5 |
| 6 | 7 | 8 | 9 | 10 | 11 | 12 |
| 13 | 14 | 15 | 16 | 17 | 18 | 19 |
| 20 | 21 | 22 | 23 | 24 | 25 | 26 |
| 27 | 28 | 29 | 30 | 31 |  |  |

# January 13–19

*It is awfully important to know what is and what is not your business.*
~Gertrude Stein

| Date | Qtr. | Sign | Activity |
|------|------|------|----------|
| Jan 14, 1:31 pm–<br>Jan 16, 8:00 pm | 2nd | Taurus | Plant annuals for hardiness. Trim to increase growth. |
| Jan 18, 10:44 pm–<br>Jan 20, 10:54 pm | 2nd | Cancer | Plant grains, leafy annuals. Fertilize (chemical). Graft or bud plants. Irrigate. Trim to increase growth. |

Don't know what to give someone for Christmas and they already have more 'stuff" than they can handle? Consider things like a unique flower arrangement, a loaf of homemade bread or jar of homemade raspberry jam, a gift certificate for a pedicure, a subscription for a weekly car wash, or a monthly date at the local coffee shop, or a bag of an exotic coffee or tea. These are all useful and don't weigh anyone down or require storage.

*January 14*
*1:46 am EST*

JANUARY

| S | M | T | W | T | F | S |
|---|---|---|---|---|---|---|
|   |   | 1 | 2 | 3 | 4 | 5 |
| 6 | 7 | 8 | 9 | 10 | 11 | 12 |
| 13 | 14 | 15 | 16 | 17 | 18 | 19 |
| 20 | 21 | 22 | 23 | 24 | 25 | 26 |
| 27 | 28 | 29 | 30 | 31 |   |   |

## January 20–26 ~~~

*Those who bring sunshine into the lives of others cannot keep
it from themselves.*

　　　　　　　　　　　　　　　　　~J. M. BARRIE

| Date | Qtr. | Sign | Activity |
|------|------|------|----------|
| Jan 21, 12:16 am–<br>Jan 22, 10:22 pm | 3rd | Leo | Cultivate. Destroy weeds and pests. Harvest fruits and root crops for food. Trim to retard growth. |
| Jan 22, 10:22 pm–<br>Jan 24, 11:02 pm | 3rd | Virgo | Cultivate, especially medicinal plants. Destroy weeds and pests. Trim to retard growth. |

Start a reading program for yourself. For one year, read a different book each month. Decide on twelve areas before you start, for example: a biography, poetry, something political, something on health or nutrition, an interesting book about new technology and how it will change our lives, life in pre-Columbian America, a book focused on nature, something that deals with the brain or consciousness, a history of the Goddess religion, a history of ancient Europe, or any other topic you're interested in. Read in any order and share what you're learning with a friend!

<br>

---

<br>

---

<br>

---

○
*January 21
12:16 am EST*

JANUARY

| S | M | T | W | T | F | S |
|---|---|---|---|---|---|---|
|   |   | 1 | 2 | 3 | 4 | 5 |
| 6 | 7 | 8 | 9 | 10 | 11 | 12 |
| 13 | 14 | 15 | 16 | 17 | 18 | 19 |
| 20 | 21 | 22 | 23 | 24 | 25 | 26 |
| 27 | 28 | 29 | 30 | 31 |   |   |

# ♒ February

## January 27–February 2

*The mind is not a vessel to be filled, but a fire to be kindled.*

~Plutarch

| Date | Qtr. | Sign | Activity |
|------|------|------|----------|
| Jan 27, 2:31 am–<br>Jan 27, 4:10 pm | 3rd | Scorpio | Plant biennials, perennials, bulbs and roots. Prune. Irrigate. Fertilize (organic). |
| Jan 27, 4:10 pm–<br>Jan 29, 9:33 am | 4th | Scorpio | Plant biennials, perennials, bulbs and roots. Prune. Irrigate. Fertilize (organic). |
| Jan 29, 9:33 am–<br>Jan 31, 7:47 pm | 4th | Sagittarius | Cultivate. Destroy weeds and pests. Harvest fruits and root crops for food. Trim to retard growth. |
| Jan 31, 7:47 pm–<br>Feb 3, 8:03 am | 4th | Capricorn | Plant potatoes and tubers. Trim to retard growth. |

Reconnect with Mother Nature by going outside, sitting on a blanket, and just observing the bugs, birds, and other creatures that cross your path. Resist the urge to scream, swat, or panic if one of these creatures lands on you. Consider trying to communicate and learn instead.

_____

_____

_____

_____

◑

*January 27*
*4:10 pm EST*

FEBRUARY

| S | M | T | W | T | F | S |
|---|---|---|---|---|---|---|
|   |   |   |   |   | 1 | 2 |
| 3 | 4 | 5 | 6 | 7 | 8 | 9 |
| 10 | 11 | 12 | 13 | 14 | 15 | 16 |
| 17 | 18 | 19 | 20 | 21 | 22 | 23 |
| 24 | 25 | 26 | 27 | 28 |   |   |

## February 3–9 〜〜

*Trying to define yourself is like trying to bite your own teeth.*

~ALAN WATTS

| Date | Qtr. | Sign | Activity |
|------|------|------|----------|
| Feb 3, 8:03 am–Feb 4, 4:04 pm | 4th | Aquarius | Cultivate. Destroy weeds and pests. Harvest fruits and root crops for food. Trim to retard growth. |
| Feb 5, 9:02 pm–Feb 8, 9:34 am | 1st | Pisces | Plant grains, leafy annuals. Fertilize (chemical). Graft or bud plants. Irrigate. Trim to increase growth. |

If you have dry skin problems in winter, try a castor oil–olive oil sweat bath. Mix 1 tbsp of castor oil with 1 tbsp of olive oil. Rub over entire body except hair and soles of feet. Get in a tub of the hottest water you can stand and stay until sweating. Get out, dress immediately—without cooling—in sweat pants, sweatshirt, and socks. Get into bed (protected with a plastic shower curtain or plastic bags), cover up, sweating some more until you are completely cooled. Then shower with mild soap, and you will feel like a million bucks with skin like a baby!

*February 4*
*4:04 pm EST*

FEBRUARY

| S | M | T | W | T | F | S |
|---|---|---|---|---|---|---|
|   |   |   |   |   | 1 | 2 |
| 3 | 4 | 5 | 6 | 7 | 8 | 9 |
| 10 | 11 | 12 | 13 | 14 | 15 | 16 |
| 17 | 18 | 19 | 20 | 21 | 22 | 23 |
| 24 | 25 | 26 | 27 | 28 |   |   |

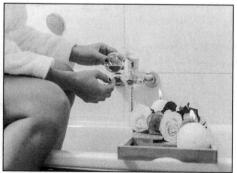

## ～～ **February 10–16**

*The art of being wise is the art of knowing what to overlook.*

~William James

| Date | Qtr. | Sign | Activity |
|------|------|------|----------|
| Feb 10, 8:28 pm–<br>Feb 12, 5:26 pm | 1st | Taurus | Plant annuals for hardiness. Trim to increase growth. |
| Feb 12, 5:26 pm–<br>Feb 13, 4:32 am | 2nd | Taurus | Plant annuals for hardiness. Trim to increase growth. |
| Feb 15, 9:03 am–<br>Feb 17, 10:21 am | 2nd | Cancer | Plant grains, leafy annuals. Fertilize (chemical). Graft or bud plants. Irrigate. Trim to increase growth. |

There's a myth out there that says that the natural sugar in fruit is the same as processed white sugar or high-fructose corn syrup. This simply isn't true and even those with diabetes could eat much more fruit, especially berries. Over the summer, make an effort to collect and freeze strawberries, raspberries, blueberries, cherries, blackberries, peaches, pears, and any other fruit you can get your hands on. Use these in smoothies over the winter to maintain good health and keep your polyphenols up and your weight down.

*February 12*
*5:26 pm EST*

| | | | February | | | |
|---|---|---|---|---|---|---|
| S | M | T | W | T | F | S |
| | | | | | 1 | 2 |
| 3 | 4 | 5 | 6 | 7 | 8 | 9 |
| 10 | 11 | 12 | 13 | 14 | 15 | 16 |
| 17 | 18 | 19 | 20 | 21 | 22 | 23 |
| 24 | 25 | 26 | 27 | 28 | | |

## February 17–23 〜〜

*It's hard to beat a person who never gives up.*

~BABE RUTH

| Date | Qtr. | Sign | Activity |
|------|------|------|----------|
| Feb 19, 10:54 am–Feb 21, 9:17 am | 3rd | Virgo | Cultivate, especially medicinal plants. Destroy weeds and pests. Trim to retard growth. |
| Feb 23, 10:56 am–Feb 25, 4:19 pm | 3rd | Scorpio | Plant biennials, perennials, bulbs and roots. Prune. Irrigate. Fertilize (organic). |

Coffee filters are so useful when gardening, indoors and out. Line a plant pot with a coffee filter. It will help the soil to contain the moisture, and slow the water down from seeping (or even flooding) through the bottom drainage holes. It's not infallible, though, so remember to set your pot on a saucer.

2018 © ArtSvitlyna Image from BigStockPhoto.com

○
*February 19*
*10:54 am EST*

FEBRUARY

| S | M | T | W | T | F | S |
|---|---|---|---|---|---|---|
|   |   |   |   |   | 1 | 2 |
| 3 | 4 | 5 | 6 | 7 | 8 | 9 |
| 10 | 11 | 12 | 13 | 14 | 15 | 16 |
| 17 | 18 | 19 | 20 | 21 | 22 | 23 |
| 24 | 25 | 26 | 27 | 28 |   |   |

# ♓ March
### February 24–March 2

*We all need help with our homework. We're all pleading for
someone to listen. We're all desperate.*   ～CHARLIE BROWN

| Date | Qtr. | Sign | Activity |
|------|------|------|----------|
| Feb 25, 4:19 pm–<br>Feb 26, 6:28 am | 3rd | Sagittarius | Cultivate. Destroy weeds and pests. Harvest fruits and root crops for food. Trim to retard growth. |
| Feb 26, 6:28 am–<br>Feb 28, 1:48 am | 4th | Sagittarius | Cultivate. Destroy weeds and pests. Harvest fruits and root crops for food. Trim to retard growth. |
| Feb 28, 1:48 am–<br>Mar 2, 2:06 pm | 4th | Capricorn | Plant potatoes and tubers. Trim to retard growth. |
| Mar 2, 2:06 pm–<br>Mar 5, 3:11 am | 4th | Aquarius | Cultivate. Destroy weeds and pests. Harvest fruits and root crops for food. Trim to retard growth. |

If you've been interested in astrology, consider taking a class in which you can learn to create and read someone's chart even if it's only your own. Get a book that has color photographs of many constellations, not just the usual ones, and study it as you learn astrology.

_____

_____

_____

◗
*February 26*
*6:28 am EST*

MARCH

| S | M | T | W | T | F | S |
|---|---|---|---|---|---|---|
|   |   |   |   |   | 1 | 2 |
| 3 | 4 | 5 | 6 | 7 | 8 | 9 |
| 10 | 11 | 12 | 13 | 14 | 15 | 16 |
| 17 | 18 | 19 | 20 | 21 | 22 | 23 |
| 24 | 25 | 26 | 27 | 28 | 29 | 30 |
| 31 |   |   |   |   |   |   |

# March 3–9

*Society teaches us that having feelings and crying is bad and wrong. Well, that's baloney, because grief isn't wrong. There's such a thing as good grief. Just ask Charlie Brown.*

~MICHAEL SCOTT, *THE OFFICE*

| Date | Qtr. | Sign | Activity |
|------|------|------|----------|
| Mar 5, 3:11 am–<br>Mar 6, 11:04 am | 4th | Pisces | Plant biennials, perennials, bulbs and roots. Prune. Irrigate. Fertilize (organic). |
| Mar 6, 11:04 am–<br>Mar 7, 3:27 pm | 1st | Pisces | Plant grains, leafy annuals. Fertilize (chemical). Graft or bud plants. Irrigate. Trim to increase growth. |

Want to grow veggies or herbs but live in an apartment? Try growing in large, deep containers on a deck or patio that gets at least 8 hours of sun per day. Containers should be 12–15" deep for plants that produce fruit above ground such as peppers, herbs, beans, lettuce, etc. They should be 24–30" deep for tomatoes, potatoes, okra, beets, carrots, cabbage, cucumber, etc. Put a 1" layer of pea gravel in the bottom of the container, fill with good soil, and plant.

2018 © makistock Image from BigStockPhoto.com

*March 6*
*11:04 am EST*

MARCH

| S | M | T | W | T | F | S |
|---|---|---|---|---|---|---|
| | | | | | 1 | 2 |
| 3 | 4 | 5 | 6 | 7 | 8 | 9 |
| 10 | 11 | 12 | 13 | 14 | 15 | 16 |
| 17 | 18 | 19 | 20 | 21 | 22 | 23 |
| 24 | 25 | 26 | 27 | 28 | 29 | 30 |
| 31 | | | | | | |

**March 10–16**

*Happiness is having a loving, close knit family in another city.*

~GEORGE BURNS

| Date | Qtr. | Sign | Activity |
|------|------|------|----------|
| Mar 10, 3:10 am–Mar 12, 11:48 am | 1st | Taurus | Plant annuals for hardiness. Trim to increase growth. |
| Mar 14, 5:49 pm–Mar 16, 8:57 pm | 2nd | Cancer | Plant grains, leafy annuals. Fertilize (chemical). Graft or bud plants. Irrigate. Trim to increase growth. |

Need a simple, natural, bug deterrent? Soap and salt to the rescue! Add ¼ cup salt to 2 quarts of soapy water (I use Dr Bronner's eucalyptus soap, about 2 T per quart) and spray it over your brassicas. The caterpillars, moths, and other problem insects don't like it at all. Repeat every couple of weeks, and after rainfall.

*Daylight Saving Time begins*
*March 10, 2:00 am*

*March 14, 6:27 am EDT*

| | | | MARCH | | | |
|---|---|---|---|---|---|---|
| S | M | T | W | T | F | S |
| | | | | | 1 | 2 |
| 3 | 4 | 5 | 6 | 7 | 8 | 9 |
| 10 | 11 | 12 | 13 | 14 | 15 | 16 |
| 17 | 18 | 19 | 20 | 21 | 22 | 23 |
| 24 | 25 | 26 | 27 | 28 | 29 | 30 |
| 31 | | | | | | |

# March 17–23

*Our faith obliges us to bind wounds, not to make blood run.*
~PETR CHELCICKÝ

| Date | Qtr. | Sign | Activity |
|------|------|------|----------|
| Mar 20, 9:28 pm–<br>Mar 20, 9:43 pm | 2nd | Libra | Plant annuals for fragrance and beauty. Trim to increase growth. |
| Mar 22, 10:16 pm–<br>Mar 25, 2:06 am | 3rd | Scorpio | Plant biennials, perennials, bulbs and roots. Prune. Irrigate. Fertilize (organic). |

I f you had a bad crop one year, don't give up hope. You might find that different plants do better in different areas of your garden. Make sure you test your soil, and that you've checked out the light for the plant's needs. Remember the garden buddies, too. Companion planting helps to attract the beneficial bugs and deter the pests. For example, tomatoes should be planted with onions, peppers, basil, lettuce, and carrots, among a list of others.

2018 © Vitalily73 Image from BigStockPhoto.com

○
*March 20*
*9:43 pm EDT*

MARCH

| S | M | T | W | T | F | S |
|---|---|---|---|---|---|---|
|   |   |   |   |   | 1 | 2 |
| 3 | 4 | 5 | 6 | 7 | 8 | 9 |
| 10 | 11 | 12 | 13 | 14 | 15 | 16 |
| 17 | 18 | 19 | 20 | 21 | 22 | 23 |
| 24 | 25 | 26 | 27 | 28 | 29 | 30 |
| 31 |   |   |   |   |   |   |

# ♈ March 24–30

*If I had to choose, I would rather have birds than airplanes.*

~CHARLES LINDBERGH

| Date | Qtr. | Sign | Activity |
|---|---|---|---|
| Mar 25, 2:06 am–<br>Mar 27, 10:07 am | 3rd | Sagittarius | Cultivate. Destroy weeds and pests. Harvest fruits and root crops for food. Trim to retard growth. |
| Mar 27, 10:07 am–<br>Mar 28, 12:10 am | 3rd | Capricorn | Plant potatoes and tubers. Trim to retard growth. |
| Mar 28, 12:10 am–<br>Mar 29, 9:46 pm | 4th | Capricorn | Plant potatoes and tubers. Trim to retard growth. |
| Mar 29, 9:46 pm–<br>Apr 1, 10:48 am | 4th | Aquarius | Cultivate. Destroy weeds and pests. Harvest fruits and root crops for food. Trim to retard growth. |

Research has shown that blueberries are your go-to fruit for lowering cholesterol, fighting certain cancers, sharpening memory, and protecting healthy cells from environmental damage. With only 84 calories per cup, blueberries also provide plenty of insoluble fiber for easing constipation.

_____

_____

_____

_____

◑
*March 28*
*12:10 am EDT*

MARCH

| S | M | T | W | T | F | S |
|---|---|---|---|---|---|---|
|  |  |  |  |  | 1 | 2 |
| 3 | 4 | 5 | 6 | 7 | 8 | 9 |
| 10 | 11 | 12 | 13 | 14 | 15 | 16 |
| 17 | 18 | 19 | 20 | 21 | 22 | 23 |
| 24 | 25 | 26 | 27 | 28 | 29 | 30 |
| 31 |  |  |  |  |  |  |

# April ♈

## March 31–April 6

*Worry is the stomach's worst poison.*    ~ALFRED NOBEL

| Date | Qtr. | Sign | Activity |
|------|------|------|----------|
| Apr 1, 10:48 am–<br>Apr 3, 10:56 pm | 4th | Pisces | Plant biennials, perennials, bulbs and roots. Prune. Irrigate. Fertilize (organic). |
| Apr 3, 10:56 pm–<br>Apr 5, 4:50 am | 4th | Aries | Cultivate. Destroy weeds and pests. Harvest fruits and root crops for food. Trim to retard growth. |
| Apr 6, 9:06 am–<br>Apr 8, 5:15 pm | 1st | Taurus | Plant annuals for hardiness. Trim to increase growth. |

Even though the bulb of an onion grows underground, it still needs the Sun! Sunlight is what determines the size of the bulb, and not the maturity of the plant. The type of onion planted will also influence the eventual circumference of the onion, but if you want them to grow big, ensure they get lots of daylight!

_____

_____

_____

_____

2018 © Paul Wish Image from BigStockPhoto.com

*April 5*
*4:50 am EDT*

APRIL

| S | M | T | W | T | F | S |
|---|---|---|---|---|---|---|
|   | 1 | 2 | 3 | 4 | 5 | 6 |
| 7 | 8 | 9 | 10 | 11 | 12 | 13 |
| 14 | 15 | 16 | 17 | 18 | 19 | 20 |
| 21 | 22 | 23 | 24 | 25 | 26 | 27 |
| 28 | 29 | 30 |   |   |   |   |

**April 7–13**

*How we spend our days is, of course, how we spend our lives.*
~ANNIE DILLARD

| Date | Qtr. | Sign | Activity |
|---|---|---|---|
| Apr 10, 11:31 pm–<br>Apr 12, 3:06 pm | 1st | Cancer | Plant grains, leafy annuals. Fertilize (chemical). Graft or bud plants. Irrigate. Trim to increase growth. |
| Apr 12, 3:06 pm–<br>Apr 13, 3:50 am | 2nd | Cancer | Plant grains, leafy annuals. Fertilize (chemical). Graft or bud plants. Irrigate. Trim to increase growth. |

Beets are loaded with antioxidants that protect the body's healthy cells against free radical damage. With 58 calories per cup, the potassium in beets benefits heart-health and blood pressure regulation. Whether juiced, pickled, raw, or canned, beet it to your local grocer or farmer's market and load up on beets today.

_____

_____

_____

_____

April 12
3:06 pm EDT

APRIL

| S | M | T | W | T | F | S |
|---|---|---|---|---|---|---|
|  | 1 | 2 | 3 | 4 | 5 | 6 |
| 7 | 8 | 9 | 10 | 11 | 12 | 13 |
| 14 | 15 | 16 | 17 | 18 | 19 | 20 |
| 21 | 22 | 23 | 24 | 25 | 26 | 27 |
| 28 | 29 | 30 |  |  |  |  |

# April 14–20 ♈

*Too much rest is rust.*          ~WALTER SCOTT

| Date | Qtr. | Sign | Activity |
|------|------|------|----------|
| Apr 17, 7:22 am–<br>Apr 19, 7:12 am | 2nd | Libra | Plant annuals for fragrance and beauty. Trim to increase growth. |
| Apr 19, 8:41 am–<br>Apr 21, 11:59 am | 3rd | Scorpio | Plant biennials, perennials, bulbs and roots. Prune. Irrigate. Fertilize (organic). |

Cats are man's best friend when it comes to killing mosquitoes. The essential oil nepetalactone in catnip is roughly ten times more powerful than commercial deterrents. Place catnip in satchels around the house or arm yourself with catnip tea from a spray bottle and take out these pests posthaste.

_____

_____

_____

_____

○
*April 19*
*7:12 am EDT*

APRIL

| S | M | T | W | T | F | S |
|---|---|---|---|---|---|---|
|   |   |   |   |   |   |   |
|   | 1 | 2 | 3 | 4 | 5 | 6 |
| 7 | 8 | 9 | 10 | 11 | 12 | 13 |
| 14 | 15 | 16 | 17 | 18 | 19 | 20 |
| 21 | 22 | 23 | 24 | 25 | 26 | 27 |
| 28 | 29 | 30 |   |   |   |   |

2018 © gvictoria Image from BigStockPhoto.com

## April 21–27

*Shall we make a new rule of life from tonight: always to try to be a little kinder than is necessary?*    ∼J. M. BARRIE

| Date | Qtr. | Sign | Activity |
|------|------|------|----------|
| Apr 21, 11:59 am–<br>Apr 23, 6:50 pm | 3rd | Sagittarius | Cultivate. Destroy weeds and pests. Harvest fruits and root crops for food. Trim to retard growth. |
| Apr 23, 6:50 pm–<br>Apr 26, 5:27 am | 3rd | Capricorn | Plant potatoes and tubers. Trim to retard growth. |
| Apr 26, 5:27 am–<br>Apr 26, 6:18 pm | 3rd | Aquarius | Cultivate. Destroy weeds and pests. Harvest fruits and root crops for food. Trim to retard growth. |
| Apr 26, 6:18 pm–<br>Apr 28, 6:11 pm | 4th | Aquarius | Cultivate. Destroy weeds and pests. Harvest fruits and root crops for food. Trim to retard growth. |

Consider erecting a bat house to eliminate thousands of unwanted insects from your neighborhood every night. Most garden supply stores or Amazon.com will sell a bat house for about $30. Bats don't usually bother people, but they might swoop in to drink from a nearby pool or birdbath.

---

---

---

◑
*April 26*
*6:18 pm EDT*

APRIL

| S | M | T | W | T | F | S |
|---|---|---|---|---|---|---|
|   |   | 1 | 2 | 3 | 4 | 5 | 6 |
| 7 | 8 | 9 | 10 | 11 | 12 | 13 |
| 14 | 15 | 16 | 17 | 18 | 19 | 20 |
| 21 | 22 | 23 | 24 | 25 | 26 | 27 |
| 28 | 29 | 30 |   |   |   |   |

2018 © Dave Willman Image from BigStockPhoto.com

# May ♉

## April 28–May 4

*We celebrate the past to awaken the future.*

~JOHN F. KENNEDY

| Date | Qtr. | Sign | Activity |
|------|------|------|----------|
| Apr 28, 6:11 pm– May 1, 6:24 am | 4th | Pisces | Plant biennials, perennials, bulbs and roots. Prune. Irrigate. Fertilize (organic). |
| May 1, 6:24 am– May 3, 4:18 pm | 4th | Aries | Cultivate. Destroy weeds and pests. Harvest fruits and root crops for food. Trim to retard growth. |
| May 3, 4:18 pm– May 4, 6:45 pm | 4th | Taurus | Plant potatoes and tubers. Trim to retard growth. |
| May 4, 6:45 pm– May 5, 11:40 pm | 1st | Taurus | Plant annuals for hardiness. Trim to increase growth. |

Vinegar makes a great window cleaner! Put household vinegar in a spray bottle and mist it over the glass, then dry with an old newspaper. To finish, polish with a microfiber cloth. Don't use a paper towel—this will put streaks in all your hard work. If you don't have a microfiber cloth, use a clean coffee filter!

●

*May 4*
*6:45 pm EDT*

MAY

| S | M | T | W | T | F | S |
|---|---|---|---|---|---|---|
|   |   |   | 1 | 2 | 3 | 4 |
| 5 | 6 | 7 | 8 | 9 | 10 | 11 |
| 12 | 13 | 14 | 15 | 16 | 17 | 18 |
| 19 | 20 | 21 | 22 | 23 | 24 | 25 |
| 26 | 27 | 28 | 29 | 30 | 31 |   |

**May 5–11**

*A thing is right when it tends to preserve the integrity, stability, and beauty of the biotic community. It is wrong when it tends otherwise.*                      ~ALDO LEOPOLD

| Date | Qtr. | Sign | Activity |
|------|------|------|----------|
| May 8, 5:06 am–<br>May 10, 9:14 am | 1st | Cancer | Plant grains, leafy annuals. Fertilize (chemical). Graft or bud plants. Irrigate. Trim to increase growth. |

Have your shrubs faded into the background? Use shrubs functionally to outline your property's borders, block an undesirable view or exposed foundation, dampen noise, or buffer wind. Shrubs may be positioned effectively for creating privacy, designating a specific walking path, or enhancing a home's attractiveness year-round.

*May 11*
*9:12 pm EDT*

| | | | May | | | |
|---|---|---|---|---|---|---|
| S | M | T | W | T | F | S |
| | | | 1 | 2 | 3 | 4 |
| 5 | 6 | 7 | 8 | 9 | 10 | 11 |
| 12 | 13 | 14 | 15 | 16 | 17 | 18 |
| 19 | 20 | 21 | 22 | 23 | 24 | 25 |
| 26 | 27 | 28 | 29 | 30 | 31 | |

2018 © Milkos Image from BigStockPhoto.com

## May 12–18

*A new adventure is coming up and I'm sure it will be a good one.*
~Sigurd F. Olson

| Date | Qtr. | Sign | Activity |
|------|------|------|----------|
| May 14, 2:51 pm–<br>May 16, 5:26 pm | 2nd | Libra | Plant annuals for fragrance and beauty. Trim to increase growth. |
| May 16, 5:26 pm–<br>May 18, 5:11 pm | 2nd | Scorpio | Plant grains, leafy annuals. Fertilize (chemical). Graft or bud plants. Irrigate. Trim to increase growth. |
| May 18, 5:11 pm–<br>May 18, 9:21 pm | 3rd | Scorpio | Plant biennials, perennials, bulbs and roots. Prune. Irrigate. Fertilize (organic). |
| May 18, 9:21 pm–<br>May 21, 3:56 am | 3rd | Sagittarius | Cultivate. Destroy weeds and pests. Harvest fruits and root crops for food. Trim to retard growth. |

Plant a small garden that contains these herbs: dill, basil, lavender, thyme, sage, oregano, marjoram, cilantro/coriander, parsley, sage, rosemary, and these flowers: nicotiana, and moonflower. Plant it somewhere that you can easily drag a chair to and sit in the sun for one of the most amazing aromatherapy experiences of your life.

_____

_____

_____

_____

*May 18*
*5:11 pm pm EDT*

### May

| S | M | T | W | T | F | S |
|---|---|---|---|---|---|---|
|   |   |   | 1 | 2 | 3 | 4 |
| 5 | 6 | 7 | 8 | 9 | 10 | 11 |
| 12 | 13 | 14 | 15 | 16 | 17 | 18 |
| 19 | 20 | 21 | 22 | 23 | 24 | 25 |
| 26 | 27 | 28 | 29 | 30 | 31 |   |

2018 © udo Image from BigStockPhoto.com

## May 19–25

*Every day above earth is a good day.*

~ERNEST HEMINGWAY

| Date | Qtr. | Sign | Activity |
|---|---|---|---|
| May 21, 3:56 am–<br>May 23, 1:49 pm | 3rd | Capricorn | Plant potatoes and tubers. Trim to retard growth. |
| May 23, 1:49 pm–<br>May 26, 2:08 am | 3rd | Aquarius | Cultivate. Destroy weeds and pests. Harvest fruits and root crops for food. Trim to retard growth. |

If you live in the country, go to the city for an afternoon and visit a museum. It can be any kind of museum as long as it offers a change of pace and perception. When you leave, take an awareness of the difference between your lifestyle and those who created the things in the museum. If you live in the city, go out to the country for an afternoon and visit a roadside stand. Buy some fruit, veggies, or eggs and take home not only fresh foods but an awareness of the lifestyles of those who live from the land.

MAY

| S | M | T | W | T | F | S |
|---|---|---|---|---|---|---|
| | | | 1 | 2 | 3 | 4 |
| 5 | 6 | 7 | 8 | 9 | 10 | 11 |
| 12 | 13 | 14 | 15 | 16 | 17 | 18 |
| 19 | 20 | 21 | 22 | 23 | 24 | 25 |
| 26 | 27 | 28 | 29 | 30 | 31 | |

2018 © maximkabb Image from BigStockPhoto.com

# June ♊

## May 26–June 1

*The flower is the poetry of reproduction. It is an example of*
*the eternal seductiveness of life.* ～Jean Giraudoux

| Date | Qtr. | Sign | Activity |
|------|------|------|----------|
| May 26, 2:08 am–May 26, 12:34 pm | 3rd | Pisces | Plant biennials, perennials, bulbs and roots. Prune. Irrigate. Fertilize (organic). |
| May 26, 12:34 pm–May 28, 2:32 pm | 4th | Pisces | Plant biennials, perennials, bulbs and roots. Prune. Irrigate. Fertilize (organic). |
| May 28, 2:32 pm–May 31, 12:43 am | 4th | Aries | Cultivate. Destroy weeds and pests. Harvest fruits and root crops for food. Trim to retard growth. |
| May 31, 12:43 am–Jun 2, 7:48 am | 4th | Taurus | Plant potatoes and tubers. Trim to retard growth. |

As spring unfolds into summer, consider a summer hairdo that is simple and carefree. This needn't mean cutting your hair. It can be as simple as brushing your bangs back from your face and off a sweaty forehead for a season, or braiding your hair to keep it off your neck. You can also get creative with combs, headbands, and hats.

*May 26*
*12:34 pm EDT*

JUNE

| S | M | T | W | T | F | S |
|---|---|---|---|---|---|---|
|   |   |   |   |   |   | 1 |
| 2 | 3 | 4 | 5 | 6 | 7 | 8 |
| 9 | 10 | 11 | 12 | 13 | 14 | 15 |
| 16 | 17 | 18 | 19 | 20 | 21 | 22 |
| 23 | 24 | 25 | 26 | 27 | 28 | 29 |
| 30 |   |   |   |   |   |   |

2018 © Sonjachnyj Image from BigStockPhoto.com

# June 2–8

*You can lead a horse to water but you can't make it drink.*

~ENGLISH PROVERB

| Date | Qtr. | Sign | Activity |
|------|------|------|----------|
| Jun 2, 7:48 am–<br>Jun 3, 6:02 am | 4th | Gemini | Cultivate. Destroy weeds and pests. Harvest fruits and root crops for food. Trim to retard growth. |
| Jun 4, 12:17 pm–<br>Jun 6, 3:16 pm | 1st | Cancer | Plant grains, leafy annuals. Fertilize (chemical). Graft or bud plants. Irrigate. Trim to increase growth. |

Go into your kitchen and get out your knives. Think about how often you use them and ask yourself, "Do these knives work beautifully and well, or do they bring a case of subtle frustration every time I use them?" If frustration is the case, consider getting them all professionally sharpened. If you can't find a professional, ask your hairdresser. Many salons have someone come in once a month to sharpen scissors.

*June 3*
*6:02 am EDT*

JUNE

| S | M | T | W | T | F | S |
|---|---|---|---|---|---|---|
|   |   |   |   |   |   | 1 |
| 2 | 3 | 4 | 5 | 6 | 7 | 8 |
| 9 | 10 | 11 | 12 | 13 | 14 | 15 |
| 16 | 17 | 18 | 19 | 20 | 21 | 22 |
| 23 | 24 | 25 | 26 | 27 | 28 | 29 |
| 30 |   |   |   |   |   |   |

# June 9–15

*This is the real secret of life—to be completely engaged with
what you are doing in the here and now. And instead of
calling it work, realize it is play.* ~ALAN WATTS

| Date | Qtr. | Sign | Activity |
|------|------|------|----------|
| Jun 10, 8:29 pm–Jun 13, 12:02 am | 2nd | Libra | Plant annuals for fragrance and beauty. Trim to increase growth. |
| Jun 13, 12:02 am–Jun 15, 5:03 am | 2nd | Scorpio | Plant grains, leafy annuals. Fertilize (chemical). Graft or bud plants. Irrigate. Trim to increase growth. |

One of the challenges of modern life is getting enough of the right nutrition every day. To resolve this problem, explore and experiment with smoothies. You can increase your nutritional intake dramatically while enjoying something delicious and energizing. Search for interesting recipes on Pinterest and modify them to include things like coconut oil, omega 3 oils, and various herbs and spices to reduce inflammation. You can have a dramatic effect on your health…again, give yourself permission to not drink what you made if you think it tastes awful!

2018 © TopFoodPics Image from BigStockPhoto.com

June 10
1:59 am EDT

| | | | JUNE | | | |
|---|---|---|---|---|---|---|
| S | M | T | W | T | F | S |
| | | | | | | 1 |
| 2 | 3 | 4 | 5 | 6 | 7 | 8 |
| 9 | 10 | 11 | 12 | 13 | 14 | 15 |
| 16 | 17 | 18 | 19 | 20 | 21 | 22 |
| 23 | 24 | 25 | 26 | 27 | 28 | 29 |
| 30 | | | | | | |

## June 16–22

*Pain nourishes courage. You can't be brave if you've only had wonderful things happen to you.*    ～Mary Tyler Moore

| Date | Qtr. | Sign | Activity |
|------|------|------|----------|
| Jun 17, 4:31 am–<br>Jun 17, 12:13 pm | 3rd | Sagittarius | Cultivate. Destroy weeds and pests. Harvest fruits and root crops for food. Trim to retard growth. |
| Jun 17, 12:13 pm–<br>Jun 19, 10:01 pm | 3rd | Capricorn | Plant potatoes and tubers. Trim to retard growth. |
| Jun 19, 10:01 pm–<br>Jun 22, 10:01 am | 3rd | Aquarius | Cultivate. Destroy weeds and pests. Harvest fruits and root crops for food. Trim to retard growth. |
| Jun 22, 10:01 am–<br>Jun 24, 10:38 pm | 3rd | Pisces | Plant biennials, perennials, bulbs and roots. Prune. Irrigate. Fertilize (organic). |

Whether you are 18 or 80, it's always important to pay attention to your feet. At least every two weeks soak your feet for 30 minutes to soften and rehydrate their tissues. If you tend toward headaches, put 1 tbsp dry mustard and 1 tsp of cayenne pepper in the water. It draws toxins out of the feet and helps relieve headaches. Scrape feet with a dull scraper or loofah to remove dead skin. Rub your feet with a scented oil after soaking.

○
*June 17*
*4:31 am EDT*

### June

| S | M | T | W | T | F | S |
|---|---|---|---|---|---|---|
|   |   |   |   |   |   | 1 |
| 2 | 3 | 4 | 5 | 6 | 7 | 8 |
| 9 | 10 | 11 | 12 | 13 | 14 | 15 |
| 16 | 17 | 18 | 19 | 20 | 21 | 22 |
| 23 | 24 | 25 | 26 | 27 | 28 | 29 |
| 30 |   |   |   |   |   |   |

2018 © NikiLitovImage from BigStockPhoto.com

# June 23–29

*Everything comes in time to him who knows how to wait.*

~LEO TOLSTOY

| Date | Qtr. | Sign | Activity |
|------|------|------|----------|
| Jun 24, 10:38 pm–<br>Jun 25, 5:46 am | 3rd | Aries | Cultivate. Destroy weeds and pests. Harvest fruits and root crops for food. Trim to retard growth. |
| Jun 25, 5:46 am–<br>Jun 27, 9:32 am | 4th | Aries | Cultivate. Destroy weeds and pests. Harvest fruits and root crops for food. Trim to retard growth. |
| Jun 27, 9:32 am–<br>Jun 29, 5:09 pm | 4th | Taurus | Plant potatoes and tubers. Trim to retard growth. |
| Jun 29, 5:09 pm–<br>Jul 1, 9:24 pm | 4th | Gemini | Cultivate. Destroy weeds and pests. Harvest fruits and root crops for food. Trim to retard growth. |

Felted wool makes an excellent fabric softener in the dryer. Wind 100% wool yarn into a ball, and secure the end. Make several, and toss in a laundry bag. Wash them a few times in hot water, then throw them in the dryer. You've made your own laundry balls! A drop of your favorite essential oil can be added before you put them in the dryer with your clothes.

2018 © elizaveta66 Image from BigStockPhoto.com

*June 25*
*5:46 am EDT*

JUNE

| S | M | T | W | T | F | S |
|---|---|---|---|---|---|---|
| | | | | | | 1 |
| 2 | 3 | 4 | 5 | 6 | 7 | 8 |
| 9 | 10 | 11 | 12 | 13 | 14 | 15 |
| 16 | 17 | 18 | 19 | 20 | 21 | 22 |
| 23 | 24 | 25 | 26 | 27 | 28 | 29 |
| 30 | | | | | | |

# ♋ July

## June 30–July 6

*If you wish to make an apple pie from scratch, you must first invent the universe.*
~CARL SAGAN

| Date | Qtr. | Sign | Activity |
|------|------|------|----------|
| Jul 1, 9:24 pm–Jul 2, 3:16 pm | 4th | Cancer | Plant biennials, perennials, bulbs and roots. Prune. Irrigate. Fertilize (organic). |
| Jul 2, 3:16 pm–Jul 3, 11:19 pm | 1st | Cancer | Plant grains, leafy annuals. Fertilize (chemical). Graft or bud plants. Irrigate. Trim to increase growth. |

Shopping at farmer's markets is great, but you still need to be diligent. Sometimes vendors purchase their goods from surplus markets for resale rather than growing it themselves. Always take the time to ask questions. Is it local grown? Is it organic? Is it heirloom? What pesticides or herbicides were used? What's the expected shelf life? A little time here could save you a lot of disappointment later.

---

●
*July 2*
*3:16 pm EDT*

JULY

| S | M | T | W | T | F | S |
|---|---|---|---|---|---|---|
|   | 1 | 2 | 3 | 4 | 5 | 6 |
| 7 | 8 | 9 | 10 | 11 | 12 | 13 |
| 14 | 15 | 16 | 17 | 18 | 19 | 20 |
| 21 | 22 | 23 | 24 | 25 | 26 | 27 |
| 28 | 29 | 30 | 31 |   |   |   |

2018 © elenathewise Image from BigStockPhoto.com

# July 7–13

*Success always demands a greater effort.*

~WINSTON CHURCHILL

| Date | Qtr. | Sign | Activity |
|------|------|------|----------|
| Jul 8, 2:07 am–Jul 9, 6:55 am | 1st | Libra | Plant annuals for fragrance and beauty. Trim to increase growth. |
| Jul 9, 6:55 am–Jul 10, 5:29 am | 2nd | Libra | Plant annuals for fragrance and beauty. Trim to increase growth. |
| Jul 10, 5:29 am–Jul 12, 11:05 am | 2nd | Scorpio | Plant grains, leafy annuals. Fertilize (chemical). Graft or bud plants. Irrigate. Trim to increase growth. |

Clean out your closets, and as you take each item out of your life, spend a moment recalling the memories associated with that item—good or bad—and why you were hanging onto it. Thank the item for having been part of your life, then put it in the box or bag that is going to Goodwill or your local donation charity. You might even write down the items along with your thoughts and feelings, leaving a small written legacy for children and grandchildren.

*July 9*
*6:55 am EDT*

JULY

| S | M | T | W | T | F | S |
|---|---|---|---|---|---|---|
|   | 1 | 2 | 3 | 4 | 5 | 6 |
| 7 | 8 | 9 | 10 | 11 | 12 | 13 |
| 14 | 15 | 16 | 17 | 18 | 19 | 20 |
| 21 | 22 | 23 | 24 | 25 | 26 | 27 |
| 28 | 29 | 30 | 31 |   |   |   |

**July 14–20**

*I would trade all of my technology for an afternoon with Socrates.*
                                        ~STEVE JOBS

| Date | Qtr. | Sign | Activity |
|------|------|------|----------|
| Jul 14, 7:05 pm–<br>Jul 16, 5:38 pm | 2nd | Capricorn | Graft or bud plants. Trim to increase growth. |
| Jul 16, 5:38 pm–<br>Jul 17, 5:19 am | 3rd | Capricorn | Plant potatoes and tubers. Trim to retard growth. |
| Jul 17, 5:19 am–<br>Jul 19, 5:19 pm | 3rd | Aquarius | Cultivate. Destroy weeds and pests. Harvest fruits and root crops for food. Trim to retard growth. |
| Jul 19, 5:19 pm–<br>Jul 22, 6:02 am | 3rd | Pisces | Plant biennials, perennials, bulbs and roots. Prune. Irrigate. Fertilize (organic). |

Some people are more tasty to mosquitoes. If they find you particularly appealing, you can help to deter them from snacking on you by reducing your alcohol consumption, cutting down on sugar and salty foods, avoiding too much potassium, eating loads of garlic, and waiting until you're inside before applying any fragrances you like to wear. Darker clothing might help, too.

_____

_____

_____

_____

O
*July 16*
*5:38 pm EDT*

JULY

| S | M | T | W | T | F | S |
|---|---|---|---|---|---|---|
|   | 1 | 2 | 3 | 4 | 5 | 6 |
| 7 | 8 | 9 | 10 | 11 | 12 | 13 |
| 14 | 15 | 16 | 17 | 18 | 19 | 20 |
| 21 | 22 | 23 | 24 | 25 | 26 | 27 |
| 28 | 29 | 30 | 31 |   |   |   |

2018 © parinyabinsuk Image from BigStockPhoto.com

# July 21–27

*I rest in the grace of the world, and am free.*

~Wendell Berry

| Date | Qtr. | Sign | Activity |
|------|------|------|----------|
| Jul 22, 6:02 am–<br>Jul 24, 5:42 pm | 3rd | Aries | Cultivate. Destroy weeds and pests. Harvest fruits and root crops for food. Trim to retard growth. |
| Jul 24, 5:42 pm–<br>Jul 24, 9:18 pm | 3rd | Taurus | Plant potatoes and tubers. Trim to retard growth. |
| Jul 24, 9:18 pm–<br>Jul 27, 2:29 am | 4th | Taurus | Plant potatoes and tubers. Trim to retard growth. |
| Jul 27, 2:29 am–<br>Jul 29, 7:31 am | 4th | Gemini | Cultivate. Destroy weeds and pests. Harvest fruits and root crops for food. Trim to retard growth. |

Baking soda and vinegar will keep your drains fresh and clean. Make a "vinegar bomb" by pouring half a cup of baking soda down the drain, followed by half a cup of household vinegar. It will erupt—a fun lesson for the kids! Flush with hot water after about 5 minutes.

2018 © eskay lim Image from BigStockPhoto.com

July 24
9:18 pm EDT

JULY

| S | M | T | W | T | F | S |
|---|---|---|---|---|---|---|
|   | 1 | 2 | 3 | 4 | 5 | 6 |
| 7 | 8 | 9 | 10 | 11 | 12 | 13 |
| 14 | 15 | 16 | 17 | 18 | 19 | 20 |
| 21 | 22 | 23 | 24 | 25 | 26 | 27 |
| 28 | 29 | 30 | 31 |   |   |   |

# ♌ August

## July 28–August 3

*A fox should not be of the jury at a goose's trial.*

~Thomas Fuller

| Date | Qtr. | Sign | Activity |
|------|------|------|----------|
| Jul 29, 7:31 am–Jul 31, 9:18 am | 4th | Cancer | Plant biennials, perennials, bulbs and roots. Prune. Irrigate. Fertilize (organic). |
| Jul 31, 9:18 am–Jul 31, 11:12 pm | 4th | Leo | Cultivate. Destroy weeds and pests. Harvest fruits and root crops for food. Trim to retard growth. |

Need a change of pace in terms of diet? Make it a project to cook one totally new and different dish every month. Go to the bookstore for a cookbook or search online for an interesting recipe. Make a shopping list of ingredients, assemble the necessary items and utensils, and experiment as if you are Julia Child reincarnated. Give yourself permission to not eat what you've made if you think it tastes awful!

*July 31*
*11:12 pm EDT*

### August

| S | M | T | W | T | F | S |
|---|---|---|---|---|---|---|
|   |   |   |   | 1 | 2 | 3 |
| 4 | 5 | 6 | 7 | 8 | 9 | 10 |
| 11 | 12 | 13 | 14 | 15 | 16 | 17 |
| 18 | 19 | 20 | 21 | 22 | 23 | 24 |
| 25 | 26 | 27 | 28 | 29 | 30 | 31 |

# August 4–10

*A dream you dream alone is only a dream. A dream you dream together is reality.*

~Yoko Ono

| Date | Qtr. | Sign | Activity |
|------|------|------|----------|
| Aug 4, 9:30 am–Aug 6, 11:31 am | 1st | Libra | Plant annuals for fragrance and beauty. Trim to increase growth. |
| Aug 6, 11:31 am–Aug 7, 1:31 pm | 1st | Scorpio | Plant grains, leafy annuals. Fertilize (chemical). Graft or bud plants. Irrigate. Trim to increase growth. |
| Aug 7, 1:31 pm–Aug 8, 4:35 pm | 2nd | Scorpio | Plant grains, leafy annuals. Fertilize (chemical). Graft or bud plants. Irrigate. Trim to increase growth. |

Don't throw out your old essential oil bottles. Even though they're empty, they're still useful. The fragrance will linger for a long time. Put one in a drawer or a cupboard as an air freshener, or with your plant seeds and on windowsills as a natural bug repellent. Leave an empty bottle in your epsom salts for a few weeks to make an aromatic foot soak.

2018 © Nataliia Image from BigStockPhoto.com

*August 7*
*1:31 pm EDT*

### August

| S | M | T | W | T | F | S |
|---|---|---|---|---|---|---|
|   |   |   |   | 1 | 2 | 3 |
| 4 | 5 | 6 | 7 | 8 | 9 | 10 |
| 11 | 12 | 13 | 14 | 15 | 16 | 17 |
| 18 | 19 | 20 | 21 | 22 | 23 | 24 |
| 25 | 26 | 27 | 28 | 29 | 30 | 31 |

# ♋ **August 11–17**

*A rainy day is the perfect time for a walk in the woods.*

~RACHEL CARSON

| Date | Qtr. | Sign | Activity |
|------|------|------|----------|
| Aug 11, 12:50 am–<br>Aug 13, 11:35 am | 2nd | Capricorn | Graft or bud plants. Trim to increase growth. |
| Aug 15, 8:29 am–<br>Aug 15, 11:49 pm | 3rd | Aquarius | Cultivate. Destroy weeds and pests. Harvest fruits and root crops for food. Trim to retard growth. |
| Aug 15, 11:49 pm–<br>Aug 18, 12:33 pm | 3rd | Pisces | Plant biennials, perennials, bulbs and roots. Prune. Irrigate. Fertilize (organic). |

Old fashioned epsom salts (hydrated magnesium sulfate) are your friend in the garden! The magnesium in them helps to deter leaves from fading and curling. Fruits and fruiting veg tastes sweeter when epsom salts are added to the soil. Roses simply adore them. Simply sprinkle the salts around your plants. The salts will dissolve in water, so you'll have to repeat this after a rainfall.

O
August 15
8:29 am EDT

AUGUST

| S | M | T | W | T | F | S |
|---|---|---|---|---|---|---|
|   |   |   |   | 1 | 2 | 3 |
| 4 | 5 | 6 | 7 | 8 | 9 | 10 |
| 11 | 12 | 13 | 14 | 15 | 16 | 17 |
| 18 | 19 | 20 | 21 | 22 | 23 | 24 |
| 25 | 26 | 27 | 28 | 29 | 30 | 31 |

2018 © Sebastian Studio Image from BigStockPhoto.com

## August 18–24

*The Eskimo has fifty-two names for snow because it is*
*important to them; there ought to be as many for love.*

~MARGARET ATWOOD

| Date | Qtr. | Sign | Activity |
|------|------|------|----------|
| Aug 18, 12:33 pm–Aug 21, 12:37 am | 3rd | Aries | Cultivate. Destroy weeds and pests. Harvest fruits and root crops for food. Trim to retard growth. |
| Aug 21, 12:37 am–Aug 23, 10:34 am | 3rd | Taurus | Plant potatoes and tubers. Trim to retard growth. |
| Aug 23, 10:34 am–Aug 23, 10:56 am | 3rd | Gemini | Cultivate. Destroy weeds and pests. Harvest fruits and root crops for food. Trim to retard growth. |
| Aug 23, 10:56 am–Aug 25, 5:05 pm | 4th | Gemini | Cultivate. Destroy weeds and pests. Harvest fruits and root crops for food. Trim to retard growth. |

Because dust mites are killed by direct sunlight, place uphol-stered furniture in the sun for a few hours to kill residents. Change and wash bedding weekly in water at least 120 degrees F. Place plush stuffed animals in plastic bags in the freezer for 24 hours.

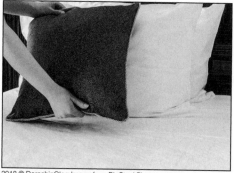

2018 © DoroshinOleg Image from BigStockPhoto.com

*August 23*
*10:56 am EDT*

AUGUST

| S | M | T | W | T | F | S |
|---|---|---|---|---|---|---|
| | | | | 1 | 2 | 3 |
| 4 | 5 | 6 | 7 | 8 | 9 | 10 |
| 11 | 12 | 13 | 14 | 15 | 16 | 17 |
| 18 | 19 | 20 | 21 | 22 | 23 | 24 |
| 25 | 26 | 27 | 28 | 29 | 30 | 31 |

# ♍ August 25–31

*Between every two pine trees there is a door leading to a new way of life.*                                    ~JOHN MUIR

| Date | Qtr. | Sign | Activity |
|---|---|---|---|
| Aug 25, 5:05 pm–<br>Aug 27, 7:53 pm | 4th | Cancer | Plant biennials, perennials, bulbs and roots. Prune. Irrigate. Fertilize (organic). |
| Aug 27, 7:53 pm–<br>Aug 29, 7:57 pm | 4th | Leo | Cultivate. Destroy weeds and pests. Harvest fruits and root crops for food. Trim to retard growth. |
| Aug 29, 7:57 pm–<br>Aug 30, 6:37 am | 4th | Virgo | Cultivate, especially medicinal plants. Destroy weeds and pests. Trim to retard growth. |
| Aug 31, 7:08 pm–<br>Sep 2, 7:35 pm | 1st | Libra | Plant annuals for fragrance and beauty. Trim to increase growth. |

If your children have flown the nest, get a birdfeeder and take care of a new family of feathered ones over the winter. Hang the feeder on the side of your house near a door or window so you can see who comes to visit. Few things are as calming, instructive, or educational as watching the interactions of birds around the feeder.

*August 30*
*6:37 am EDT*

AUGUST

| S | M | T | W | T | F | S |
|---|---|---|---|---|---|---|
|   |   |   |   | 1 | 2 | 3 |
| 4 | 5 | 6 | 7 | 8 | 9 | 10 |
| 11 | 12 | 13 | 14 | 15 | 16 | 17 |
| 18 | 19 | 20 | 21 | 22 | 23 | 24 |
| 25 | 26 | 27 | 28 | 29 | 30 | 31 |

2018 © Michael Schultz Image from BigStockPhoto.com

# September ♍

## September 1–7

*I can't say as ever I was lost, but I was bewildered once for three days.*

~DANIEL BOONE

| Date | Qtr. | Sign | Activity |
|------|------|------|----------|
| Sep 2, 7:35 pm–Sep 4, 11:08 pm | 1st | Scorpio | Plant grains, leafy annuals. Fertilize (chemical). Graft or bud plants. Irrigate. Trim to increase growth. |
| Sep 7, 6:37 am–Sep 9, 5:24 pm | 2nd | Capricorn | Graft or bud plants. Trim to increase growth. |

Save your plastic forks when you get takeaway meals, or look for old silverware at yard sales. Plant them in with your vegetables. It may look odd, but it will deter rabbits and other animals who would hop along to help themselves, undoing all your hard work and putting your crop in jeopardy.

*September 5*
*11:10 pm EDT*

### SEPTEMBER

| S | M | T | W | T | F | S |
|---|---|---|---|---|---|---|
| 1 | 2 | 3 | 4 | 5 | 6 | 7 |
| 8 | 9 | 10 | 11 | 12 | 13 | 14 |
| 15 | 16 | 17 | 18 | 19 | 20 | 21 |
| 22 | 23 | 24 | 25 | 26 | 27 | 28 |
| 29 | 30 | | | | | |

2018 © Maren Winter Image from BigStockPhoto.com

# ♍ **September 8–14**

*A purpose of human life, no matter who is controlling it, is to love whoever is around to be loved.* ~Kurt Vonnegut

| Date | Qtr. | Sign | Activity |
|------|------|------|----------|
| Sep 12, 5:52 am–<br>Sep 14, 12:33 am | 2nd | Pisces | Plant grains, leafy annuals. Fertilize (chemical). Graft or bud plants. Irrigate. Trim to increase growth. |
| Sep 14, 12:33 am–<br>Sep 14, 6:32 pm | 3rd | Pisces | Plant biennials, perennials, bulbs and roots. Prune. Irrigate. Fertilize (organic). |
| Sep 14, 6:32 pm–<br>Sep 17, 6:31 am | 3rd | Aries | Cultivate. Destroy weeds and pests. Harvest fruits and root crops for food. Trim to retard growth. |

Recycle your old flannel bedding by making reusable dryer sheets. Cut the cloth into strips; 4" × 6" is good. Add a few drops of your favorite essential oil to 1 cup white vinegar, and decant into an amber glass spray bottle. Spray a dryer sheet lightly before you dry your clothes. When the cycle is complete, store the sheet with the spray bottle to be used again next time.

○
*September 14*
*12:33 am EDT*

Sᴇᴘᴛᴇᴍʙᴇʀ

| S | M | T | W | T | F | S |
|---|---|---|---|---|---|---|
| 1 | 2 | 3 | 4 | 5 | 6 | 7 |
| 8 | 9 | 10 | 11 | 12 | 13 | 14 |
| 15 | 16 | 17 | 18 | 19 | 20 | 21 |
| 22 | 23 | 24 | 25 | 26 | 27 | 28 |
| 29 | 30 | | | | | |

## September 15–21 ♍

*What, is the jay more precious than the lark,*
*Because his feathers are more beautiful?*
~WILLIAM SHAKESPEARE

| Date | Qtr. | Sign | Activity |
|------|------|------|----------|
| Sep 17, 6:31 am–Sep 19, 4:58 pm | 3rd | Taurus | Plant potatoes and tubers. Trim to retard growth. |
| Sep 19, 4:58 pm–Sep 21, 10:41 pm | 3rd | Gemini | Cultivate. Destroy weeds and pests. Harvest fruits and root crops for food. Trim to retard growth. |
| Sep 21, 10:41 pm–Sep 22, 12:50 am | 4th | Gemini | Cultivate. Destroy weeds and pests. Harvest fruits and root crops for food. Trim to retard growth. |

Gourds are easy to grow and fun to use. They come in all shapes and sizes, and their uses are many and varied—some are even edible! Gourds that are hardened on the vine seem more robust than those that are brought inside to dry. Plant different types, and use them to make ladles, birdhouses, and interesting decorations.

*September 21*
*10:41 pm EDT*

2018 © TasiPas Image from BigStockPhoto.com

SEPTEMBER

| S | M | T | W | T | F | S |
|---|---|---|---|---|---|---|
| 1 | 2 | 3 | 4 | 5 | 6 | 7 |
| 8 | 9 | 10 | 11 | 12 | 13 | 14 |
| 15 | 16 | 17 | 18 | 19 | 20 | 21 |
| 22 | 23 | 24 | 25 | 26 | 27 | 28 |
| 29 | 30 | | | | | |

**September 22–28**

*The only business of the head in the world is to bow a
ceaseless obeisance to the heart.*                    ~W. B. YEATS

| Date | Qtr. | Sign | Activity |
|------|------|------|----------|
| Sep 22, 12:50 am–<br>Sep 24, 5:19 am | 4th | Cancer | Plant biennials, perennials, bulbs and roots. Prune. Irrigate. Fertilize (organic). |
| Sep 24, 5:19 am–<br>Sep 26, 6:37 am | 4th | Leo | Cultivate. Destroy weeds and pests. Harvest fruits and root crops for food. Trim to retard growth. |
| Sep 26, 6:37 am–<br>Sep 28, 6:03 am | 4th | Virgo | Cultivate, especially medicinal plants. Destroy weeds and pests. Trim to retard growth. |
| Sep 28, 2:26 pm–<br>Sep 30, 5:42 am | 1st | Libra | Plant annuals for fragrance and beauty. Trim to increase growth. |

Autumn is the best time to create a compost pile. Pick a spot that's out of the way, dump your leaves, weeds, and yard wastes there, wet the pile with water, and let it set until early spring. Then turn the pile over, let it set again until late spring when it should be ready to use. Sprinkle a little bit around flowers, fruit trees, vegetables, or houseplants to give them amazing health, stamina, and fabulous taste.

*September 28*
*2:26 pm EDT*

### SEPTEMBER

| S | M | T | W | T | F | S |
|---|---|---|---|---|---|---|
|   |   |   |   |   |   | 1 |
| 2 | 3 | 4 | 5 | 6 | 7 | 8 |
| 9 | 10 | 11 | 12 | 13 | 14 | 15 |
| 16 | 17 | 18 | 19 | 20 | 21 | 22 |
| 23 | 24 | 25 | 26 | 27 | 28 | 29 |
| 30 |   |   |   |   |   |   |

2018 © singkham Image from BigStockPhoto.com

# October ♎

## September 29–October 5

*If something ever happens to me, people are gonna be like "we knew a croc would get him!"*    ∼STEVE IRWIN

| Date | Qtr. | Sign | Activity |
|------|------|------|----------|
| Sep 30, 5:42 am–Oct 2, 7:44 am | 1st | Scorpio | Plant grains, leafy annuals. Fertilize (chemical). Graft or bud plants. Irrigate. Trim to increase growth. |
| Oct 4, 1:43 pm–Oct 5, 12:47 pm | 1st | Capricorn | Graft or bud plants. Trim to increase growth. |
| Oct 5, 12:47 pm–Oct 6, 11:42 pm | 2nd | Capricorn | Graft or bud plants. Trim to increase growth. |

Homemade toothpaste is environmentally friendly, economical, and so easy to make. Mix 4 tablespoons of baking soda with a tablespoon of sea salt, and add 20 or more drops of peppermint oil. Keep this in a small lidded glass jar in your bathroom to use when you brush.

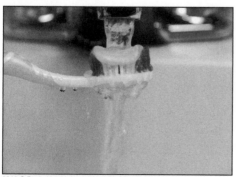

2018 © Rachel Lerch Image from BigStockPhoto.com

October 5
12:47 pm EDT

### OCTOBER

| S | M | T | W | T | F | S |
|---|---|---|---|---|---|---|
| | | 1 | 2 | 3 | 4 | 5 |
| 6 | 7 | 8 | 9 | 10 | 11 | 12 |
| 13 | 14 | 15 | 16 | 17 | 18 | 19 |
| 20 | 21 | 22 | 23 | 24 | 25 | 26 |
| 27 | 28 | 29 | 30 | 31 | | |

# ⟳ October 6–12

*Every individual has a place to fill in the world, and is*
*important, in some respect, whether he chooses to be so or not.*

⟲NATHANIAL HAWTHORNE

| Date | Qtr. | Sign | Activity |
|------|------|------|----------|
| Oct 9, 12:05 pm–<br>Oct 12, 12:46 am | 2nd | Pisces | Plant grains, leafy annuals. Fertilize (chemical). Graft or bud plants. Irrigate. Trim to increase growth. |

Baking soda (bicarbonate of soda) has so many uses around the house. Pop an open box in your fridge or your closet to keep it fresh smelling. Change it monthly. Don't discard it though; put the baking soda in your sneakers after a sweaty session, and it will keep them fresh smelling too! Simply tap it out before putting them on again.

---

---

---

---

OCTOBER

| S | M | T | W | T | F | S |
|---|---|---|---|---|---|---|
|   |   | 1 | 2 | 3 | 4 | 5 |
| 6 | 7 | 8 | 9 | 10 | 11 | 12 |
| 13 | 14 | 15 | 16 | 17 | 18 | 19 |
| 20 | 21 | 22 | 23 | 24 | 25 | 26 |
| 27 | 28 | 29 | 30 | 31 |   |   |

## October 13–19 ♎

*Stupidity is an attempt to iron out all differences, and not to
use or value them creatively.* ~BILL MOLLISON

| Date | Qtr. | Sign | Activity |
|------|------|------|----------|
| Oct 13, 5:08 pm–Oct 14, 12:24 pm | 3rd | Aries | Cultivate. Destroy weeds and pests. Harvest fruits and root crops for food. Trim to retard growth. |
| Oct 14, 12:24 pm–Oct 16, 10:30 pm | 3rd | Taurus | Plant potatoes and tubers. Trim to retard growth. |
| Oct 16, 10:30 pm–Oct 19, 6:43 am | 3rd | Gemini | Cultivate. Destroy weeds and pests. Harvest fruits and root crops for food. Trim to retard growth. |
| Oct 19, 6:43 am–Oct 21, 8:39 am | 3rd | Cancer | Plant biennials, perennials, bulbs and roots. Prune. Irrigate. Fertilize (organic). |

For a heart-healthy substitution, consider replacing mashed or pureed avocado, with its healthy unsaturated fats and creamy texture, for half the oil in baked goods recipes. Muffins and other quick breads are a good way to add heart-healthy avocado into recipes; find California Avocado Commission online for recipes.

October 13
5:08 pm EDT

OCTOBER

| S | M | T | W | T | F | S |
|---|---|---|---|---|---|---|
| | | 1 | 2 | 3 | 4 | 5 |
| 6 | 7 | 8 | 9 | 10 | 11 | 12 |
| 13 | 14 | 15 | 16 | 17 | 18 | 19 |
| 20 | 21 | 22 | 23 | 24 | 25 | 26 |
| 27 | 28 | 29 | 30 | 31 | | |

2018 © weyo Image from BigStockPhoto.com

## ♎ October 20–26

*He that breaks a thing to find out what it is has left the path of wisdom.*    ~*J. R. R. TOLKEIN, FELLOWSHIP OF THE RING*

| Date | Qtr. | Sign | Activity |
|------|------|------|----------|
| Oct 21, 8:39 am–<br>Oct 21, 12:29 pm | 4th | Cancer | Plant biennials, perennials, bulbs and roots. Prune. Irrigate. Fertilize (organic). |
| Oct 21, 12:29 pm–<br>Oct 23, 3:29 pm | 4th | Leo | Cultivate. Destroy weeds and pests. Harvest fruits and root crops for food. Trim to retard growth. |
| Oct 23, 3:29 pm–<br>Oct 25, 4:20 pm | 4th | Virgo | Cultivate, especially medicinal plants. Destroy weeds and pests. Trim to retard growth. |

Pumpkin is far more than just a Halloween decoration! With only 30 calories per cup, pumpkin's potassium is heart-healthy, and its color indicates the presence of beta carotene, an antioxidant that protects the body from damaging free radicals, and also benefits skin and sharpens eyesight.

_____

_____

_____

_____

◐
*October 21*
*8:39 am EDT*

### OCTOBER

| S | M | T | W | T | F | S |
|---|---|---|---|---|---|---|
|   |   | 1 | 2 | 3 | 4 | 5 |
| 6 | 7 | 8 | 9 | 10 | 11 | 12 |
| 13 | 14 | 15 | 16 | 17 | 18 | 19 |
| 20 | 21 | 22 | 23 | 24 | 25 | 26 |
| 27 | 28 | 29 | 30 | 31 |   |   |

# November ♏

## October 27–November 2

*To be good and lead a good life means to give to others more
than one takes from them.*                    ∼LEO TOLSTOY

| Date | Qtr. | Sign | Activity |
|------|------|------|----------|
| Oct 27, 4:29 pm–<br>Oct 27, 11:39 pm | 4th | Scorpio | Plant biennials, perennials, bulbs and roots. Prune. Irrigate. Fertilize (organic). |
| Oct 27, 11:39 pm–<br>Oct 29, 5:58 pm | 1st | Scorpio | Plant grains, leafy annuals. Fertilize (chemical). Graft or bud plants. Irrigate. Trim to increase growth. |
| Oct 31, 10:38 pm–<br>Nov 3, 6:19 am | 1st | Capricorn | Graft or bud plants. Trim to increase growth. |

If you're trying to train roses up a trellis, give them some protection against winter cold by stopping any "feeding" after August so they shut down. Then use Styrofoam cones to cover each rose to protect against severe cold and winter winds. You'll find you don't have to start over every year regrowing the same lengths lost to Old Man Winter.

―――――――――――――――――――――――

―――――――――――――――――――――――

―――――――――――――――――――――――

―――――――――――――――――――――――

*October 27
11:39 pm EDT*

### NOVEMBER

| S | M | T | W | T | F | S |
|---|---|---|---|---|---|---|
|   |   |   |   |   | 1 | 2 |
| 3 | 4 | 5 | 6 | 7 | 8 | 9 |
| 10 | 11 | 12 | 13 | 14 | 15 | 16 |
| 17 | 18 | 19 | 20 | 21 | 22 | 23 |
| 24 | 25 | 26 | 27 | 28 | 29 | 30 |

2018 © ZoomTravels Image from BigStockPhoto.com

# ♏ November 3–9

*Today is only one day in all the days that will ever be. But what will happen in all the other days that ever come can depend on what you do today.* ∼ERNEST HEMINGWAY

| Date | Qtr. | Sign | Activity |
|------|------|------|----------|
| Nov 5, 6:08 pm–<br>Nov 8, 6:49 am | 2nd | Pisces | Plant grains, leafy annuals. Fertilize (chemical). Graft or bud plants. Irrigate. Trim to increase growth. |

If your garden is struggling with mildew on zucchini or melon plants, get your hands on some raw milk and spray the plants with it. Raw milk is full of enzymes that simply kill molds and mildew, often overnight. It also has excellent minerals that nurture the plants. Pasteurized milk will not do anything except make your garden smell like sour milk for a while, but raw milk makes all plants healthy, shiny, and disease-free.

_____

_____

_____

_____

*Daylight Saving Time ends November 3, 2:00 am*

*November 4, 5:23 am EST*

NOVEMBER

| S | M | T | W | T | F | S |
|---|---|---|---|---|---|---|
|   |   |   |   |   | 1 | 2 |
| 3 | 4 | 5 | 6 | 7 | 8 | 9 |
| 10 | 11 | 12 | 13 | 14 | 15 | 16 |
| 17 | 18 | 19 | 20 | 21 | 22 | 23 |
| 24 | 25 | 26 | 27 | 28 | 29 | 30 |

2018 © AlterPhoto Image from BigStockPhoto.com

## November 10–16 ♏

*The creator of the new composition in the arts is an outlaw*
*until he is a classic.*                                    ~GERTRUDE STEIN

| Date | Qtr. | Sign | Activity |
|------|------|------|----------|
| Nov 10, 6:18 pm–<br>Nov 12, 8:34 am | 2nd | Taurus | Plant annuals for hardiness. Trim to increase growth. |
| Nov 12, 8:34 am–<br>Nov 13, 3:46 am | 3rd | Taurus | Plant potatoes and tubers. Trim to retard growth. |
| Nov 13, 3:46 am–<br>Nov 15, 11:15 am | 3rd | Gemini | Cultivate. Destroy weeds and pests. Harvest fruits and root crops for food. Trim to retard growth. |
| Nov 15, 11:15 am–<br>Nov 17, 4:57 pm | 3rd | Cancer | Plant biennials, perennials, bulbs and roots. Prune. Irrigate. Fertilize (organic). |

Before winter sets in, go for a walk with all your senses turned on. Deeply enjoy the colors, sounds, smells, and feel of late autumn. When you return, make yourself a cup of warm cider with a dash of cinnamon on top. The whole experience from walk to cider and cinnamon benefits the entire self.

_____

_____

_____

_____

○
*November 12*
*8:34 am EST*

NOVEMBER

| S | M | T | W | T | F | S |
|---|---|---|---|---|---|---|
|   |   |   |   |   | 1 | 2 |
| 3 | 4 | 5 | 6 | 7 | 8 | 9 |
| 10 | 11 | 12 | 13 | 14 | 15 | 16 |
| 17 | 18 | 19 | 20 | 21 | 22 | 23 |
| 24 | 25 | 26 | 27 | 28 | 29 | 30 |

2018 © Dreamframer Image from BigStockPhoto.com

**November 17–23**

*It does not matter much whom we live with in this world, but it matters a great deal whom we dream of.*

~WILLA CATHER

| Date | Qtr. | Sign | Activity |
|------|------|------|----------|
| Nov 17, 4:57 pm–<br>Nov 19, 4:11 pm | 3rd | Leo | Cultivate. Destroy weeds and pests. Harvest fruits and root crops for food. Trim to retard growth. |
| Nov 19, 4:11 pm–<br>Nov 19, 8:54 pm | 4th | Leo | Cultivate. Destroy weeds and pests. Harvest fruits and root crops for food. Trim to retard growth. |
| Nov 19, 8:54 pm–<br>Nov 21, 11:20 pm | 4th | Virgo | Cultivate, especially medicinal plants. Destroy weeds and pests. Trim to retard growth. |

Some of your kitchen utensils can be used for more than just their labeled use. For example, an apple corer can be used to cut potatoes into perfect wedges for baking or frying. An apple peeler can be used to slice potatoes for a modified Hasselback potato recipe.

---

---

◖

*November 19*
*4:11 pm EST*

NOVEMBER

| S | M | T | W | T | F | S |
|---|---|---|---|---|---|---|
| | | | | | 1 | 2 |
| 3 | 4 | 5 | 6 | 7 | 8 | 9 |
| 10 | 11 | 12 | 13 | 14 | 15 | 16 |
| 17 | 18 | 19 | 20 | 21 | 22 | 23 |
| 24 | 25 | 26 | 27 | 28 | 29 | 30 |

# November 24–30

*Death is nature's way of saying, "Your table is ready."*
~ROBIN WILLIAMS

| Date | Qtr. | Sign | Activity |
|------|------|------|----------|
| Nov 24, 12:58 am–<br>Nov 26, 3:11 am | 4th | Scorpio | Plant biennials, perennials, bulbs and roots. Prune. Irrigate. Fertilize (organic). |
| Nov 26, 3:11 am–<br>Nov 26, 10:06 am | 4th | Sagittarius | Cultivate. Destroy weeds and pests. Harvest fruits and root crops for food. Trim to retard growth. |
| Nov 28, 7:33 am–<br>Nov 30, 3:13 pm | 1st | Capricorn | Graft or bud plants. Trim to increase growth. |

While it won't knock you out like Ambien, magnesium's calming effect helps to relieve mild anxiety that keeps you up at night. Magnesium has also been shown to help muscles relax, soothe achy muscles, and ward off migraines. Look for magnesium in veggies, brown rice, and nut butters.

2018 © Yastremska Image from BigStockPhoto.com

*November 26*
*10:06 am EST*

### NOVEMBER

| S | M | T | W | T | F | S |
|---|---|---|---|---|---|---|
|   |   |   |   |   | 1 | 2 |
| 3 | 4 | 5 | 6 | 7 | 8 | 9 |
| 10 | 11 | 12 | 13 | 14 | 15 | 16 |
| 17 | 18 | 19 | 20 | 21 | 22 | 23 |
| 24 | 25 | 26 | 27 | 28 | 29 | 30 |

#  December

## December 1–7

*When one door of happiness closes, another opens; but often we look so long at the closed door that we do not see the one which has been opened for us.*    ~HELEN KELLER

| Date | Qtr. | Sign | Activity |
|------|------|------|----------|
| Dec 3, 2:11 am–<br>Dec 4, 1:58 am | 1st | Pisces | Plant grains, leafy annuals. Fertilize (chemical). Graft or bud plants. Irrigate. Trim to increase growth. |
| Dec 4, 1:58 am–<br>Dec 5, 2:44 pm | 2nd | Pisces | Plant grains, leafy annuals. Fertilize (chemical). Graft or bud plants. Irrigate. Trim to increase growth. |

If you didn't or couldn't send out Christmas cards this year, don't feel bad. Many people are now sending holiday greetings via text message or email. If you really miss the traditional holiday card exchange, surprise your favorite people with a Valentine's card containing a cheery or newsworthy message.

*December 4*
*1:58 am EST*

DECEMBER

| S | M | T | W | T | F | S |
|---|---|---|---|---|---|---|
| 1 | 2 | 3 | 4 | 5 | 6 | 7 |
| 8 | 9 | 10 | 11 | 12 | 13 | 14 |
| 15 | 16 | 17 | 18 | 19 | 20 | 21 |
| 22 | 23 | 24 | 25 | 26 | 27 | 28 |
| 29 | 30 | 31 | | | | |

2018 © stockasso Image from BigStockPhoto.com

# December 8–14

*The teachers are everywhere. What is wanted is a learner.*
~WENDELL BERRY

| Date | Qtr. | Sign | Activity |
|------|------|------|----------|
| Dec 8, 2:29 am–Dec 10, 11:47 am | 2nd | Taurus | Plant annuals for hardiness. Trim to increase growth. |
| Dec 12, 12:12 am–Dec 12, 6:23 pm | 3rd | Gemini | Cultivate. Destroy weeds and pests. Harvest fruits and root crops for food. Trim to retard growth. |
| Dec 12, 6:23 pm–Dec 14, 10:56 pm | 3rd | Cancer | Plant biennials, perennials, bulbs and roots. Prune. Irrigate. Fertilize (organic). |
| Dec 14, 10:56 pm–Dec 17, 2:16 am | 3rd | Leo | Cultivate. Destroy weeds and pests. Harvest fruits and root crops for food. Trim to retard growth. |

Potatoes aren't just for the table! If your eyes are tired, bloodshot, or puffy, cut two slices of raw potato. Rest comfortably and place one slice over each eye. Relax for ten minutes or so and let the spud do its work! The naturally astringent properties of the potato are soothing, but they're not a substitute for a doctor's advice.

○
December 12
12:12 am EST

DECEMBER

| S | M | T | W | T | F | S |
|---|---|---|---|---|---|---|
| 1 | 2 | 3 | 4 | 5 | 6 | 7 |
| 8 | 9 | 10 | 11 | 12 | 13 | 14 |
| 15 | 16 | 17 | 18 | 19 | 20 | 21 |
| 22 | 23 | 24 | 25 | 26 | 27 | 28 |
| 29 | 30 | 31 | | | | |

# December 15–21

*The civility which money will purchase is rarely extended to those who have none.*   ∼*Charles Dickens*

| Date | Qtr. | Sign | Activity |
|------|------|------|----------|
| Dec 17, 2:16 am–<br>Dec 18, 11:57 pm | 3rd | Virgo | Cultivate, especially medicinal plants. Destroy weeds and pests. Trim to retard growth. |
| Dec 18, 11:57 pm–<br>Dec 19, 5:04 am | 4th | Virgo | Cultivate, especially medicinal plants. Destroy weeds and pests. Trim to retard growth. |
| Dec 21, 7:57 am–<br>Dec 23, 11:34 am | 4th | Scorpio | Plant biennials, perennials, bulbs and roots. Prune. Irrigate. Fertilize (organic). |

The planet is full of people who have entirely different cultures. Choose an unfamiliar culture and learn as much as you can about their food, their geography, their finances, education system, values, and worldview. You will help bring the world together just a tiny bit by doing so.

_____

_____

_____

_____

◑

*December 18*
*11:57 pm EST*

### DECEMBER

| S | M | T | W | T | F | S |
|---|---|---|---|---|---|---|
|   |   |   |   |   |   |   |
| 1 | 2 | 3 | 4 | 5 | 6 | 7 |
| 8 | 9 | 10 | 11 | 12 | 13 | 14 |
| 15 | 16 | 17 | 18 | 19 | 20 | 21 |
| 22 | 23 | 24 | 25 | 26 | 27 | 28 |
| 29 | 30 | 31 |   |   |   |   |

2018 © Rawpixel.com Image from BigStockPhoto.com

# December 22–28

*Understanding is a two-way street.*

~*Eleanor Roosevelt*

| Date | Qtr. | Sign | Activity |
|------|------|------|----------|
| Dec 23, 11:34 am–<br>Dec 25, 4:45 pm | 4th | Sagittarius | Cultivate. Destroy weeds and pests. Harvest fruits and root crops for food. Trim to retard growth. |
| Dec 25, 4:45 pm–<br>Dec 26, 12:13 am | 4th | Capricorn | Plant potatoes and tubers. Trim to retard growth. |
| Dec 26, 12:13 am–<br>Dec 28, 12:21 am | 1st | Capricorn | Graft or bud plants. Trim to increase growth. |

Many people are now taking reusable bags to the store in an effort to reduce the dependency on plastic. Some cafes give you a discount if you bring your own reusable mug. Most people don't think about their drinking straws though, which are a huge plastic litter problem. Say no, next time, or if you must use a straw, look into the reusable plastic or aluminum alternatives.

*December 26*
*12:13 am EST*

2018 © Nickeline Image from BigStockPhoto.com

### December

| S | M | T | W | T | F | S |
|---|---|---|---|---|---|---|
| 1 | 2 | 3 | 4 | 5 | 6 | 7 |
| 8 | 9 | 10 | 11 | 12 | 13 | 14 |
| 15 | 16 | 17 | 18 | 19 | 20 | 21 |
| 22 | 23 | 24 | 25 | 26 | 27 | 28 |
| 29 | 30 | 31 | | | | |

# December 29–January 4, 2020

*Oft it may chance that old wives keep in memory word of things that once were needful for the wise to know.*

~J. R. R. TOLKEIN

| Date | Qtr. | Sign | Activity |
|------|------|------|----------|
| Jan 4, 11:15 am–Jan 6, 9:11 pm | 2nd | Taurus | Plant annuals for hardiness. Trim to increase growth. |

Do you experience a big letdown every year after the winter holidays? Consider the possibility that you could end your post-holiday drop by planning something new and different for yourself to start the first or second week in January. Sign up for a weaving or woodworking class, attend a conference on something you're interested in, or go on a trip just to see some neat physical features—sequoias, caves, mountains, architecture, the Great Lakes, waterfalls, or amazing dams.

January 2
8:45 pm EST

### DECEMBER

| S | M | T | W | T | F | S |
|---|---|---|---|---|---|---|
|   | 1 | 2 | 3 | 4 | 5 | 6 | 7 |
| 8 | 9 | 10 | 11 | 12 | 13 | 14 |
| 15 | 16 | 17 | 18 | 19 | 20 | 21 |
| 22 | 23 | 24 | 25 | 26 | 27 | 28 |
| 29 | 30 | 31 |   |   |   |   |

# Gardening by the Moon

Today, people often reject the notion of gardening according to the Moon's phase and sign. The usual nonbeliever is not a scientist but the city dweller who has never had any real contact with nature and little experience of natural rhythms.

Camille Flammarion, the French astronomer, testifies to the success of Moon planting, though:

"Cucumbers increase at Full Moon, as well as radishes, turnips, leeks, lilies, horseradish, and saffron; onions, on the contrary, are much larger and better nourished during the decline and old age of the Moon than at its increase, during its youth and fullness, which is the reason the Egyptians abstained from onions, on account of their antipathy to the Moon. Herbs gathered while the Moon increases are of great efficiency. If the vines are trimmed at night when the Moon is in the sign of the Lion, Sagittarius, the Scorpion, or the Bull, it will save them from field rats, moles, snails, flies, and other animals."

Dr. Clark Timmins is one of the few modern scientists to have conducted tests in Moon planting. Following is a summary of his experiments:

**Beets:** When sown with the Moon in Scorpio, the germination rate was 71 percent; when sown in Sagittarius, the germination rate was 58 percent.

**Scotch marigold:** When sown with the Moon in Cancer, the germination rate was 90 percent; when sown in Leo, the rate was 32 percent.

**Carrots:** When sown with the Moon in Scorpio, the germination rate was 64 percent; when sown with the Moon in Sagittarius, the germination rate was 47 percent.

**Tomatoes:** When sown with the Moon in Cancer, the germination rate was 90 percent; but when sown with the Moon in Leo, the germination rate was 58 percent.

Two things should be emphasized. First, remember that this is only a summary of the results of the experiments; the experiments themselves were conducted in a scientific manner to eliminate any variation in soil, temperature, moisture, and so on, so that only the Moon sign is varied. Second, note that these astonishing results were obtained without regard to the phase of the Moon—the other factor we use in Moon planting, and which presumably would have increased the differential in germination rates.

Dr. Timmins also tried transplanting Cancer- and Leo-planted tomato seedlings while the Cancer Moon was waxing. The result was 100 percent survival. When transplanting was done with the waning Sagittarius Moon, there was 0 percent survival. Dr. Timmins's tests show that the Cancer-planted tomatoes had blossoms twelve days earlier than those planted under Leo; the Cancer-planted tomatoes had an average height of twenty inches at that time compared to fifteen inches for the Leo-planted; the first ripe tomatoes were gathered from the Cancer plantings eleven days ahead of the Leo plantings; and a count of the hanging fruit and its size and weight shows an advantage to the Cancer plants over the Leo plants of 45 percent.

Dr. Timmins also observed that there have been similar tests that did not indicate results favorable to the Moon planting theory. As a scientist, he asked why one set of experiments indicated a positive verification of Moon planting, and others did not. He checked these other tests and found that the experimenters had not followed the geocentric system for determining the Moon sign positions, but the heliocentric. When the times used in these other tests were converted to the geocentric system, the dates chosen often were found to be in barren, rather than fertile, signs. Without going into a technical explanation, it is sufficient to point out that geocentric and heliocentric positions often vary by as much as four days. This is a large enough differential to place the Moon in Cancer, for example, in the heliocentric system, and at the same time in Leo by the geocentric system.

Most almanacs and calendars show the Moon's signs heliocentrically—and thus incorrectly for Moon planting—while the *Moon Sign Book* is calculated correctly for planting purposes, using the geocentric system. Some readers are confused because the *Moon Sign Book* talks about first, second, third, and fourth quarters, while other almanacs refer to these same divisions as New Moon, first quarter, Full Moon, and fourth quarter. Thus the almanacs say first quarter when the *Moon Sign Book* says second quarter.

There is nothing complicated about using astrology in agriculture and horticulture in order to increase both pleasure and profit, but there is one very important rule that is often neglected—use common sense! Of course this is one rule that should be remembered in every activity we undertake, but in the case of gardening and farming by the Moon, if it is not possible to use the best dates for planting or harvesting, we must select the next best and just try to do the best we can.

This brings up the matter of the other factors to consider in your gardening work. The dates we give as best for a certain activity apply to the entire country (with slight time correction), but in your section of the country you may be buried under three feet of snow on a date we say is good to plant your flowers. So we have factors of weather, season, temperature, and moisture variations, soil conditions, your own available time and opportunity, and so forth. Some astrologers like to think it is all a matter of science, but gardening is also an art. In art, you develop an instinctive identification with your work and influence it with your feelings and wishes.

The *Moon Sign Book* gives you the place of the Moon for every day of the year so that you can select the best times once you have become familiar with the rules and practices of lunar agriculture. We give you specific, easy-to-follow directions so that you can get right down to work.

We give you the best dates for planting, and also for various related activities, including cultivation, fertilizing, harvesting, irrigation, and getting rid of weeds and pests. But we cannot tell you exactly when it's good to plant. Many of these rules were learned by observation and experience; as the body of experience grew, we could see various patterns emerging that allowed us to make judgments about new things. That's what you should do, too. After you have worked with lunar agriculture for a while and have gained a working knowledge, you will probably begin to try new things—and we hope you will share your experiments and findings with us. That's how the science grows.

Here's an example of what we mean. Years ago Llewellyn George suggested we try to combine our bits of knowledge about what to expect in planting under each of the Moon signs in order to benefit from several lunar factors in one plant. From this came our rule for developing "thoroughbred seed." To develop thoroughbred seed, save the seed for three successive years from plants grown by the correct Moon sign and phase. You can plant in the first quarter phase and in the sign of Cancer for fruitfulness; the second year, plant seeds from the first year plants in Libra for beauty; and in the third year, plant the seeds from the second year plants in Taurus to produce hardiness. In a similar manner you can combine the fruitfulness of Cancer, the good root growth of Pisces, and the sturdiness and good vine growth of Scorpio. And don't forget the characteristics of Capricorn: hardy like Taurus, but drier and perhaps more resistant to drought and disease.

Unlike common almanacs, we consider both the Moon's phase and the Moon's sign in making our calculations for the proper timing of our work. It is perhaps a little easier to understand this if we remind you that we are all living in the center of a vast electromagnetic field that is Earth and its environment in space. Everything that occurs within this electromagnetic field has an effect on everything else within the field. The Moon and the Sun are the most important of the factors affecting the life of Earth, and it is their relative positions to Earth that we project for each day of the year.

Many people claim that not only do they achieve larger crops gardening by the Moon, but that their fruits and vegetables are much tastier. A number of organic gardeners have also become lunar gardeners using the natural rhythm of life forces that we experience through the relative movements of the Sun and Moon. We provide a few basic rules and then give you day-by-day guidance for your gardening work. You will be able to choose the best dates to meet your own needs and opportunities.

## Planting by the Moon's Phases

During the increasing or waxing light—from New Moon to Full Moon—plant annuals that produce their yield above the ground. An annual is a plant that completes its entire life cycle within one growing season and has to be seeded each year. During the decreasing or waning light—from Full Moon to New Moon—plant biennials, perennials, and bulb and root plants. Biennials include crops that are planted one season to winter over and produce crops the next, such as winter wheat. Perennials and bulb and root plants include all plants that grow from the same root each year.

A simpler, less-accurate rule is to plant crops that produce above the ground during the waxing Moon, and to plant crops that produce below the ground during the waning Moon. Thus the old adage, "Plant potatoes during the dark of the Moon." Llewellyn George's system divided the lunar month into quarters. The first two from New Moon to Full Moon are the first and second quarters, and the last two from Full Moon to New Moon the third and fourth quarters. Using these divisions, we can increase our accuracy in timing our efforts to coincide with natural forces.

## First Quarter

Plant annuals producing their yield above the ground, which are generally of the leafy kind that produce their seed outside the fruit. Some examples are asparagus, broccoli, brussels sprouts, cabbage, cauliflower, celery, cress, endive, kohlrabi, lettuce, parsley, and spinach. Cucumbers are an exception, as they do best in the first quarter rather than the second, even though the seeds are inside the fruit. Also plant cereals and grains.

## Second Quarter

Plant annuals producing their yield above the ground, which are generally of the viney kind that produce their seed inside the fruit. Some examples include beans, eggplant, melons, peas, peppers, pumpkins, squash, tomatoes, etc. These are not hard-and-fast divisions. If you can't plant during the first quarter, plant during the second, and vice versa. There are many plants that seem to do equally well planted in either quarter, such as watermelon, hay, and cereals and grains.

## Third Quarter

Plant biennials, perennials, bulbs, root plants, trees, shrubs, berries, grapes, strawberries, beets, carrots, onions, parsnips, rutabagas, potatoes, radishes, peanuts, rhubarb, turnips, winter wheat, etc.

## Fourth Quarter

This is the best time to cultivate, turn sod, pull weeds, and destroy pests of all kinds, especially when the Moon is in Aries, Leo, Virgo, Gemini, Aquarius, and Sagittarius.

## The Moon in the Signs

### *Moon in Aries*

Barren, dry, fiery, and masculine. Use for destroying noxious weeds.

### *Moon in Taurus*

Productive, moist, earthy, and feminine. Use for planting many crops when hardiness is important, particularly root crops. Also used for lettuce, cabbage, and similar leafy vegetables.

### *Moon in Gemini*

Barren and dry, airy and masculine. Use for destroying noxious growths, weeds, and pests, and for cultivation.

### *Moon in Cancer*

Fruitful, moist, feminine. Use for planting and irrigation.

### *Moon in Leo*

Barren, dry, fiery, masculine. Use for killing weeds or cultivation.

### *Moon in Virgo*

Barren, dry, earthy, and feminine. Use for cultivation and destroying weeds and pests.

### Moon in Libra

Semi-fruitful, moist, and airy. Use for planting crops that need good pulp growth. A very good sign for flowers and vines. Also used for seeding hay, corn fodder, and the like.

### Moon in Scorpio

Very fruitful and moist, watery and feminine. Nearly as productive as Cancer; use for the same purposes. Especially good for vine growth and sturdiness.

### Moon in Sagittarius

Barren and dry, fiery and masculine. Use for planting onions, seeding hay, and for cultivation.

### Moon in Capricorn

Productive and dry, earthy and feminine. Use for planting potatoes and other tubers.

### Moon in Aquarius

Barren, dry, airy, and masculine. Use for cultivation and destroying noxious growths and pests.

### Moon in Pisces

Very fruitful, moist, watery, and feminine. Especially good for root growth.

# A Guide to Planting

| Plant | Quarter | Sign |
|---|---|---|
| Annuals | 1st or 2nd | |
| Apple tree | 2nd or 3rd | Cancer, Pisces, Virgo |
| Artichoke | 1st | Cancer, Pisces |
| Asparagus | 1st | Cancer, Scorpio, Pisces |
| Aster | 1st or 2nd | Virgo, Libra |
| Barley | 1st or 2nd | Cancer, Pisces, Libra, Capricorn, Virgo |
| Beans (bush & pole) | 2nd | Cancer, Taurus, Pisces, Libra |
| Beans (kidney, white & navy) | 1st or 2nd | Cancer, Pisces |
| Beech tree | 2nd or 3rd | Virgo, Taurus |
| Beets | 3rd | Cancer, Capricorn, Pisces, Libra |
| Biennials | 3rd or 4th | |
| Broccoli | 1st | Cancer, Scorpio, Pisces, Libra |
| Brussels sprouts | 1st | Cancer, Scorpio, Pisces, Libra |
| Buckwheat | 1st or 2nd | Capricorn |
| Bulbs | 3rd | Cancer, Scorpio, Pisces |
| Bulbs for seed | 2nd or 3rd | |
| Cabbage | 1st | Cancer, Scorpio, Pisces, Taurus, Libra |
| Canes (raspberry, blackberry & gooseberry) | 2nd | Cancer, Scorpio, Pisces |
| Cantaloupe | 1st or 2nd | Cancer, Scorpio, Pisces, Taurus, Libra |
| Carrots | 3rd | Cancer, Scorpio, Pisces, Taurus, Libra |
| Cauliflower | 1st | Cancer, Scorpio, Pisces, Libra |
| Celeriac | 3rd | Cancer, Scorpio, Pisces |
| Celery | 1st | Cancer, Scorpio, Pisces |
| Cereals | 1st or 2nd | Cancer, Scorpio, Pisces, Libra |
| Chard | 1st or 2nd | Cancer, Scorpio, Pisces |
| Chicory | 2nd or 3rd | Cancer, Scorpio, Pisces |
| Chrysanthemum | 1st or 2nd | Virgo |
| Clover | 1st or 2nd | Cancer, Scorpio, Pisces |

| Plant | Quarter | Sign |
|---|---|---|
| Coreopsis | 2nd or 3rd | Libra |
| Corn | 1st | Cancer, Scorpio, Pisces |
| Corn for fodder | 1st or 2nd | Libra |
| Cosmos | 2nd or 3rd | Libra |
| Cress | 1st | Cancer, Scorpio, Pisces |
| Crocus | 1st or 2nd | Virgo |
| Cucumber | 1st | Cancer, Scorpio, Pisces |
| Daffodil | 1st or 2nd | Libra, Virgo |
| Dahlia | 1st or 2nd | Libra, Virgo |
| Deciduous trees | 2nd or 3rd | Cancer, Scorpio, Pisces, Virgo, Libra |
| Eggplant | 2nd | Cancer, Scorpio, Pisces, Libra |
| Endive | 1st | Cancer, Scorpio, Pisces, Libra |
| Flowers | 1st | Cancer, Scorpio, Pisces, Libra, Taurus, Virgo |
| Garlic | 3rd | Libra, Taurus, Pisces |
| Gladiola | 1st or 2nd | Libra, Virgo |
| Gourds | 1st or 2nd | Cancer, Scorpio, Pisces, Libra |
| Grapes | 2nd or 3rd | Cancer, Scorpio, Pisces, Virgo |
| Hay | 1st or 2nd | Cancer, Scorpio, Pisces, Libra, Taurus |
| Herbs | 1st or 2nd | Cancer, Scorpio, Pisces |
| Honeysuckle | 1st or 2nd | Scorpio, Virgo |
| Hops | 1st or 2nd | Scorpio, Libra |
| Horseradish | 1st or 2nd | Cancer, Scorpio, Pisces |
| Houseplants | 1st | Cancer, Scorpio, Pisces, Libra |
| Hyacinth | 3rd | Cancer, Scorpio, Pisces |
| Iris | 1st or 2nd | Cancer, Virgo |
| Kohlrabi | 1st or 2nd | Cancer, Scorpio, Pisces, Libra |
| Leek | 2nd or 3rd | Sagittarius |
| Lettuce | 1st | Cancer, Scorpio, Pisces, Libra, Taurus |
| Lily | 1st or 2nd | Cancer, Scorpio, Pisces |
| Maple tree | 2nd or 3rd | Taurus, Virgo, Cancer, Pisces |
| Melon | 2nd | Cancer, Scorpio, Pisces |
| Moon vine | 1st or 2nd | Virgo |

| Plant | Quarter | Sign |
|-------|---------|------|
| Morning glory | 1st or 2nd | Cancer, Scorpio, Pisces, Virgo |
| Oak tree | 2nd or 3rd | Taurus, Virgo, Cancer, Pisces |
| Oats | 1st or 2nd | Cancer, Scorpio, Pisces, Libra |
| Okra | 1st or 2nd | Cancer, Scorpio, Pisces, Libra |
| Onion seed | 2nd | Cancer, Scorpio, Sagittarius |
| Onion set | 3rd or 4th | Cancer, Pisces, Taurus, Libra |
| Pansies | 1st or 2nd | Cancer, Scorpio, Pisces |
| Parsley | 1st | Cancer, Scorpio, Pisces, Libra |
| Parsnip | 3rd | Cancer, Scorpio, Taurus, Capricorn |
| Peach tree | 2nd or 3rd | Cancer, Taurus, Virgo, Libra |
| Peanuts | 3rd | Cancer, Scorpio, Pisces |
| Pear tree | 2nd or 3rd | Cancer, Scorpio, Pisces, Libra |
| Peas | 2nd | Cancer, Scorpio, Pisces, Libra |
| Peony | 1st or 2nd | Virgo |
| Peppers | 2nd | Cancer, Scorpio, Pisces |
| Perennials | 3rd | |
| Petunia | 1st or 2nd | Libra, Virgo |
| Plum tree | 2nd or 3rd | Cancer, Pisces, Taurus, Virgo |
| Poppies | 1st or 2nd | Virgo |
| Portulaca | 1st or 2nd | Virgo |
| Potatoes | 3rd | Cancer, Scorpio, Libra, Taurus, Capricorn |
| Privet | 1st or 2nd | Taurus, Libra |
| Pumpkin | 2nd | Cancer, Scorpio, Pisces, Libra |
| Quince | 1st or 2nd | Capricorn |
| Radishes | 3rd | Cancer, Scorpio, Pisces, Libra, Capricorn |
| Rhubarb | 3rd | Cancer, Pisces |
| Rice | 1st or 2nd | Scorpio |
| Roses | 1st or 2nd | Cancer, Virgo |
| Rutabaga | 3rd | Cancer, Scorpio, Pisces, Taurus |
| Saffron | 1st or 2nd | Cancer, Scorpio, Pisces |
| Sage | 3rd | Cancer, Scorpio, Pisces |

| Plant | Quarter | Sign |
|-------|---------|------|
| Salsify | 1st | Cancer, Scorpio, Pisces |
| Shallot | 2nd | Scorpio |
| Spinach | 1st | Cancer, Scorpio, Pisces |
| Squash | 2nd | Cancer, Scorpio, Pisces, Libra |
| Strawberries | 3rd | Cancer, Scorpio, Pisces |
| String beans | 1st or 2nd | Taurus |
| Sunflowers | 1st or 2nd | Libra, Cancer |
| Sweet peas | 1st or 2nd | Any |
| Tomatoes | 2nd | Cancer, Scorpio, Pisces, Capricorn |
| Trees, shade | 3rd | Taurus, Capricorn |
| Trees, ornamental | 2nd | Libra, Taurus |
| Trumpet vine | 1st or 2nd | Cancer, Scorpio, Pisces |
| Tubers for seed | 3rd | Cancer, Scorpio, Pisces, Libra |
| Tulips | 1st or 2nd | Libra, Virgo |
| Turnips | 3rd | Cancer, Scorpio, Pisces, Taurus, Capricorn, Libra |
| Valerian | 1st or 2nd | Virgo, Gemini |
| Watermelon | 1st or 2nd | Cancer, Scorpio, Pisces, Libra |
| Wheat | 1st or 2nd | Cancer, Scorpio, Pisces, Libra |

# Companion Planting Guide

| Plant | Companions | Hindered by |
|---|---|---|
| Asparagus | Tomatoes, parsley, basil | None known |
| Beans | Tomatoes, carrots, cucumbers, garlic, cabbage, beets, corn | Onions, gladiolas |
| Beets | Onions, cabbage, lettuce, mint, catnip | Pole beans |
| Broccoli | Beans, celery, potatoes, onions | Tomatoes |
| Cabbage | Peppermint, sage, thyme, tomatoes | Strawberries, grapes |
| Carrots | Peas, lettuce, chives, radishes, leeks, onions, sage | Dill, anise |
| Citrus trees | Guava, live oak, rubber trees, peppers | None known |
| Corn | Potatoes, beans, peas, melon, squash, pumpkin, sunflowers, soybeans | Quack grass, wheat, straw, mulch |
| Cucumbers | Beans, cabbage, radishes, sunflowers, lettuce, broccoli, squash | Aromatic herbs |
| Eggplant | Green beans, lettuce, kale | None known |
| Grapes | Peas, beans, blackberries | Cabbage, radishes |
| Melons | Corn, peas | Potatoes, gourds |
| Onions, leeks | Beets, chamomile, carrots, lettuce | Peas, beans, sage |
| Parsnip | Peas | None known |
| Peas | Radishes, carrots, corn, cucumbers, beans, tomatoes, spinach, turnips | Onion, garlic |
| Potatoes | Beans, corn, peas, cabbage, hemp, cucumbers, eggplant, catnip | Raspberries, pumpkins, tomatoes, sunflowers |
| Radishes | Peas, lettuce, nasturtiums, cucumbers | Hyssop |
| Spinach | Strawberries | None known |
| Squash/Pumpkin | Nasturtiums, corn, mint, catnip | Potatoes |
| Tomatoes | Asparagus, parsley, chives, onions, carrots, marigolds, nasturtiums, dill | Black walnut roots, fennel, potatoes |
| Turnips | Peas, beans, brussels sprouts | Potatoes |

| Plant | Companions | Uses |
|-------|-----------|------|
| Anise | Coriander | Flavor candy, pastry, cheeses, cookies |
| Basil | Tomatoes | Dislikes rue; repels flies and mosquitoes |
| Borage | Tomatoes, squash | Use in teas |
| Buttercup | Clover | Hinders delphinium, peonies, monkshood, columbine |
| Catnip | | Repels flea beetles |
| Chamomile | Peppermint, wheat, onions, cabbage | Roman chamomile may control damping-off disease; use in herbal sprays |
| Chervil | Radishes | Good in soups and other dishes |
| Chives | Carrots | Use in spray to deter black spot on roses |
| Coriander | Plant anywhere | Hinders seed formation in fennel |
| Cosmos | | Repels corn earworms |
| Dill | Cabbage | Hinders carrots and tomatoes |
| Fennel | Plant in borders | Disliked by all garden plants |
| Horseradish | | Repels potato bugs |
| Horsetail | | Makes fungicide spray |
| Hyssop | | Attracts cabbage flies; harmful to radishes |
| Lavender | Plant anywhere | Use in spray to control insects on cotton, repels clothes moths |
| Lovage | | Lures horn worms away from tomatoes |
| Marigolds | | Pest repellent; use against Mexican bean beetles and nematodes |
| Mint | Cabbage, tomatoes | Repels ants, flea beetles, cabbage worm butterflies |
| Morning glory | Corn | Helps melon germination |
| Nasturtium | Cabbage, cucumbers | Deters aphids, squash bugs, pumpkin beetles |
| Okra | Eggplant | Attracts leafhopper (lure insects from other plants) |
| Parsley | Tomatoes, asparagus | Freeze chopped-up leaves to flavor foods |
| Purslane | | Good ground cover |
| Rosemary | | Repels cabbage moths, bean beetles, carrot flies |
| Savory | | Plant with onions for added sweetness |
| Tansy | | Deters Japanese beetles, striped cucumber beetles, squash bugs |
| Thyme | | Repels cabbage worms |
| Yarrow | | Increases essential oils of neighbors |

# Moon Void-of-Course

*By Kim Rogers-Gallagher*

The Moon circles the Earth in about twenty-eight days, moving through each zodiac sign in two-and-a-half days. As she passes through the thirty degrees of each sign, she "visits" with the planets in numerical order, forming aspects with them. Because she moves one degree in just two to two and a half hours, her influence on each planet lasts only a few hours. She eventually reaches the planet that's in the highest degree of any sign and forms what will be her final aspect before leaving the sign. From this point until she enters the next sign, she is referred to as void-of-course.

Think of it this way: the Moon is the emotional "tone" of the day, carrying feelings with her particular to the sign she's "wearing" at the moment. After she has contacted each of the planets, she symbolically "rests" before changing her costume, so her instinct is temporarily on hold. It's during this time that many people feel "fuzzy" or "vague." Plans or decisions made now often do not pan out. Without the instinctual "knowing" the Moon provides as she touches each planet, we tend to be unrealistic or exercise poor judgment. The traditional definition of the void Moon is that "nothing will come of this." Actions initiated under a void Moon are often wasted, irrelevant, or incorrect—usually because information is hidden, missing, or has been overlooked.

Although it's not a good time to initiate plans, routine tasks seem to go along just fine. This period is ideal for reflection. On the lighter side, remember there are good uses for the void Moon. It is the period when the universe seems to be most open to loopholes. It's a great time to make plans you don't want to fulfill or schedule things you don't want to do. See the tables on pages 76–81 for a schedule of the Moon's void-of-course times.

## Last Aspect                    Moon Enters New Sign

| | | | January | | |
|---|---|---|---|---|---|
| 1 | 5:26 pm | 2 | Sagittarius | 3:58 am |
| 4 | 12:41 pm | 4 | Capricorn | 1:55 pm |
| 7 | 1:20 am | 7 | Aquarius | 1:46 am |
| 9 | 11:53 am | 9 | Pisces | 2:44 pm |
| 11 | 9:25 am | 12 | Aries | 3:18 am |
| 14 | 10:56 am | 14 | Taurus | 1:31 pm |
| 16 | 1:34 pm | 16 | Gemini | 8:00 pm |
| 18 | 8:32 pm | 18 | Cancer | 10:44 pm |
| 20 | 8:50 pm | 20 | Leo | 10:54 pm |
| 22 | 8:19 pm | 22 | Virgo | 10:22 pm |
| 24 | 8:50 am | 24 | Libra | 11:02 pm |
| 27 | 12:21 am | 27 | Scorpio | 2:31 am |
| 28 | 5:39 pm | 29 | Sagittarius | 9:33 am |
| 31 | 5:33 pm | 31 | Capricorn | 7:47 pm |
| | | | February | | |
| 3 | 5:53 am | 3 | Aquarius | 8:03 am |
| 5 | 6:59 pm | 5 | Pisces | 9:02 pm |
| 7 | 5:14 pm | 8 | Aries | 9:34 am |
| 10 | 6:48 pm | 10 | Taurus | 8:28 pm |
| 12 | 5:26 pm | 13 | Gemini | 4:32 am |
| 15 | 7:48 am | 15 | Cancer | 9:03 am |
| 17 | 9:17 am | 17 | Leo | 10:21 am |
| 19 | 8:51 am | 19 | Virgo | 9:47 am |
| 20 | 8:52 pm | 21 | Libra | 9:17 am |
| 23 | 10:11 am | 23 | Scorpio | 10:56 am |
| 25 | 7:14 am | 25 | Sagittarius | 4:19 pm |
| 28 | 1:17 am | 28 | Capricorn | 1:48 am |

| **Last Aspect** | | **Moon Enters New Sign** | | |
|---|---|---|---|---|
| | | **March** | | |
| 2 | 1:47 pm | 2 | Aquarius | 2:06 pm |
| 5 | 3:05 am | 5 | Pisces | 3:11 am |
| 7 | 2:08 pm | 7 | Aries | 3:27 pm |
| 9 | 12:14 pm | 10 | Taurus | 3:10 am |
| 12 | 5:31 am | 12 | Gemini | 11:48 am |
| 14 | 8:30 am | 14 | Cancer | 5:49 pm |
| 16 | 2:03 pm | 16 | Leo | 8:57 pm |
| 18 | 11:19 am | 18 | Virgo | 9:41 pm |
| 20 | 11:22 am | 20 | Libra | 9:28 pm |
| 22 | 2:10 pm | 22 | Scorpio | 10:16 pm |
| 24 | 10:24 pm | 25 | Sagittarius | 2:06 am |
| 26 | 10:37 pm | 27 | Capricorn | 10:07 am |
| 29 | 8:05 pm | 29 | Aquarius | 9:46 pm |
| 31 | 11:02 pm | 4/1 | Pisces | 10:48 am |
| | | **April** | | |
| 3 | 11:36 am | 3 | Aries | 10:56 pm |
| 5 | 10:15 pm | 6 | Taurus | 9:06 am |
| 8 | 4:29 am | 8 | Gemini | 5:15 pm |
| 10 | 1:27 pm | 10 | Cancer | 11:31 pm |
| 12 | 7:33 pm | 13 | Leo | 3:50 am |
| 14 | 9:38 pm | 15 | Virgo | 6:14 am |
| 17 | 12:29 am | 17 | Libra | 7:22 am |
| 19 | 7:12 am | 19 | Scorpio | 8:41 am |
| 21 | 12:00 am | 21 | Sagittarius | 11:59 am |
| 23 | 7:44 am | 23 | Capricorn | 6:50 pm |
| 25 | 3:48 pm | 26 | Aquarius | 5:27 am |
| 28 | 5:44 am | 28 | Pisces | 6:11 pm |
| 30 | 5:57 pm | 5/1 | Aries | 6:24 am |

**Last Aspect**                    **Moon Enters New Sign**

| | | | | |
|---|---|---|---|---|
| **May** | | | | |
| 3 | 4:47 am | 3 | Taurus | 4:18 pm |
| 5 | 11:10 am | 5 | Gemini | 11:40 pm |
| 7 | 7:50 pm | 8 | Cancer | 5:06 am |
| 9 | 10:06 pm | 10 | Leo | 9:14 am |
| 12 | 8:24 am | 12 | Virgo | 12:22 pm |
| 14 | 1:19 pm | 14 | Libra | 2:51 pm |
| 16 | 5:37 am | 16 | Scorpio | 5:26 pm |
| 18 | 5:11 pm | 18 | Sagittarius | 9:21 pm |
| 20 | 1:05 pm | 21 | Capricorn | 3:56 am |
| 22 | 11:58 pm | 23 | Aquarius | 1:49 pm |
| 25 | 8:51 am | 26 | Pisces | 2:08 am |
| 28 | 12:21 am | 28 | Aries | 2:32 pm |
| 30 | 11:08 am | 31 | Taurus | 12:43 am |
| **June** | | | | |
| 1 | 6:53 pm | 2 | Gemini | 7:48 am |
| 4 | 11:42 am | 4 | Cancer | 12:17 pm |
| 6 | 10:10 am | 6 | Leo | 3:16 pm |
| 8 | 5:23 pm | 8 | Virgo | 5:45 pm |
| 10 | 8:01 am | 10 | Libra | 8:29 pm |
| 12 | 11:15 am | 13 | Scorpio | 12:02 am |
| 14 | 3:46 pm | 15 | Sagittarius | 5:03 am |
| 17 | 4:31 am | 17 | Capricorn | 12:13 pm |
| 19 | 7:19 am | 19 | Aquarius | 10:01 pm |
| 21 | 10:02 am | 22 | Pisces | 10:01 am |
| 24 | 7:10 pm | 24 | Aries | 10:38 pm |
| 27 | 3:51 am | 27 | Taurus | 9:32 am |
| 29 | 2:38 pm | 29 | Gemini | 5:09 pm |

| Last Aspect | | Moon Enters New Sign | | |
|---|---|---|---|---|
| | | July | | |
| 1 | 5:48 pm | 1 | Cancer | 9:24 pm |
| 3 | 10:25 am | 3 | Leo | 11:19 pm |
| 5 | 2:24 am | 6 | Virgo | 12:25 am |
| 7 | 12:50 pm | 8 | Libra | 2:07 am |
| 9 | 3:36 pm | 10 | Scorpio | 5:29 am |
| 11 | 8:28 pm | 12 | Sagittarius | 11:05 am |
| 13 | 9:30 pm | 14 | Capricorn | 7:05 pm |
| 16 | 5:38 pm | 17 | Aquarius | 5:19 am |
| 18 | 11:53 am | 19 | Pisces | 5:19 pm |
| 22 | 4:34 am | 22 | Aries | 6:02 am |
| 24 | 10:48 am | 24 | Taurus | 5:42 pm |
| 27 | 12:28 am | 27 | Gemini | 2:29 am |
| 28 | 11:24 am | 29 | Cancer | 7:31 am |
| 30 | 11:32 pm | 31 | Leo | 9:18 am |
| | | August | | |
| 1 | 4:48 pm | 2 | Virgo | 9:20 am |
| 4 | 12:27 am | 4 | Libra | 9:30 am |
| 6 | 3:36 am | 6 | Scorpio | 11:31 am |
| 8 | 10:58 am | 8 | Sagittarius | 4:35 pm |
| 10 | 3:50 pm | 11 | Capricorn | 12:50 am |
| 12 | 6:11 pm | 13 | Aquarius | 11:35 am |
| 15 | 9:02 pm | 15 | Pisces | 11:49 pm |
| 17 | 6:35 pm | 18 | Aries | 12:33 pm |
| 21 | 12:06 am | 21 | Taurus | 12:37 am |
| 22 | 5:33 pm | 23 | Gemini | 10:34 am |
| 25 | 2:58 am | 25 | Cancer | 5:05 pm |
| 27 | 4:55 am | 27 | Leo | 7:53 pm |
| 28 | 8:07 pm | 29 | Virgo | 7:57 pm |
| 31 | 4:46 am | 31 | Libra | 7:08 pm |

**Last Aspect**                    **Moon Enters New Sign**

| | | September | | |
|---|---|---|---|---|
| 2 | 4:34 am | 2 | Scorpio | 7:35 pm |
| 4 | 6:58 am | 4 | Sagittarius | 11:08 pm |
| 6 | 12:03 pm | 7 | Capricorn | 6:37 am |
| 9 | 4:30 am | 9 | Aquarius | 5:24 pm |
| 11 | 1:22 am | 12 | Pisces | 5:52 am |
| 14 | 12:33 am | 14 | Aries | 6:32 pm |
| 16 | 12:03 pm | 17 | Taurus | 6:31 am |
| 19 | 9:57 am | 19 | Gemini | 4:58 pm |
| 21 | 10:41 pm | 22 | Cancer | 12:50 am |
| 23 | 6:05 pm | 24 | Leo | 5:19 am |
| 25 | 12:14 pm | 26 | Virgo | 6:37 am |
| 27 | 11:58 pm | 28 | Libra | 6:03 am |
| 29 | 10:06 pm | 30 | Scorpio | 5:42 am |
| | | October | | |
| 2 | 5:46 am | 2 | Sagittarius | 7:44 am |
| 4 | 3:34 am | 4 | Capricorn | 1:43 pm |
| 6 | 7:25 pm | 6 | Aquarius | 11:42 pm |
| 8 | 2:27 pm | 9 | Pisces | 12:05 pm |
| 11 | 5:55 am | 12 | Aries | 12:46 am |
| 13 | 5:59 pm | 14 | Taurus | 12:24 pm |
| 16 | 4:37 am | 16 | Gemini | 10:30 pm |
| 18 | 10:14 pm | 19 | Cancer | 6:43 am |
| 21 | 8:39 am | 21 | Leo | 12:29 pm |
| 23 | 5:14 am | 23 | Virgo | 3:29 pm |
| 25 | 9:00 am | 25 | Libra | 4:20 pm |
| 27 | 4:22 am | 27 | Scorpio | 4:29 pm |
| 29 | 1:34 pm | 29 | Sagittarius | 5:58 pm |
| 31 | 10:30 am | 31 | Capricorn | 10:38 pm |

**Last Aspect**　　　　　**Moon Enters New Sign**

| | | | | |
|---|---|---|---|---|
| **November** | | | | |
| 3 | 1:46 am | 3 | Aquarius | 6:19 am |
| 5 | 9:37 am | 5 | Pisces | 6:08 pm |
| 7 | 8:13 pm | 8 | Aries | 6:49 am |
| 10 | 9:00 am | 10 | Taurus | 6:18 pm |
| 12 | 10:48 am | 13 | Gemini | 3:46 am |
| 15 | 6:40 am | 15 | Cancer | 11:15 am |
| 17 | 3:14 pm | 17 | Leo | 4:57 pm |
| 19 | 4:11 pm | 19 | Virgo | 8:54 pm |
| 21 | 10:31 pm | 21 | Libra | 11:20 pm |
| 23 | 9:49 pm | 24 | Scorpio | 12:58 am |
| 25 | 12:30 pm | 26 | Sagittarius | 3:11 am |
| 28 | 5:50 am | 28 | Capricorn | 7:33 am |
| 29 | 10:57 pm | 30 | Aquarius | 3:13 pm |
| **December** | | | | |
| 2 | 7:27 am | 3 | Pisces | 2:11 am |
| 5 | 3:15 am | 5 | Aries | 2:44 pm |
| 7 | 10:01 am | 8 | Taurus | 2:29 am |
| 9 | 8:13 pm | 10 | Gemini | 11:47 am |
| 12 | 12:12 am | 12 | Cancer | 6:23 pm |
| 14 | 10:57 am | 14 | Leo | 10:56 pm |
| 16 | 5:10 pm | 17 | Virgo | 2:16 am |
| 19 | 3:07 am | 19 | Libra | 5:04 am |
| 21 | 6:45 am | 21 | Scorpio | 7:57 am |
| 22 | 10:27 pm | 23 | Sagittarius | 11:34 am |
| 25 | 6:18 am | 25 | Capricorn | 4:45 pm |
| 27 | 4:03 pm | 28 | Aquarius | 12:21 am |
| 30 | 5:24 am | 30 | Pisces | 10:41 am |

# The Moon's Rhythm

The Moon journeys around Earth in an elliptical orbit that takes about 27.33 days, which is known as a sidereal month (period of revolution of one body about another). She can move up to 15 degrees or as few as 11 degrees in a day, with the fastest motion occurring when the Moon is at perigee (closest approach to Earth). The Moon is never retrograde, but when her motion is slow, the effect is similar to a retrograde period.

Astrologers have observed that people born on a day when the Moon is fast will process information differently from those who are born when the Moon is slow in motion. People born when the Moon is fast process information quickly and tend to react quickly, while those born during a slow Moon will be more deliberate.

The time from New Moon to New Moon is called the synodic month (involving a conjunction), and the average time span between this Sun-Moon alignment is 29.53 days. Since 29.53

won't divide into 365 evenly, we can have a month with two Full Moons or two New Moons.

## Moon Aspects

The aspects the Moon will make during the times you are considering are also important. A trine or sextile, and sometimes a conjunction, are considered favorable aspects. A trine or sextile between the Sun and Moon is an excellent foundation for success. Whether or not a conjunction is considered favorable depends upon the planet the Moon is making a conjunction to. If it's joining the Sun, Venus, Mercury, Jupiter, or even Saturn, the aspect is favorable. If the Moon joins Pluto or Mars, however, that would not be considered favorable. There may be exceptions, but it would depend on what you are electing to do. For example, a trine to Pluto might hasten the end of a relationship you want to be free of.

It is important to avoid times when the Moon makes an aspect to or is conjoining any retrograde planet, unless, of course, you want the thing started to end in failure.

After the Moon has completed an aspect to a planet, that planetary energy has passed. For example, if the Moon squares Saturn at 10:00 am, you can disregard Saturn's influence on your activity if it will occur after that time. You should always look ahead at aspects the Moon will make on the day in question, though, because if the Moon opposes Mars at 11:30 pm on that day, you can expect events that stretch into the evening to be affected by the Moon-Mars aspect. A testy conversation might lead to an argument, or more.

## Moon Signs

Much agricultural work is ruled by earth signs—Virgo, Capricorn, and Taurus. The air signs—Gemini, Aquarius, and Libra—rule flying and intellectual pursuits.

Each planet has one or two signs in which its characteristics are enhanced or "dignified," and the planet is said to "rule" that sign. The Sun rules Leo and the Moon rules Cancer, for example. The ruling planet for each sign is listed below. These should not be considered complete lists. We recommend that you purchase a book of planetary rulerships for more complete information.

### Aries Moon

The energy of an Aries Moon is masculine, dry, barren, and fiery. Aries provides great start-up energy, but things started at this time may be the result of impulsive action that lacks research or necessary support. Aries lacks staying power.

Use this assertive, outgoing Moon sign to initiate change, but have a plan in place for someone to pick up the reins when you're impatient to move on to the next thing. Work that requires skillful but not necessarily patient use of tools—cutting down trees, hammering, etc.—is appropriate in Aries. Expect things to occur rapidly but to also quickly pass. If you are prone to injury or accidents, exercise caution and good judgment in Aries-related activities.

RULER: Mars

IMPULSE: Action

RULES: Head and face

### Taurus Moon

A Taurus Moon's energy is feminine, semi-fruitful, and earthy. The Moon is exalted—very strong—in Taurus. Taurus is known as the farmer's sign because of its associations with farmland and precipitation that is the typical day-long "soaker" variety. Taurus energy is good to incorporate into your plans when patience, practicality, and perseverance are needed. Be aware, though, that you may also experience stubbornness in this sign.

Things started in Taurus tend to be long lasting and to increase in value. This can be very supportive energy in a marriage election. On the downside, the fixed energy of this sign resists change or the letting go of even the most difficult situations. A divorce following a marriage that occurred during a Taurus Moon may be difficult and costly to end. Things begun now tend to become habitual and hard to alter. If you want to make changes in something you started, it would be better to wait for Gemini. This is a good time to get a loan, but expect the people in charge of money to be cautious and slow to make decisions.

RULER: Venus

IMPULSE: Stability

RULES: Neck, throat, and voice

### Gemini Moon

A Gemini Moon's energy is masculine, dry, barren, and airy. People are more changeable than usual and may prefer to follow intellectual pursuits and play mental games rather than apply themselves to practical concerns.

This sign is not favored for agricultural matters, but it is an excellent time to prepare for activities, to run errands, and write letters. Plan to use a Gemini Moon to exchange ideas, meet people, go on vacations that include walking or biking, or be in situations that require versatility and quick thinking on your feet.

RULER: Mercury

IMPULSE: Versatility

RULES: Shoulders, hands, arms, lungs, and nervous system

### Cancer Moon

A Cancer Moon's energy is feminine, fruitful, moist, and very strong. Use this sign when you want to grow things—flowers, fruits, vegetables, commodities, stocks, or collections—for example. This sensitive sign stimulates rapport between people. Considered the most fertile of the signs, it is often associated with mothering. You can use this moontime to build personal friendships that support mutual growth.

Cancer is associated with emotions and feelings. Prominent Cancer energy promotes growth, but it can also turn people pouty and prone to withdrawing into their shells.

RULER: The Moon

IMPULSE: Tenacity

RULES: Chest area, breasts, and stomach

### Leo Moon

A Leo Moon's energy is masculine, hot, dry, fiery, and barren. Use it whenever you need to put on a show, make a presentation, or entertain colleagues or guests. This is a proud yet playful energy that exudes self-confidence and is often associated with romance.

This is an excellent time for fundraisers and ceremonies or to be straightforward, frank, and honest about something. It is advisable not to put yourself in a position of needing public approval or where you might have to cope with underhandedness, as trouble in these areas can bring out the worst Leo traits. There is a tendency in this sign to become arrogant or self-centered.

RULER: The Sun

IMPULSE: I am

RULES: Heart and upper back

### Virgo Moon

A Virgo Moon is feminine, dry, barren, earthy energy. It is favorable for anything that needs painstaking attention—especially those things where exactness rather than innovation is preferred.

Use this sign for activities when you must analyze information or when you must determine the value of something. Virgo is the sign of bargain hunting. It's friendly toward agricultural matters with an emphasis on animals and harvesting vegetables. It is an excellent time to care for animals, especially training them and veterinary work.

This sign is most beneficial when decisions have already been made and now need to be carried out. The inclination here is to see details rather than the bigger picture.

There is a tendency in this sign to overdo. Precautions should be taken to avoid becoming too dull from all work and no play. Build a little relaxation and pleasure into your routine from the beginning.

RULER: Mercury

IMPULSE: Discriminating

RULES: Abdomen and intestines

### Libra Moon

A Libra Moon's energy is masculine, semi-fruitful, and airy. This energy will benefit any attempt to bring beauty to a place or thing. Libra is considered good energy for starting things of an intellectual nature. Libra is the sign of partnership and unions, which makes it an excellent time to form partnerships of any kind, to make agreements, and to negotiate. Even though this sign is good for initiating things, it is crucial to work with a partner who will provide incentive and encouragement, however. A Libra Moon accentuates teamwork (particularly teams of two) and artistic work (especially work that involves color). Make use of this sign when you are decorating your home or shopping for better-quality clothing.

RULER: Venus

IMPULSE: Balance

RULES: Lower back, kidneys, and buttocks

### Scorpio Moon

The Scorpio Moon is feminine, fruitful, cold, and moist. It is useful when intensity (that sometimes borders on obsession) is needed. Scorpio is considered a very psychic sign. Use this Moon sign when you must back up something you strongly believe in, such as union or employer relations. There is strong group loyalty here, but a Scorpio Moon is also a good time to end connections thoroughly. This is also a good time to conduct research.

The desire nature is so strong here that there is a tendency to manipulate situations to get what one wants or to not see one's responsibility in an act.

RULER: Pluto, Mars (traditional)

IMPULSE: Transformation

RULES: Reproductive organs, genitals, groin, and pelvis

### Sagittarius Moon

The Moon's energy is masculine, dry, barren, and fiery in Sagittarius, encouraging flights of imagination and confidence in the flow of life. Sagittarius is the most philosophical sign. Candor and honesty are enhanced when the Moon is here. This is an excellent time to "get things off your chest" and to deal with institutions of higher learning, publishing companies, and the law. It's also a good time for sport and adventure.

Sagittarians are the crusaders of this world. This is a good time to tackle things that need improvement, but don't try to be the diplomat while influenced by this energy. Opinions can run strong, and the tendency to proselytize is increased.

RULER: Jupiter

IMPULSE: Expansion

RULES: Thighs and hips

### Capricorn Moon

In Capricorn the Moon's energy is feminine, semi-fruitful, and earthy. Because Cancer and Capricorn are polar opposites, the Moon's energy is thought to be weakened here. This energy encourages the need for structure, discipline, and organization. This is a good time to set goals and plan for the future, tend to family business, and to take care of details requiring patience or a businesslike manner. Institutional activities are favored. This sign should be avoided if you're seeking favors, as those in authority can be insensitive under this influence.

RULER: Saturn

IMPULSE: Ambitious

RULES: Bones, skin, and knees

## Aquarius Moon

An Aquarius Moon's energy is masculine, barren, dry, and airy. Activities that are unique, individualistic, concerned with humanitarian issues, society as a whole, and making improvements are favored under this Moon. It is this quality of making improvements that has caused this sign to be associated with inventors and new inventions.

An Aquarius Moon promotes the gathering of social groups for friendly exchanges. People tend to react and speak from an intellectual rather than emotional viewpoint when the Moon is in this sign.

RULER: Uranus and Saturn

IMPULSE: Reformer

RULES: Calves and ankles

## Pisces Moon

A Pisces Moon is feminine, fruitful, cool, and moist. This is an excellent time to retreat, meditate, sleep, pray, or make that dreamed-of escape into a fantasy vacation. However, things are not always what they seem to be with the Moon in Pisces. Personal boundaries tend to be fuzzy, and you may not be seeing things clearly. People tend to be idealistic under this sign, which can prevent them from seeing reality.

There is a live-and-let-live philosophy attached to this sign, which in the idealistic world may work well enough, but chaos is frequently the result. That's why this sign is also associated with alcohol and drug abuse, drug trafficking, and counterfeiting. On the lighter side, many musicians and artists are ruled by Pisces. It's only when they move too far away from reality that the dark side of substance abuse, suicide, or crime takes away life.

RULER: Jupiter and Neptune

IMPULSE: Empathetic

RULES: Feet

## More About Zodiac Signs

### *Element (Triplicity)*

Each of the zodiac signs is classified as belonging to an element; these are the four basic elements:

**Fire Signs**

Aries, Sagittarius, and Leo are action-oriented, outgoing, energetic, and spontaneous.

**Earth Signs**

Taurus, Capricorn, and Virgo are stable, conservative, practical, and oriented to the physical and material realm.

**Air Signs**

Gemini, Aquarius, and Libra are sociable and critical, and they tend to represent intellectual responses rather than feelings.

**Water Signs**

Cancer, Scorpio, and Pisces are emotional, receptive, intuitive, and can be very sensitive.

### *Quality (Quadruplicity)*

Each zodiac sign is further classified as being cardinal, mutable, or fixed. There are four signs in each quadruplicity, one sign from each element.

**Cardinal Signs**

Aries, Cancer, Libra, and Capricorn represent beginnings and newly initiated action. They initiate each new season in the cycle of the year.

**Fixed Signs**

Taurus, Leo, Scorpio, and Aquarius want to maintain the status quo through stubbornness and persistence; they represent that "between" time. For example, Leo is the month when summer really feels like summer.

**Mutable Signs**

Pisces, Gemini, Virgo, and Sagittarius adapt to change and tolerate situations. They represent the last month of each season, when things are changing in preparation for the coming season.

## *Nature and Fertility*

In addition to a sign's element and quality, each sign is further classified as either fruitful, semi-fruitful, or barren. This classification is the most important for readers who use the gardening information in the *Moon Sign Book* because the timing of most events depends on the fertility of the sign occupied by the Moon. The water signs of Cancer, Scorpio, and Pisces are the most fruitful. The semi-fruitful signs are the earth signs Taurus and Capricorn, and the air sign Libra. The barren signs correspond to fire-signs Aries, Leo, and Sagittarius; air-signs Gemini and Aquarius; and earth-sign Virgo.

2018 © Andrey Khokhlov Image from BigStockPhoto.com

# Good Timing

*By Sharon Leah*

Electional astrology is the art of electing times to begin any undertaking. Say, for example, you want to start a business. That business will experience ups and downs, as well as reach its potential, according to the promise held in the universe at the time the business was started—its birth time. The horoscope (birth chart) set for the date, time, and place that a business starts would indicate the outcome—its potential to succeed.

So, you might ask yourself the question: If the horoscope for a business start can show success or failure, why not begin at a time that is more favorable to the venture? Well, you can.

While no time is perfect, there are better times and better days to undertake specific activities. There are thousands of examples that prove electional astrology is not only practical, but that it can make a difference in our lives. There are rules for electing times to begin various activities—even shopping. You'll find detailed instructions about how to make elections beginning on page 107.

## Personalizing Elections

The election rules in this almanac are based upon the planetary positions at the time for which the election is made. They do not depend on any type of birth chart. However, a birth chart based upon the time, date, and birthplace of an event has advantages. No election is effective for every person. For example, you may leave home to begin a trip at the same time as a friend, but each of you will have a different experience according to whether or not your birth chart favors the trip.

Not all elections require a birth chart, but the timing of very important events—business starts, marriages, etc.—would benefit from the additional accuracy a birth chart provides. To order a birth chart for yourself or a planned event, visit our Web site at www .llewellyn.com.

### Some Things to Consider

You've probably experienced good timing in your life. Maybe you were at the right place at the right time to meet a friend whom you hadn't seen in years. Frequently, when something like that happens, it is the result of following an intuitive impulse—that "gut instinct." Consider for a moment that you were actually responding to planetary energies. Electional astrology is a tool that can help you to align with energies, present and future, that are available to us through planetary placements.

### Significators

Decide upon the important significators (planet, sign, and house ruling the matter) for which the election is being made. The Moon is the most important significator in any election, so the Moon should always be fortified (strong by sign and making favorable aspects to other planets). The Moon's aspects to other planets are more important than the sign the Moon is in.

Other important considerations are the significators of the Ascendant and Midheaven—the house ruling the election matter and the ruler of the sign on that house cusp. Finally, any planet or sign that has a general rulership over the matter in question should be taken into consideration.

### Nature and Fertility

Determine the general nature of the sign that is appropriate for your election. For example, much agricultural work is ruled by the earth signs of Virgo, Capricorn, and Taurus; while the air signs—Gemini, Aquarius, and Libra—rule intellectual pursuits.

### One Final Comment

Use common sense. If you must do something, like plant your garden or take an airplane trip on a day that doesn't have the best aspects, proceed anyway, but try to minimize problems. For example, leave early for the airport to avoid being left behind due to delays in the security lanes. When you have no other choice, do the best that you can under the circumstances at the time.

If you want to personalize your elections, please turn to page 107 for more information. If you want a quick and easy answer, you can refer to Llewellyn's Astro Almanac on the following pages.

## Llewellyn's Astro Almanac

The Astro Almanac tables, beginning on the next page, can help you find the dates best suited to particular activities. The dates provided are determined from the Moon's sign, phase, and aspects to other planets. Please note that the Astro Almanac does not take personal factors, such as your Sun and Moon sign, into account. The dates are general, and they will apply for everyone. Some activities will not have ideal dates during a particular month.

| Activity | January |
|---|---|
| Animals (Neuter or spay) | 2–5, 30, 31 |
| Animals (Sell or buy) | 7, 13 |
| Automobile (Buy) | 5, 18, 23 |
| Brewing | 1, 27, 28 |
| Build (Start foundation) | no ideal dates |
| Business (Conducting for self and others) | 11, 16, 25, 30 |
| Business (Start new) | 15 |
| Can Fruits and Vegetables | 1, 27, 28 |
| Can Preserves | 1, 27, 28 |
| Concrete (Pour) | 21, 22 |
| Construction (Begin new) | 8, 13, 16, 22, 25, 26, 30 |
| Consultants (Begin work with) | 3, 4, 8, 10, 13, 15, 22, 25, 26, 30 |
| Contracts (Bid on) | 8, 10, 13, 15 |
| Cultivate | no ideal dates |
| Decorating | 7–9, 17, 18 |
| Demolition | 2, 3, 21, 29, 30 |
| Electronics (Buy) | 9, 18, 25 |
| Entertain Guests | no ideal dates |
| Floor Covering (Laying new) | 2,1–27 |
| Habits (Break) | no ideal dates |
| Hair (Cut to increase growth) | 6, 7, 10, 11, 14–17 |
| Hair (Cut to decrease growth) | 2–5, 29–31 |
| Harvest (Grain for storage) | 22 |
| Harvest (Root crops) | 2–4, 21, 29–31 |
| Investments (New) | 16, 25 |
| Loan (Ask for) | 15, 16, 20, 21 |
| Massage (Relaxing) | 21, 26 |
| Mow Lawn (Decrease growth) | 1–4, 22–31 |
| Mow Lawn (Increase growth) | 6–19 |
| Mushrooms (Pick) | 20–22 |
| Negotiate (Business for the elderly) | 10, 15, 23 |
| Prune for Better Fruit | 1, 2, 27–31 |
| Prune to Promote Healing | 5 |
| Wean Children | 2–9, 30, 31 |
| Wood Floors (Installing) | 4, 5 |
| Write Letters or Contracts | 4, 9, 18, 22, 31 |

| Activity | February |
|---|---|
| Animals (Neuter or spay) | 2, 3, 26–28 |
| Animals (Sell or buy) | 6, 9, 11, 18 |
| Automobile (Buy) | 2, 15, 20 |
| Brewing | 24, 25 |
| Build (Start foundation) | 7, 12 |
| Business (Conducting for self and others) | 10, 15, 23, 28 |
| Business (Start new) | 12 |
| Can Fruits and Vegetables | 24, 25 |
| Can Preserves | 2, 25 |
| Concrete (Pour) | no ideal dates |
| Construction (Begin new) | 4, 9, 10, 15, 18, 22, 28 |
| Consultants (Begin work with) | 4, 5, 9, 10, 16, 18, 22, 25, 27 |
| Contracts (Bid on) | 5, 9, 10, 16, 18 |
| Cultivate | no ideal dates |
| Decorating | 4, 5, 13–15 |
| Demolition | 25–28 |
| Electronics (Buy) | 5, 15 |
| Entertain Guests | no ideal dates |
| Floor Covering (Laying new) | 3, 2—23 |
| Habits (Break) | 3, 28 |
| Hair (Cut to increase growth) | 6, 7, 10–14, 17 |
| Hair (Cut to decrease growth) | 2, 25–28 |
| Harvest (Grain for storage) | 25 |
| Harvest (Root crops) | 3, 25–27 |
| Investments (New) | 15, 23 |
| Loan (Ask for) | 10–13, 17, 18 |
| Massage (Relaxing) | 11 |
| Mow Lawn (Decrease growth) | 2, 3, 20–28 |
| Mow Lawn (Increase growth) | 5–18 |
| Mushrooms (Pick) | 18–20 |
| Negotiate (Business for the elderly) | 20, 24 |
| Prune for Better Fruit | 23–27 |
| Prune to Promote Healing | 2, 3, 28 |
| Wean Children | 2–5, 26–28 |
| Wood Floors (Installing) | 2, 3, 28 |
| Write Letters or Contracts | 5, 15, 19, 28 |

| Activity | March |
|---|---|
| Animals (Neuter or spay) | 1, 2, 28, 29 |
| Animals (Sell or buy) | 8, 9, 13 |
| Automobile (Buy) | 1, 2, 18, 20, 27–29 |
| Brewing | 23 |
| Build (Start foundation) | 11 |
| Business (Conducting for self and others) | 11, 16, 25, 30 |
| Business (Start new) | 11, 20 |
| Can Fruits and Vegetables | 6, 23 |
| Can Preserves | 23 |
| Concrete (Pour) | 3, 4, 30, 31 |
| Construction (Begin new) | 4, 9, 11, 16, 18, 22, 25, 30, 31 |
| Consultants (Begin work with) | 2, 4, 7, 9, 12, 16, 18, 22, 24, 26, 28, 31 |
| Contracts (Bid on) | 7, 9, 12, 16, 18 |
| Cultivate | 3, 4, 25, 26, 30, 31 |
| Decorating | 12–14 |
| Demolition | 25, 26 |
| Electronics (Buy) | 5 |
| Entertain Guests | 22 |
| Floor Covering (Laying new) | 2–5, 21, 22, 30, 31 |
| Habits (Break) | 1, 2, 4, 5, 28–31 |
| Hair (Cut to increase growth) | 6, 10–13, 16 |
| Hair (Cut to decrease growth) | 1, 25–28 |
| Harvest (Grain for storage) | 25, 26 |
| Harvest (Root crops) | 2–4, 25, 26, 30, 31 |
| Investments (New) | 16, 25 |
| Loan (Ask for) | 10–12, 161–18 |
| Massage (Relaxing) | 2, 22 |
| Mow Lawn (Decrease growth) | 1–5, 21–31 |
| Mow Lawn (Increase growth) | 7–19 |
| Mushrooms (Pick) | 19–21 |
| Negotiate (Business for the elderly) | 6, 11 |
| Prune for Better Fruit | 22–24, 26 |
| Prune to Promote Healing | 1, 2, 27–29 |
| Wean Children | 1–5, 25–31 |
| Wood Floors (Installing) | 1, 2, 27–29 |
| Write Letters or Contracts | 5, 7, 18, 27 |

| Activity | April |
|---|---|
| Animals (Neuter or spay) | 1–3, 29, 30 |
| Animals (Sell or buy) | 7, 14, 18 |
| Automobile (Buy) | 15, 16, 23, 25 |
| Brewing | 2, 3, 20, 29, 30 |
| Build (Start foundation) | 7 |
| Business (Conducting for self and others) | 10, 14, 24, 29 |
| Business (Start new) | 7, 16 |
| Can Fruits and Vegetables | 2, 3, 20, 29, 30 |
| Can Preserves | 20 |
| Concrete (Pour) | 27, 28 |
| Construction (Begin new) | 5, 10, 14, 18, 24, 28 |
| Consultants (Begin work with) | 2, 5, 8, 12, 14, 18, 21, 23, 27, 28 |
| Contracts (Bid on) | 8, 12, 14, 18 |
| Cultivate | 4, 5, 22, 23, 27, 28 |
| Decorating | 8–10, 17–19 |
| Demolition | 4, 5, 21, 22 |
| Electronics (Buy) | 27 |
| Entertain Guests | no ideal dates |
| Floor Covering (Laying new) | 1, 26–28 |
| Habits (Break) | 4, 27, 28 |
| Hair (Cut to increase growth) | 6–9, 13 |
| Hair (Cut to decrease growth) | 1, 2, 21–25, 29, 30 |
| Harvest (Grain for storage) | 21–23, 26 |
| Harvest (Root crops) | 4, 21, 22, 23, 26–28 |
| Investments (New) | 14, 24 |
| Loan (Ask for) | 6–8, 13–15 |
| Massage (Relaxing) | 7, 12, 26 |
| Mow Lawn (Decrease growth) | 1–4, 20–30 |
| Mow Lawn (Increase growth) | 6–18 |
| Mushrooms (Pick) | 18–20 |
| Negotiate (Business for the elderly) | 7, 16, 20, 30 |
| Prune for Better Fruit | 19–22 |
| Prune to Promote Healing | 24, 25 |
| Wean Children | 22–28 |
| Wood Floors (Installing) | 23–25 |
| Write Letters or Contracts | 1, 2, 11, 15, 23, 29 |

| Activity | May |
|---|---|
| Animals (Neuter or spay) | 26–28 |
| Animals (Sell or buy) | 12, 16 |
| Automobile (Buy) | 12, 13, 21, 22 |
| Brewing | 26–28 |
| Build (Start foundation) | 5 |
| Business (Conducting for self and others) | 9, 14, 23, 29 |
| Business (Start new) | 5, 13, 14 |
| Can Fruits and Vegetables | 26, 27 |
| Can Preserves | 4, 31 |
| Concrete (Pour) | 24, 31 |
| Construction (Begin new) | 3, 9, 12, 14, 16, 23, 25, 29, 30 |
| Consultants (Begin work with) | 3, 8, 12, 13, 16, 20, 24, 25, 30 |
| Contracts (Bid on) | 8, 12, 13, 16 |
| Cultivate | 1–3, 19, 20, 29, 30 |
| Decorating | 6, 7, 14–16 |
| Demolition | 1, 2, 19–21, 29, 30 |
| Electronics (Buy) | 24 |
| Entertain Guests | 12 |
| Floor Covering (Laying new) | 3, 4, 23–25, 31 |
| Habits (Break) | 1, 3 |
| Hair (Cut to increase growth) | 5–7, 10 |
| Hair (Cut to decrease growth) | 3, 4, 19–22, 26, 27, 31 |
| Harvest (Grain for storage) | 19–21, 23, 24 |
| Harvest (Root crops) | 1–3, 19, 20, 23–25, 29, 30 |
| Investments (New) | 14, 23 |
| Loan (Ask for) | 5, 10–12 |
| Massage (Relaxing) | 12 |
| Mow Lawn (Decrease growth) | 1–3, 19–31 |
| Mow Lawn (Increase growth) | 5–17 |
| Mushrooms (Pick) | 17–19 |
| Negotiate (Business for the elderly) | 13, 27 |
| Prune for Better Fruit | 18–20 |
| Prune to Promote Healing | 21, 22 |
| Wean Children | 19—25 |
| Wood Floors (Installing) | 21, 22 |
| Write Letters or Contracts | 3, 8, 12, 21, 26 |

| Activity | June |
|---|---|
| Animals (Neuter or spay) | no ideal dates |
| Animals (Sell or buy) | 6, 8 |
| Automobile (Buy) | 4, 9, 10, 17, 18, 29 |
| Brewing | 23, 24 |
| Build (Start foundation) | no ideal dates |
| Business (Conducting for self and others) | 7, 12, 22, 27 |
| Business (Start new) | 10 |
| Can Fruits and Vegetables | 23, 24 |
| Can Preserves | 1, 28, 29 |
| Concrete (Pour) | 1, 20, 21, 28, 29 |
| Construction (Begin new) | 7, 8, 12, 21, 26, 27 |
| Consultants (Begin work with) | 4, 8, 9, 12, 14, 16, 21, 24, 26, 29 |
| Contracts (Bid on) | 4, 8, 9, 12, 14, 16 |
| Cultivate | 25–27, 30 |
| Decorating | 3, 4, 11, 12 |
| Demolition | 25, 26 |
| Electronics (Buy) | 4, 29 |
| Entertain Guests | 11, 31 |
| Floor Covering (Laying new) | 27–30 |
| Habits (Break) | 2, 29, 30 |
| Hair (Cut to increase growth) | 3, 6, 15, 16 |
| Hair (Cut to decrease growth) | 1, 2, 18, 23, 27–30 |
| Harvest (Grain for storage) | 19–21, 24 |
| Harvest (Root crops) | 2, 17, 20, 21, 25, 26, 29, 30 |
| Investments (New) | 12, 22 |
| Loan (Ask for) | 6–8 |
| Massage (Relaxing) | 1, 6, 11, 21 |
| Mow Lawn (Decrease growth) | 1, 2, 18–30 |
| Mow Lawn (Increase growth) | 4–16 |
| Mushrooms (Pick) | 16–18 |
| Negotiate (Business for the elderly) | 1, 14, 23, 28 |
| Prune for Better Fruit | no ideal dates |
| Prune to Promote Healing | 17–19 |
| Wean Children | 15–22 |
| Wood Floors (Installing) | 17–19 |
| Write Letters or Contracts | 4, 9, 17, 22 |

| Activity | July |
|----------|------|
| Animals (Neuter or spay) | no ideal dates |
| Animals (Sell or buy) | 5, 6 |
| Automobile (Buy) | 6, 7, 15, 16 |
| Brewing | 20, 21, 30 |
| Build (Start foundation) | 7 |
| Business (Conducting for self and others) | 7, 11, 22, 27 |
| Business (Start new) | 7 |
| Can Fruits and Vegetables | 2, 20, 21, 30 |
| Can Preserves | 2, 25, 30 |
| Concrete (Pour) | 18, 19, 25 |
| Construction (Begin new) | 5, 7, 9, 18, 23, 27 |
| Consultants (Begin work with) | 4, 5, 8, 9, 12, 13, 18, 22, 23, 26, 30 |
| Contracts (Bid on) | 4, 5, 8, 9, 12, 13 |
| Cultivate | 1, 27, 28 |
| Decorating | 8, 9 |
| Demolition | 22, 23, 31 |
| Electronics (Buy) | 8 |
| Entertain Guests | 31 |
| Floor Covering (Laying new) | 17, 18, 24–28, 31 |
| Habits (Break) | 1, 27, 28 |
| Hair (Cut to increase growth) | 3, 12–16 |
| Hair (Cut to decrease growth) | 19–21, 24–28, 31 |
| Harvest (Grain for storage) | 17–19, 22–24 |
| Harvest (Root crops) | 1, 17–19, 22–24, 27, 28 |
| Investments (New) | 11, 22 |
| Loan (Ask for) | 3–5 |
| Massage (Relaxing) | 27, 31 |
| Mow Lawn (Decrease growth) | 1, 17–30 |
| Mow Lawn (Increase growth) | 3–15 |
| Mushrooms (Pick) | 15–17 |
| Negotiate (Business for the elderly) | 11 |
| Prune for Better Fruit | no ideal dates |
| Prune to Promote Healing | 16 |
| Wean Children | 13–19 |
| Wood Floors (Installing) | 16 |
| Write Letters or Contracts | 2, 6, 15, 20, 29 |

| Activity | August |
|---|---|
| Animals (Neuter or spay) | no ideal dates |
| Animals (Sell or buy) | 5, 9, 14 |
| Automobile (Buy) | 2–4, 11, 12, 25, 29, 30 |
| Brewing | 16–18, 26, 27 |
| Build (Start foundation) | 3, 30 |
| Business (Conducting for self and others) | 5, 10, 20, 25 |
| Business (Start new) | 3, 30 |
| Can Fruits and Vegetables | 16, 17, 26, 27 |
| Can Preserves | 21, 22, 26, 27 |
| Concrete (Pour) | 21, 22, 28, 29 |
| Construction (Begin new) | 1, 5, 10, 14, 19, 20, 25, 28 |
| Consultants (Begin work with) | 1, 4, 5, 8, 9, 14, 19, 25, 28, 29 |
| Contracts (Bid on) | 1, 4, 5, 8, 9, 14 |
| Cultivate | 24, 25, 28–30 |
| Decorating | 4–6, 13, 14 |
| Demolition | 18–21, 28 |
| Electronics (Buy) | 25 |
| Entertain Guests | 5 |
| Floor Covering (Laying new) | 21–24, 28–30 |
| Habits (Break) | 24, 25, 28, 29 |
| Hair (Cut to increase growth) | 8–12 |
| Hair (Cut to decrease growth) | 16, 17, 21–24, 27 |
| Harvest (Grain for storage) | 18, 19 |
| Harvest (Root crops) | 15, 18–21, 23–25, 28, 29 |
| Investments (New) | 10, 20 |
| Loan (Ask for) | 1 |
| Massage (Relaxing) | 5, 26 |
| Mow Lawn (Decrease growth) | 16–29 |
| Mow Lawn (Increase growth) | 1–14, 31 |
| Mushrooms (Pick) | 14–16 |
| Negotiate (Business for the elderly) | 3, 7, 30 |
| Prune for Better Fruit | no ideal dates |
| Prune to Promote Healing | no ideal dates |
| Wean Children | 9–15 |
| Wood Floors (Installing) | no ideal dates |
| Write Letters or Contracts | 2, 11, 26, 29, 30 |

| Activity | September |
|---|---|
| Animals (Neuter or spay) | no ideal dates |
| Animals (Sell or buy) | 1, 4, 9, 11, 29 |
| Automobile (Buy) | 7, 8, 20, 26, 27 |
| Brewing | 22, 23 |
| Build (Start foundation) | 3 |
| Business (Conducting for self and others) | 3, 8, 19, 24 |
| Business (Start new) | no ideal dates |
| Can Fruits and Vegetables | 22, 23 |
| Can Preserves | 18, 19, 22, 23 |
| Concrete (Pour) | 18, 19, 25 |
| Construction (Begin new) | 1, 8, 11, 16, 19, 24, 25, 29 |
| Consultants (Begin work with) | 1, 3, 6, 8, 11, 16, 20, 25, 29 |
| Contracts (Bid on) | 1, 3, 6, 8, 11, 29 |
| Cultivate | 24–27 |
| Decorating | 1, 2, 9–11, 28, 29 |
| Demolition | 14–16, 24, 25 |
| Electronics (Buy) | 20, 29 |
| Entertain Guests | 29 |
| Floor Covering (Laying new) | 17–21, 24–28 |
| Habits (Break) | 24–26 |
| Hair (Cut to increase growth) | 5–8, 12 |
| Hair (Cut to decrease growth) | 17–21, 24 |
| Harvest (Grain for storage) | 15, 16, 19, 20 |
| Harvest (Root crops) | 14–16, 20, 21, 24, 25 |
| Investments (New) | 8, 19 |
| Loan (Ask for) | no ideal dates |
| Massage (Relaxing) | 25, 29 |
| Mow Lawn (Decrease growth) | 15–27 |
| Mow Lawn (Increase growth) | 1–12, 29, 30 |
| Mushrooms (Pick) | 13–15 |
| Negotiate (Business for the elderly) | 3, 13, 18 |
| Prune for Better Fruit | no ideal dates |
| Prune to Promote Healing | no ideal dates |
| Wean Children | 5–11 |
| Wood Floors (Installing) | no ideal dates |
| Write Letters or Contracts | 7, 12, 22, 26, 29 |

| Activity | October |
|---|---|
| Animals (Neuter or spay) | no ideal dates |
| Animals (Sell or buy) | 8, 9 |
| Automobile (Buy) | 4, 5, 23–25 |
| Brewing | 20, 21 |
| Build (Start foundation) | 1, 28 |
| Business (Conducting for self and others) | 3, 8, 18, 23 |
| Business (Start new) | no ideal dates |
| Can Fruits and Vegetables | 20 |
| Can Preserves | 15, 16, 20 |
| Concrete (Pour) | 15, 16, 22, 23 |
| Construction (Begin new) | 3, 8, 13, 18, 23, 27 |
| Consultants (Begin work with) | 3, 4, 8, 10, 13, 20, 23, 25, 27, 29 |
| Contracts (Bid on) | 3, 4, 8, 10, 13, 29, 31 |
| Cultivate | 22–25 |
| Decorating | 7, 8 |
| Demolition | 13, 21, 22 |
| Electronics (Buy) | no ideal dates |
| Entertain Guests | no ideal dates |
| Floor Covering (Laying new) | 14–18, 21–27 |
| Habits (Break) | 22, 23 |
| Hair (Cut to increase growth) | 2–5, 10, 11, 29–31 |
| Hair (Cut to decrease growth) | 14–18, 21 |
| Harvest (Grain for storage) | 16–18 |
| Harvest (Root crops) | 17, 18, 21–23 |
| Investments (New) | 8, 18 |
| Loan (Ask for) | no ideal dates |
| Massage (Relaxing) | 20 |
| Mow Lawn (Decrease growth) | 14–26 |
| Mow Lawn (Increase growth) | 1–12, 28–31 |
| Mushrooms (Pick) | 12–14 |
| Negotiate (Business for the elderly) | 10, 15, 24, 28 |
| Prune for Better Fruit | 27 |
| Prune to Promote Healing | no ideal dates |
| Wean Children | 2–8, 30, 31 |
| Wood Floors (Installing) | no ideal dates |
| Write Letters or Contracts | 5, 9, 19, 23, 29 |

| Activity | November |
|---|---|
| Animals (Neuter or spay) | no ideal dates |
| Animals (Sell or buy) | 5, 9 |
| Automobile (Buy) | 1–3, 20, 21, 28, 29 |
| Brewing | 16, 17, 24, 25 |
| Build (Start foundation) | 2, 29 |
| Business (Conducting for self and others) | 1, 6, 17, 21 |
| Business (Start new) | 12 |
| Can Fruits and Vegetables | 16, 17, 24, 25 |
| Can Preserves | 16, 17, 24, 25 |
| Concrete (Pour) | 18, 19 |
| Construction (Begin new) | 1, 5, 10, 17, 19, 21, 23 |
| Consultants (Begin work with) | 3, 5, 7, 10, 16, 19, 20, 23, 24, 28, 29 |
| Contracts (Bid on) | 3, 5, 7, 10, 28, 29 |
| Cultivate | 20, 21 |
| Decorating | 4, 5, 30 |
| Demolition | 17, 18, 26 |
| Electronics (Buy) | no ideal dates |
| Entertain Guests | 19, 23 |
| Floor Covering (Laying new) | 13, 14, 17–23 |
| Habits (Break) | no ideal dates |
| Hair (Cut to increase growth) | 13, 14, 17 |
| Hair (Cut to decrease growth) | 1, 2, 6, 7, 10, 11, 28, 29 |
| Harvest (Grain for storage) | 13, 14, 17–19 |
| Harvest (Root crops) | 13, 14, 17–19 |
| Investments (New) | 6, 17 |
| Loan (Ask for) | 10, 11 |
| Massage (Relaxing) | 3, 19, 23 |
| Mow Lawn (Decrease growth) | 13–25 |
| Mow Lawn (Increase growth) | 1–11, 27–30 |
| Mushrooms (Pick) | 11–13 |
| Negotiate (Business for the elderly) | no ideal dates |
| Prune for Better Fruit | 24, 25 |
| Prune to Promote Healing | no ideal dates |
| Wean Children | 1–5, 26–30 |
| Wood Floors (Installing) | no ideal dates |
| Write Letters or Contracts | 1, 6, 15, 20, 24, 28 |

| Activity | December |
|---|---|
| Animals (Neuter or spay) | 23–26 |
| Animals (Sell or buy) | 3, 8 |
| Automobile (Buy) | 17, 18, 25, 27 |
| Brewing | 13, 14, 22 |
| Build (Start foundation) | 4, 27 |
| Business (Conducting for self and others) | 1, 6, 16, 21, 31 |
| Business (Start new) | 8, 9 |
| Can Fruits and Vegetables | 13, 14, 22 |
| Can Preserves | 13, 14, 22 |
| Concrete (Pour) | 15 |
| Construction (Begin new) | 1, 6, 8, 16, 17, 21 |
| Consultants (Begin work with) | 3, 5, 8, 15, 17, 20, 21, 25, 26, 30 |
| Contracts (Bid on) | 3, 5, 8, 30 |
| Cultivate | 19 |
| Decorating | 1, 2, 10, 11, 28, 30 |
| Demolition | 15, 16, 23, 24 |
| Electronics (Buy) | 20 |
| Entertain Guests | no ideal dates |
| Floor Covering (Laying new) | 15–21 |
| Habits (Break) | no ideal dates |
| Hair (Cut to increase growth) | 4, 8–10, 26, 27, 30, 31 |
| Hair (Cut to decrease growth) | 14, 23–25 |
| Harvest (Grain for storage) | 14–16 |
| Harvest (Root crops) | 12, 15, 16, 23, 24 |
| Investments (New) | 6, 16 |
| Loan (Ask for) | 8–10 |
| Massage (Relaxing) | 9, 28 |
| Mow Lawn (Decrease growth) | 13–24 |
| Mow Lawn (Increase growth) | 1–10, 27, 28, 30, 31 |
| Mushrooms (Pick) | 11–13 |
| Negotiate (Business for the elderly) | 4, 9, 18, 22 |
| Prune for Better Fruit | 21–24 |
| Prune to Promote Healing | no ideal dates |
| Wean Children | 1, 2, 24–30 |
| Wood Floors (Installing) | 25 |
| Write Letters or Contracts | 3, 12, 17, 25, 30 |

# Choose the Best Time for Your Activities

When rules for elections refer to "favorable" and "unfavorable" aspects to your Sun or other planets, please refer to the Favorable and Unfavorable Days Tables and Lunar Aspectarian for more information. You'll find instructions beginning on page 129 and the tables beginning on page 136.

The material in this section came from several sources including: *The New A to Z Horoscope Maker and Delineator* by Llewellyn George (Llewellyn, 1999), *Moon Sign Book* (Llewellyn, 1945), and *Electional Astrology* by Vivian Robson (Slingshot Publishing, 2000). Robson's book was originally published in 1937.

## Advertise (Internet)

The Moon should be conjunct, sextile, or trine Mercury or Uranus and in the sign of Gemini, Capricorn, or Aquarius.

## Advertise (Print)

Write ads on a day favorable to your Sun. The Moon should be conjunct, sextile, or trine Mercury or Venus. Avoid hard aspects to Mars and Saturn. Ad campaigns produce the best results when the Moon is well aspected in Gemini (to enhance communication) or Capricorn (to build business).

## Animals

Take home new pets when the day is favorable to your Sun, or when the Moon is trine, sextile, or conjunct Mercury, Jupiter or Venus, or in the sign of Virgo or Pisces. However, avoid days when the Moon is either square or opposing the Sun, Mars, Saturn, Uranus, Neptune, or Pluto. When selecting a pet, have the Moon well aspected by the planet that rules the animal. Cats are ruled by the Sun, dogs by Mercury, birds by Venus, horses by Jupiter, and fish by Neptune. Buy large animals when the Moon is in Sagittarius or Pisces and making favorable aspects to Jupiter or Mercury. Buy animals smaller than sheep when the Moon is in Virgo with favorable aspects to Mercury or Venus.

## Animals (Breed)

Animals are easiest to handle when the Moon is in Taurus, Cancer, Libra, or Pisces, but try to avoid the Full Moon. To encourage healthy births, animals should be mated so births occur when the Moon is increasing in Taurus, Cancer, Pisces, or Libra. Those born during a semi-fruitful sign (Taurus and Capricorn) will produce leaner meat. Libra yields beautiful animals for showing and racing.

## Animals (Declaw)

Declaw cats for medical purposes in the dark of the Moon. Avoid the week before and after the Full Moon and the sign of Pisces.

## Animals (Neuter or Spay)

Have livestock and pets neutered or spayed when the Moon is in Sagittarius, Capricorn, or Pisces, after it has passed through Scorpio, the sign that rules reproductive organs. Avoid the week before and after the Full Moon.

## Animals (Sell or Buy)

In either buying or selling, it is important to keep the Moon and Mercury free from any aspect to Mars. Aspects to Mars will create discord and increase the likelihood of wrangling over price and quality. The Moon should be passing from the first quarter to full and sextile or trine Venus or Jupiter. When buying racehorses, let the Moon be in an air sign. The Moon should be in air signs when you buy birds. If the birds are to be pets, let the Moon be in good aspect to Venus.

## Animals (Train)

Train pets when the Moon is in Virgo or trine to Mercury.

## Animals (Train Dogs to Hunt)

Let the Moon be in Aries in conjunction with Mars, which makes them courageous and quick to learn. But let Jupiter also be in aspect to preserve them from danger in hunting.

## Automobiles

When buying an automobile, select a time when the Moon is conjunct, sextile, or trine to Mercury, Saturn, or Uranus and in the sign of Gemini or Capricorn. Avoid times when Mercury is in retrograde motion.

## Baking Cakes

Your cakes will have a lighter texture if you see that the Moon is in Gemini, Libra, or Aquarius and in good aspect to Venus or Mercury. If you are decorating a cake or confections are being made, have the Moon placed in Libra.

## Beauty Treatments (Massage, etc.)

See that the Moon is in Taurus, Cancer, Leo, Libra, or Aquarius and in favorable aspect to Venus. In the case of plastic surgery, aspects to Mars should be avoided, and the Moon should not be in the sign ruling the part to be operated on.

## Borrow (Money or Goods)

See that the Moon is not placed between 15 degrees Libra and 15 degrees Scorpio. Let the Moon be waning and in Leo, Scorpio (16 to 30 degrees), Sagittarius, or Pisces. Venus should be in good aspect to the Moon, and the Moon should not be square, opposing, or conjunct either Saturn or Mars.

## Brewing

Start brewing during the third or fourth quarter, when the Moon is in Cancer, Scorpio, or Pisces.

## Build (Start Foundation)

Turning the first sod for the foundation marks the beginning of the building. For best results, excavate the site when the Moon is in the first quarter of a fixed sign and making favorable aspects to Saturn.

## Business (Start New)

When starting a business, have the Moon be in Taurus, Virgo, or Capricorn and increasing. The Moon should be sextile or trine Jupiter or Saturn, but avoid oppositions or squares. The planet ruling the business should be well aspected, too.

## Buy Goods

Buy during the third quarter, when the Moon is in Taurus for quality or in a mutable sign (Gemini, Sagittarius, Virgo, or Pisces) for savings. Good aspects to Venus or the Sun are desirable. If you are buying for yourself, it is good if the day is favorable for your Sun sign. You may also apply rules for buying specific items.

## Canning

Can fruits and vegetables when the Moon is in either the third or fourth quarter and in the water sign Cancer or Pisces. Preserves and jellies use the same quarters and the signs Cancer, Pisces, or Taurus.

## Clothing

Buy clothing on a day that is favorable for your Sun sign and when Venus or Mercury is well aspected. Avoid aspects to Mars and Saturn. Buy your clothing when the Moon is in Taurus if you want to remain satisfied. Do not buy clothing or jewelry when the Moon is in Scorpio or Aries. See that the Moon is sextile or trine the Sun during the first or second quarters.

## Collections

Try to make collections on days when your natal Sun is well aspected. Avoid days when the Moon is opposing or square Mars or Saturn. If possible, the Moon should be in a cardinal sign (Aries, Cancer, Libra, or Capricorn). It is more difficult to collect when the Moon is in Taurus or Scorpio.

## Concrete

Pour concrete when the Moon is in the third quarter of the fixed sign Taurus, Leo, or Aquarius.

## Construction (Begin New)

The Moon should be sextile or trine Jupiter. According to Hermes, no building should be begun when the Moon is in Scorpio or Pisces. The best time to begin building is when the Moon is in Aquarius.

## Consultants (Work with)

The Moon should be conjunct, sextile, or trine Mercury or Jupiter.

## Contracts (Bid On)

The Moon should be in Gemini or Capricorn and either the Moon or Mercury should be conjunct, sextile, or trine Jupiter.

## Copyrights/Patents

The Moon should be conjunct, trine, or sextile either Mercury or Jupiter.

## Coronations and Installations

Let the Moon be in Leo and in favorable aspect to Venus, Jupiter, or Mercury. The Moon should be applying to these planets.

## Cultivate

Cultivate when the Moon is in a barren sign and waning, ideally the fourth quarter in Aries, Gemini, Leo, Virgo, or Aquarius. The third quarter in the sign of Sagittarius will also work.

## Cut Timber

Timber cut during the waning Moon does not become worm-eaten; it will season well and not warp, decay, or snap during burning. Cut when the Moon is in Taurus, Gemini, Virgo, or Capricorn—especially in August. Avoid the water signs. Look for favorable aspects to Mars.

## Decorating or Home Repairs

Have the Moon waxing and in the sign of Libra, Gemini, or Aquarius. Avoid squares or oppositions to either Mars or Saturn. Venus in good aspect to Mars or Saturn is beneficial.

## Demolition

Let the waning Moon be in Leo, Sagittarius, or Aries.

## Dental and Dentists

Visit the dentist when the Moon is in Virgo, or pick a day marked favorable for your Sun sign. Mars should be marked sextile, conjunct, or trine; avoid squares or oppositions to Saturn, Uranus, or Jupiter.

Teeth are best removed when the Moon is in Gemini, Virgo, Sagittarius, or Pisces and during the first or second quarter. Avoid the Full Moon! The day should be favorable for your lunar cycle, and Mars and Saturn should be marked conjunct, trine, or sextile. Fillings should be done in the third or fourth quarters in the sign of Taurus, Leo, Scorpio, or Pisces. The same applies for dentures.

## Dressmaking

William Lilly wrote in 1676: "Make no new clothes, or first put them on when the Moon is in Scorpio or afflicted by Mars, for they will be apt to be torn and quickly worn out." Design, repair, and sew clothes in the first and second quarters of Taurus, Leo, or Libra on a day marked favorable for your Sun sign. Venus, Jupiter, and Mercury should be favorably aspected, but avoid hard aspects to Mars or Saturn.

## Egg-Setting (see p. 161)

Eggs should be set so chicks will hatch during fruitful signs. To set eggs, subtract the number of days given for incubation or

2018 © Okrasyuk Image from BigStockPhoto.com

gestation from the fruitful dates. Chickens incubate in twenty-one days, turkeys and geese in twenty-eight days.

A freshly laid egg loses quality rapidly if it is not handled properly. Use plenty of clean litter in the nests to reduce the number of dirty or cracked eggs. Gather eggs daily in mild weather and at least two times daily in hot or cold weather. The eggs should be placed in a cooler immediately after gathering and stored at 50 to 55°F. Do not store eggs with foods or products that give off pungent odors since eggs may absorb the odors.

Eggs saved for hatching purposes should not be washed. Only clean and slightly soiled eggs should be saved for hatching. Dirty eggs should not be incubated. Eggs should be stored in a cool place with the large ends up. It is not advisable to store the eggs longer than one week before setting them in an incubator.

## Electricity and Gas (Install)
The Moon should be in a fire sign, and there should be no squares, oppositions, or conjunctions with Uranus (ruler of electricity), Neptune (ruler of gas), Saturn, or Mars. Hard aspects to Mars can cause fires.

## Electronics (Buying)
Choose a day when the Moon is in an air sign (Gemini, Libra, Aquarius) and well aspected by Mercury and/or Uranus when buying electronics.

## Electronics (Repair)
The Moon should be sextile or trine Mars or Uranus and in a fixed sign (Taurus, Leo, Scorpio, Aquarius).

## Entertain Friends
Let the Moon be in Leo or Libra and making good aspects to Venus. Avoid squares or oppositions to either Mars or Saturn by the Moon or Venus.

# Eyes and Eyeglasses

Have your eyes tested and glasses fitted on a day marked favorable for your Sun sign, and on a day that falls during your favorable lunar cycle. Mars should not be in aspect with the Moon. The same applies for any treatment of the eyes, which should also be started during the Moon's first or second quarter.

# Fence Posts

Set posts when the Moon is in the third or fourth quarter of the fixed sign Taurus or Leo.

# Fertilize and Compost

Fertilize when the Moon is in a fruitful sign (Cancer, Scorpio, Pisces). Organic fertilizers are best when the Moon is waning. Use chemical fertilizers when the Moon is waxing. Start compost when the Moon is in the fourth quarter in a water sign.

# Find Hidden Treasure

Let the Moon be in good aspect to Jupiter or Venus. If you erect a horoscope for this election, place the Moon in the Fourth House.

# Find Lost Articles

Search for lost articles during the first quarter and when your Sun sign is marked favorable. Also check to see that the planet ruling the lost item is trine, sextile, or conjunct the Moon. The Moon rules household utensils; Mercury rules letters and books; and Venus rules clothing, jewelry, and money.

# Fishing

During the summer months, the best time of the day to fish is from sunrise to three hours after and from two hours before sunset until one hour after. Fish do not bite in cooler months until the air is warm, from noon to three pm. Warm, cloudy days are good. The most favorable winds are from the south and southwest. Easterly winds are unfavorable. The best days of the month for fishing are when the Moon changes quarters, especially if the change occurs on a day when the Moon is in a water sign (Cancer, Scorpio, Pisces). The best period in any month is the day after the Full Moon.

## Friendship

The need for friendship is greater when the Moon is in Aquarius or when Uranus aspects the Moon. Friendship prospers when Venus or Uranus is trine, sextile, or conjunct the Moon. The Moon in Gemini facilitates the chance meeting of acquaintances and friends.

## Grafting or Budding

Grafting is the process of introducing new varieties of fruit on less desirable trees. For this process you should use the increasing phase of the Moon in fruitful signs such as Cancer, Scorpio, or Pisces. Capricorn may be used, too. Cut your grafts while

trees are dormant, from December to March. Keep them in a cool, dark place, not too dry or too damp. Do the grafting before the sap starts to flow and while the Moon is waxing, preferably while it is in Cancer, Scorpio, or Pisces. The type of plant should determine both cutting and planting times.

## Habit (Breaking)

To end an undesirable habit, and this applies to ending everything from a bad relationship to smoking, start on a day when the Moon is in the fourth quarter and in the barren sign of Gemini, Leo, or Aquarius. Aries, Virgo, and Capricorn may be suitable as well, depending on the habit you want to be rid of. Make sure that your lunar cycle is favorable. Avoid lunar aspects to Mars or Jupiter. However, favorable aspects to Pluto are helpful.

## Haircuts

Cut hair when the Moon is in Gemini, Sagittarius, Pisces, Taurus, or Capricorn, but not in Virgo. Look for favorable aspects to Venus. For faster growth, cut hair when the Moon is increasing in Cancer or Pisces. To make hair grow thicker, cut when the Moon is full in the signs of Taurus, Cancer, or Leo. If you want your hair to grow more slowly, have the Moon be decreasing in Aries, Gemini, or Virgo, and have the Moon square or opposing Saturn.

Permanents, straightening, and hair coloring will take well if the Moon is in Taurus or Leo and trine or sextile Venus. Avoid hair treatments if Mars is marked as square or in opposition, especially if heat is to be used. For permanents, a trine to Jupiter is helpful. The Moon also should be in the first quarter. Check the lunar cycle for a favorable day in relation to your Sun sign.

## Harvest Crops

Harvest root crops when the Moon is in a dry sign (Aries, Leo, Sagittarius, Gemini, Aquarius) and waning. Harvest grain for storage just after the Full Moon, avoiding Cancer, Scorpio, or

Pisces. Harvest in the third and fourth quarters in dry signs. Dry crops in the third quarter in fire signs.

## Health

A diagnosis is more likely to be successful when the Moon is in Aries, Cancer, Libra, or Capricorn and less so when in Gemini, Sagittarius, Pisces, or Virgo. Begin a recuperation program or enter a hospital when the Moon is in a cardinal or fixed sign and the day is favorable to your Sun sign. For surgery, see "Surgical Procedures." Buy medicines when the Moon is in Virgo or Scorpio.

## Home (Buy New)

If you desire a permanent home, buy when the New Moon is in a fixed sign—Taurus or Leo, for example. Each sign will affect your decision in a different way. A house bought when the Moon is in Taurus is likely to be more practical and have a country look—right down to the split-rail fence. A house purchased when the Moon is in Leo will more likely be a real showplace.

If you're buying for speculation and a quick turnover, be certain that the Moon is in a cardinal sign (Aries, Cancer, Libra, Capricorn). Avoid buying when the Moon is in a fixed sign (Leo, Scorpio, Aquarius, Taurus).

## Home (Make Repairs)

In all repairs, avoid squares, oppositions, or conjunctions to the planet ruling the place or thing to be repaired. For example, bathrooms are ruled by Scorpio and Cancer. You would not want to start a project in those rooms when the Moon or Pluto is receiving hard aspects. The front entrance, hall, dining room, and porch are ruled by the Sun. So you would want to avoid times when Saturn or Mars are square, opposing, or conjunct the Sun. Also, let the Moon be waxing.

# Home (Sell)

Make a strong effort to list your property for sale when the Sun is marked favorable in your sign and in good aspect to Jupiter. Avoid adverse aspects to as many planets as possible.

# Home Furnishings (Buy New)

Saturn days (Saturday) are good for buying, and Jupiter days (Thursday) are good for selling. Items bought on days when Saturn is well aspected tend to wear longer and purchases tend to be more conservative.

# Job (Start New)

Jupiter and Venus should be sextile, trine, or conjunct the Moon. A day when your Sun is receiving favorable aspects is preferred.

# Legal Matters

Good Moon-Jupiter aspects improve the outcome in legal decisions. To gain damages through a lawsuit, begin the process during the increasing Moon. To avoid paying damages, a court date during the decreasing Moon is desirable. Good Moon-Sun aspects strengthen your chance of success. A well-aspected Moon in Cancer or Leo, making good aspects to the Sun, brings the best results in custody cases. In divorce cases, a favorable Moon-Venus aspect is best.

# Loan (Ask For)

A first and second quarter phase favors the lender, the third and fourth quarters favor the borrower. Good aspects of Jupiter and Venus to the Moon are favorable to both, as is having the Moon in Leo or Taurus.

# Machinery, Appliances, or Tools (Buy)

Tools, machinery, and other implements should be bought on days when your lunar cycle is favorable and when Mars and

Uranus are trine, sextile, or conjunct the Moon. Any quarter of the Moon is suitable. When buying gas or electrical appliances, the Moon should be in Aquarius.

## Make a Will

Let the Moon be in a fixed sign (Taurus, Leo, Scorpio, or Aquarius) to ensure permanence. If the Moon is in a cardinal sign (Aries, Cancer, Libra, or Capricorn), the will could be altered. Let the Moon be waxing—increasing in light—and in good aspect to Saturn, Venus, or Mercury. In case the will is made in an emergency during illness and the Moon is slow in motion, void-of-course, combust, or under the Sun's beams, the testator will die and the will remain unaltered. There is some danger that it will be lost or stolen, however.

## Marriage

The best time for marriage to take place is when the Moon is increasing, but not yet full. Good signs for the Moon to be in are Taurus, Cancer, Leo, or Libra.

The Moon in Taurus produces the most steadfast marriages, but if the partners later want to separate, they may have a difficult time. Make sure that the Moon is well aspected, especially to Venus or Jupiter. Avoid aspects to Mars, Uranus, or Pluto and the signs Aries, Gemini, Virgo, Scorpio, or Aquarius.

The values of the signs are as follows:

- Aries is not favored for marriage
- Taurus from 0 to 19 degrees is good, the remaining degrees are less favorable
- Cancer is unfavorable unless you are marrying a widow
- Leo is favored, but it may cause one party to deceive the other as to his or her money or possessions
- Virgo is not favored except when marrying a widow
- Libra is good for engagements but not for marriage

- Scorpio from 0 to 15 degrees is good, but the last 15 degrees are entirely unfortunate. The woman may be fickle, envious, and quarrelsome
- Sagittarius is neutral
- Capricorn, from 0 to 10 degrees, is difficult for marriage; however, the remaining degrees are favorable, especially when marrying a widow
- Aquarius is not favored
- Pisces is favored, although marriage under this sign can incline a woman to chatter a lot

These effects are strongest when the Moon is in the sign. If the Moon and Venus are in a cardinal sign, happiness between the couple may not continue long.

On no account should the Moon apply to Saturn or Mars, even by good aspect.

## Medical Treatment for the Eyes

Let the Moon be increasing in light and motion and making favorable aspects to Venus or Jupiter and be unaspected by Mars. Keep the Moon out of Taurus, Capricorn, or Virgo. If an aspect between the Moon and Mars is unavoidable, let it be separating.

## Medical Treatment for the Head

If possible, have Mars and Saturn free of hard aspects. Let the Moon be in Aries or Taurus, decreasing in light, in conjunction or aspect with Venus or Jupiter and free of hard aspects. The Sun should not be in any aspect to the Moon.

## Medical Treatment for the Nose

Let the Moon be in Cancer, Leo, or Virgo and not aspecting Mars or Saturn and also not in conjunction with a retrograde or weak planet.

# Mining

Saturn rules mining. Begin work when Saturn is marked conjunct, trine, or sextile. Mine for gold when the Sun is marked conjunct, trine, or sextile. Mercury rules quicksilver, Venus rules copper, Jupiter rules tin, Saturn rules lead and coal, Uranus rules radioactive elements, Neptune rules oil, the Moon rules water. Mine for these items when the ruling planet is marked conjunct, trine, or sextile.

# Move to New Home

If you have a choice, and sometimes you don't, make sure that Mars is not aspecting the Moon. Move on a day favorable to your Sun sign or when the Moon is conjunct, sextile, or trine the Sun.

# Mow Lawn

Mow in the first and second quarters (waxing phase) to increase growth and lushness, and in the third and fourth quarters (waning phase) to decrease growth.

# Negotiate

When you are choosing a time to negotiate, consider what the meeting is about and what you want to have happen. If it is agreement or compromise between two parties that you desire, have the Moon be in the sign of Libra. When you are making contracts, it is best to have the Moon in the same element. For example, if your concern is communication, then elect a time when the Moon is in an air sign. If, on the other hand, your concern is about possessions, an earth sign would be more appropriate. Fixed signs are unfavorable, with the exception of Leo; so are cardinal signs, except for Capricorn. If you are negotiating the end of something, use the rules that apply to ending habits.

## Occupational Training

When you begin training, see that your lunar cycle is favorable that day and that the planet ruling your occupation is marked conjunct or trine.

## Paint

Paint buildings during the waning Libra or Aquarius Moon. If the weather is hot, paint when the Moon is in Taurus. If the weather is cold, paint when the Moon is in Leo. Schedule the painting to start in the fourth quarter as the wood is drier and paint will penetrate wood better. Avoid painting around the New Moon, though, as the wood is likely to be damp, making the paint subject to scalding when hot weather hits it. If the temperature is below 70°F, it is not advisable to paint while the Moon is in Cancer, Scorpio, or Pisces as the paint is apt to creep, check, or run.

## Party (Host or Attend)

A party timed so the Moon is in Gemini, Leo, Libra, or Sagittarius, with good aspects to Venus and Jupiter, will be fun and well attended. There should be no aspects between the Moon and Mars or Saturn.

## Pawn

Do not pawn any article when Jupiter is receiving a square or opposition from Saturn or Mars or when Jupiter is within 17 degrees of the Sun, for you will have little chance to redeem the items.

## Pick Mushrooms

Mushrooms, one of the most promising traditional medicines in the world, should be gathered at the Full Moon.

## Plant

Root crops, like carrots and potatoes, are best if planted in the sign Taurus or Capricorn. Beans, peas, tomatoes, peppers, and other fruit-bearing plants are best if planted in a sign that supports seed growth. Leaf plants, like lettuce, broccoli, or cauliflower, are best planted when the Moon is in a water sign.

It is recommended that you transplant during a decreasing Moon, when forces are streaming into the lower part of the plant. This helps root growth.

## Promotion (Ask For)

Choose a day favorable to your Sun sign. Mercury should be marked conjunct, trine, or sextile. Avoid days when Mars or Saturn is aspected.

## Prune

Prune during the third and fourth quarter of a Scorpio Moon to retard growth and to promote better fruit. Prune when the Moon is in cardinal Capricorn to promote healing.

## Reconcile with People

If the reconciliation is with a woman, let Venus be strong and well aspected. If elders or superiors are involved, see that Saturn is receiving good aspects; if the reconciliation is between young people or between an older and younger person, see that Mercury is well aspected.

## Romance

There is less control of when a romance starts, but romances begun under an increasing Moon are more likely to be permanent or satisfying, while those begun during the decreasing Moon tend to transform the participants. The tone of the relationship can be guessed from the sign the Moon is in. Romances begun with the Moon in Aries may be impulsive. Those begun in Capricorn will take greater effort to bring to a desirable conclusion, but they may be very rewarding. Good aspects between the Moon and Venus will have a positive influence on the relationship. Avoid unfavorable aspects to Mars, Uranus, and Pluto. A decreasing Moon, particularly the fourth quarter, facilitates ending a relationship and causes the least pain.

## Roof a Building

Begin roofing a building during the third or fourth quarter, when the Moon is in Aries or Aquarius. Shingles laid during the New Moon have a tendency to curl at the edges.

## Sauerkraut

The best-tasting sauerkraut is made just after the Full Moon in the fruitful signs of Cancer, Scorpio, or Pisces.

## Select a Child's Sex

Count from the last day of menstruation to the first day of the next cycle and divide the interval between the two dates in half. Pregnancy in the first half produces females, but copulation should take place with the Moon in a feminine sign. Pregnancy in the latter half, up to three days before the beginning of menstrua-

tion, produces males, but copulation should take place with the Moon in a masculine sign. The three-day period before the next period again produces females.

## Sell or Canvass

Begin these activities during a day favorable to your Sun sign. Otherwise, sell on days when Jupiter, Mercury, or Mars is trine, sextile, or conjunct the Moon. Avoid days when Saturn is square or opposing the Moon, for that always hinders business and causes discord. If the Moon is passing from the first quarter to full, it is best to have the Moon swift in motion and in good aspect with Venus and/or Jupiter.

## Sign Papers

Sign contracts or agreements when the Moon is increasing in a fruitful sign and on a day when the Moon is making favorable aspects to Mercury. Avoid days when Mars, Saturn, or Neptune are square or opposite the Moon.

## Spray and Weed

Spray pests and weeds during the fourth quarter when the Moon is in the barren sign Leo or Aquarius and making favorable aspects to Pluto. Weed during a waning Moon in a barren sign.

## Staff (Fire)

Have the Moon in the third or fourth quarter, but not full. The Moon should not be square any planets.

## Staff (Hire)

The Moon should be in the first or second quarter, and preferably in the sign of Gemini or Virgo. The Moon should be conjunct, trine, or sextile Mercury or Jupiter.

## Stocks (Buy)

The Moon should be in Taurus or Capricorn, and there should be a sextile or trine to Jupiter or Saturn.

## Surgical Procedures

Blood flow, like ocean tides, appears to be related to Moon phases. To reduce hemorrhage after a surgery, schedule it within one week before or after a New Moon. Schedule surgery to occur during the increase of the Moon if possible, as wounds heal better and vitality is greater than during the decrease of the Moon. Avoid surgery within one week before or after the Full Moon. Select a date when the Moon is past the sign governing the part of the body involved in the operation. For example, abdominal operations should be done when the Moon is in Sagittarius, Capricorn, or Aquarius. The further removed the Moon sign is from the sign ruling the afflicted part of the body, the better.

For successful operations, avoid times when the Moon is applying to any aspect of Mars. (This tends to promote inflammation and complications.) See the Lunar Aspectarian on odd pages 137–159 to find days with negative Mars aspects and positive Venus and Jupiter aspects. Never operate with the Moon in the same sign as a person's Sun sign or Ascendant. Let the Moon be in a fixed sign and avoid square or opposing aspects. The Moon should not be void-of-course. Cosmetic surgery should be done in the increase of the Moon, when the Moon is not square or in opposition to Mars. Avoid days when the Moon is square or opposing Saturn or the Sun.

## Travel (Air)

Start long trips when the Moon is making favorable aspects to the Sun. For enjoyment, aspects to Jupiter are preferable; for visiting, look for favorable aspects to Mercury. To prevent accidents, avoid squares or oppositions to Mars, Saturn, Uranus, or

Pluto. Choose a day when the Moon is in Sagittarius or Gemini and well aspected to Mercury, Jupiter, or Uranus. Avoid adverse aspects of Mars, Saturn, or Uranus.

## Visit

On setting out to visit a person, let the Moon be in aspect with any retrograde planet, for this ensures that the person you're visiting will be at home. If you desire to stay a long time in a place, let the Moon be in good aspect to Saturn. If you desire to leave the place quickly, let the Moon be in a cardinal sign.

## Wean Children

To wean a child successfully, do so when the Moon is in Sagittarius, Capricorn, Aquarius, or Pisces—signs that do not rule vital human organs. By observing this astrological rule, much trouble for parents and child may be avoided.

## Weight (Reduce)

If you want to lose weight, the best time to get started is when the Moon is in the third or fourth quarter and in the barren sign of Virgo. Review the section on How to Use the Moon Tables and Lunar Aspectarian beginning on page 136 to help you select a date that is favorable to begin your weight-loss program.

## Wine and Drink Other Than Beer

Start brewing when the Moon is in Pisces or Taurus. Sextiles or trines to Venus are favorable, but avoid aspects to Mars or Saturn.

## Write

Write for pleasure or publication when the Moon is in Gemini. Mercury should be making favorable aspects to Uranus and Neptune.

# How to Use the Moon Tables and Lunar Aspectarian

Timing activities is one of the most important things you can do to ensure success. In many Eastern countries, timing by the planets is so important that practically no event takes place without first setting up a chart for it. Weddings have occurred in the middle of the night because the influences were at the best then. You may not want to take it that far, but you can still make use of the influences of the Moon whenever possible. It's easy and it works!

*Llewellyn's Moon Sign Book* has information to help you plan just about any activity: weddings, fishing, making purchases, cutting your hair, traveling, and more. We provide the guidelines you need to pick the best day out of the several from which you have to choose. The Moon Tables are the *Moon Sign Book's* primary method for choosing dates. Following are instructions, examples, and directions on how to read the Moon Tables. More advanced information on using the tables containing the Lunar Aspectarian and favorable and unfavorable days (found on odd-numbered pages opposite the Moon Tables), Moon void-of-course and retrograde information to choose the dates best for you is also included.

## The Five Basic Steps

### Step 1: Directions for Choosing Dates

Look up the directions for choosing dates for the activity that you wish to begin, then go to step 2.

### Step 2: Check the Moon Tables

You'll find two tables for each month of the year beginning on page 136. The Moon Tables (on the left-hand pages) include the day, date, and sign the Moon is in; the element and nature of the sign; the Moon's phase; and when it changes sign or phase. If there is a time listed after a date, that time is the time when the Moon moves into that zodiac sign. Until then, the Moon is considered to be in the sign for the previous day.

The abbreviation Full signifies Full Moon and New signifies New Moon. The times listed with dates indicate when the Moon changes sign. The times listed after the phase indicate when the Moon changes phase.

Turn to the month you would like to begin your activity. You will be using the Moon's sign and phase information most often when you begin choosing your own dates. Use the Time Zone Map on page 164 and the Time Zone Conversions table on page 165 to convert time to your own time zone.

When you find dates that meet the criteria for the correct Moon phase and sign for your activity, you may have completed the process. For certain simple activities, such as getting a haircut, the phase and sign information is all that is needed. If the directions for your activity include information on certain lunar aspects, however, you should consult the Lunar Aspectarian. An example of this would be if the directions told you not to perform a certain activity when the Moon is square (Q) Jupiter.

### Step 3: Check the Lunar Aspectarian

On the pages opposite the Moon Tables you will find tables containing the Lunar Aspectarian and Favorable and Unfavorable Days. The Lunar Aspectarian gives the aspects (or angles) of the Moon to other planets. Some aspects are favorable, while others are not. To use the Lunar Aspectarian, find the planet that the directions list as favorable for your activity, and run down the column to the date desired. For example, you should avoid aspects to Mars if you are planning surgery. So you would look for Mars across the top and then run down that column looking for days where there are no aspects to Mars (as signified by empty boxes). If you want to find a *favorable* aspect (sextile (X) or trine (T)) to Mercury, run your finger down the column under Mercury until you find an X or T. *Adverse* aspects to planets are squares (Q) or oppositions (O). A conjunction (C) is sometimes beneficial, sometimes not, depending on the activity or planets involved.

### Step 4: Favorable and Unfavorable Days

The tables listing favorable and unfavorable days are helpful when you want to choose your personal best dates because your Sun sign is taken into consideration. The twelve Sun signs are listed on the right side of the tables. Once you have determined which days meet your criteria for phase, sign, and aspects, you can determine whether or not those days are positive for you by checking the favorable and unfavorable days for your Sun sign.

To find out if a day is positive for you, find your Sun sign and then look down the column. If it is marked F, it is very favorable.

The Moon is in the same sign as your Sun on a favorable day. If it is marked f, it is slightly favorable; U is very unfavorable; and u means slightly unfavorable. A day marked very unfavorable (U) indicates that the Moon is in the sign opposing your Sun.

Once you have selected good dates for the activity you are about to begin, you can go straight to "Using What You've Learned," beginning on the next page. To learn how to fine-tune your selections even further, read on.

### Step 5: Void-of-Course Moon and Retrogrades

This last step is perhaps the most advanced portion of the procedure. It is generally considered poor timing to make decisions, sign important papers, or start special activities during a Moon void-of-course period or during a Mercury retrograde. Once you have chosen the best date for your activity based on steps one through four, you can check the Void-of-Course tables, beginning on page 76, to find out if any of the dates you have chosen have void periods.

The Moon is said to be void-of-course after it has made its last aspect to a planet within a particular sign, but before it has moved into the next sign. Put simply, the Moon is "resting" during the void-of-course period, so activities initiated at this time generally don't come to fruition. You will notice that there are many void periods during the year, and it is nearly impossible to avoid all of them. Some people choose to ignore these altogether and do not take them into consideration when planning activities.

Next, you can check the Retrograde Planets tables on page 160 to see what planets are retrograde during your chosen date(s).

A planet is said to be retrograde when it appears to move backward in the sky as viewed from Earth. Generally, the farther a planet is away from the Sun, the longer it can stay retrograde. Some planets will retrograde for several months at a time. Avoiding retrogrades is not as important in lunar planning as avoiding the Moon void-of-course, with the exception of the planet Mercury.

Mercury rules thought and communication, so it is advisable not to sign important papers, initiate important business or legal work, or make crucial decisions during these times. As with the Moon void-of-course, it is difficult to avoid all planetary retrogrades when beginning events, and you may choose to ignore this step of the process. Following are some examples using some or all of the steps outlined above.

## Using What You've Learned

Let's say it's a new year and you want to have your hair cut. It's thin and you would like it to look fuller, so you find the directions for hair care and you see that for thicker hair you should cut hair while the Moon is Full and in the sign of Taurus, Cancer, or Leo. You should avoid the Moon in Aries, Gemini, or Virgo. Look at the January Moon Table on page 136. You see that the Full Moon is on January 21 at 12:16 am. The Moon is in Leo from 10:54 pm on the 20th and remains in Leo until January 22 at 10:22 pm, so January 21–22 meets both the phase and sign criteria.

Let's move on to a more difficult example using the sign and phase of the Moon. You want to buy a permanent home. After checking the instructions for purchasing a house: "Home (Buy New)" on page 118, you see that you should buy a home when the Moon is in Taurus, Cancer, or Leo. You need to get a loan, so you should also look under "Loan (Ask For)" on page 119. Here it says that the third and fourth quarters favor the borrower (you). You are going to buy the house in October, so go to page 154. The Moon is in the third quarter October 13–21 and fourth quarter Oct. 21–27. The Moon is in Taurus from 12:24 pm on Oct. 14 until Oct. 16 at 10:30 pm; in Cancer from 6:43 am Oct. 19 until Oct. 21 at 12:29 pm; and in Leo from Oct. 21 at 12:29 pm until Oct. 23 at 3:29 pm. The best days for obtaining a loan would be October 14-16 and 19–23.

Just match up the best sign and phase (quarter) to come up with the best date. With all activities, be sure to check the favorable and unfavorable days for your Sun sign in the table adjoining the Lunar Aspectarian. If there is a choice between several dates, pick the one most favorable for you. Because buying a home is an important business decision, you may also wish to see if the Moon is void or if Mercury is retrograde during these dates.

Now let's look at an example that uses signs, phases, and aspects. Our example is starting new home construction. We will use the month of February. Look under "Build (Start Foundation)" on page 110 and you'll see that the Moon should be in the first quarter of a fixed sign—Leo, Taurus, Aquarius, or Scorpio. You should select a time when the Moon is not making unfavorable aspects to Saturn. (Conjunctions are usually considered unfavorable if they are to Mars, Saturn, or Neptune.) Look in the February Moon Table on page 138. You will see that the Moon is in the first quarter Feb. 4–12 and in Taurus from 8:28 pm on Feb. 10 until 4:32 am on Feb. 13. Now, look to the February Lunar Aspectarian. We see that there are no unfavorable aspects between Feb. 10 and 13, and a favorable time on Feb. 12; therefore that date would be best to start a foundation.

## A Note About Time and Time Zones

All tables in the Moon Sign Book use Eastern Time. You must calculate the difference between your time zone and the Eastern Time Zone. Please refer to the Time Zone Conversions chart on page 165 for help with time conversions. The sign the Moon is in at midnight is the sign shown in the Aspectarian and Favorable and Unfavorable Days tables.

### How Does the Time Matter?

Due to the three-hour time difference between the East and West Coasts of the United States, those of you living on the East Coast may be, for example, under the influence of a Virgo Moon, while those of you living on the West Coast will still have a Leo Moon influence.

We follow a commonly held belief among astrologers: whatever sign the Moon is in at the start of a day—12:00 am Eastern Time—is considered the dominant influence of the day. That sign is indicated in the Moon Tables. If the date you select for an activity shows the Moon changing signs, you can decide how important the sign change may be for your specific election and adjust your election date and time accordingly.

### *Use Common Sense*

Some activities depend on outside factors. Obviously, you can't go out and plant when there is a foot of snow on the ground. You should adjust to the conditions at hand. If the weather was bad during the first quarter, when it was best to plant crops, do it during the second quarter while the Moon is in a fruitful sign. If the Moon is not in a fruitful sign during the first or second quarter, choose a day when it is in a semi-fruitful sign. The best advice is to choose either the sign or phase that is most favorable, when the two don't coincide.

### *To Summarize*

First, look up the activity under the proper heading, then look for the information given in the tables. Choose the best date considering the number of positive factors in effect. If most of the dates are favorable, there is no problem choosing the one that will fit your schedule. However, if there aren't any really good dates, pick the ones with the least number of negative influences. Please keep in mind that the information found here applies in the broadest sense to the events you want to plan or are considering. To be the most effective, when you use electional astrology, you should also consider your own birth chart in relation to a chart drawn for the time or times you have under consideration. The best advice we can offer you is: read the entire introduction to each section.

# January Moon Table

| Date | Sign | Element | Nature | Phase |
|------|------|---------|--------|-------|
| 1 Tue | Scorpio | Water | Fruitful | 4th |
| 2 Wed 3:58 am | Sagittarius | Fire | Barren | 4th |
| 3 Thu | Sagittarius | Fire | Barren | 4th |
| 4 Fri 1:55 pm | Capricorn | Earth | Semi-fruitful | 4th |
| 5 Sat | Capricorn | Earth | Semi-fruitful | New 8:28 pm |
| 6 Sun | Capricorn | Earth | Semi-fruitful | 1st |
| 7 Mon 1:46 am | Aquarius | Air | Barren | 1st |
| 8 Tue | Aquarius | Air | Barren | 1st |
| 9 Wed 2:44 pm | Pisces | Water | Fruitful | 1st |
| 10 Thu | Pisces | Water | Fruitful | 1st |
| 11 Fri | Pisces | Water | Fruitful | 1st |
| 12 Sat 3:18 am | Aries | Fire | Barren | 1st |
| 13 Sun | Aries | Fire | Barren | 1st |
| 14 Mon 1:31 pm | Taurus | Earth | Semi-fruitful | 2nd 1:46 am |
| 15 Tue | Taurus | Earth | Semi-fruitful | 2nd |
| 16 Wed 8:00 pm | Gemini | Air | Barren | 2nd |
| 17 Thu | Gemini | Air | Barren | 2nd |
| 18 Fri 10:44 pm | Cancer | Water | Fruitful | 2nd |
| 19 Sat | Cancer | Water | Fruitful | 2nd |
| 20 Sun 10:54 pm | Leo | Fire | Barren | 2nd |
| 21 Mon | Leo | Fire | Barren | Full 12:16 am |
| 22 Tue 10:22 pm | Virgo | Earth | Barren | 3rd |
| 23 Wed | Virgo | Earth | Barren | 3rd |
| 24 Thu 11:02 pm | Libra | Air | Semi-fruitful | 3rd |
| 25 Fri | Libra | Air | Semi-fruitful | 3rd |
| 26 Sat | Libra | Air | Semi-fruitful | 3rd |
| 27 Sun 2:31 am | Scorpio | Water | Fruitful | 4th 4:10 pm |
| 28 Mon | Scorpio | Water | Fruitful | 4th |
| 29 Tue 9:33 am | Sagittarius | Fire | Barren | 4th |
| 30 Wed | Sagittarius | Fire | Barren | 4th |
| 31 Thu 7:47 pm | Capricorn | Earth | Semi-fruitful | 4th |

# January Aspectarian/Favorable & Unfavorable Days

| Date | Sun | Mercury | Venus | Mars | Jupiter | Saturn | Uranus | Neptune | Pluto |
|---|---|---|---|---|---|---|---|---|---|
| 1 | | | C | | | | | | X |
| 2 | | | | T | | | | | |
| 3 | | | | | C | | | Q | |
| 4 | | C | | Q | | | T | | |
| 5 | C | | | | | C | | X | |
| 6 | | | | | | | Q | | C |
| 7 | | | X | X | | | | | |
| 8 | | | | X | | | | | |
| 9 | | | Q | | | | X | | |
| 10 | | X | | | Q | X | | C | |
| 11 | X | | | | | | | | X |
| 12 | | | T | C | | | | | |
| 13 | | Q | | | T | Q | | | Q |
| 14 | Q | | | | | | C | | |
| 15 | | T | | | | T | | X | |
| 16 | T | | | | | | | | T |
| 17 | | | O | X | O | | | Q | |
| 18 | | | | | | | X | | |
| 19 | | | | Q | | O | T | | |
| 20 | | O | | | | | Q | | O |
| 21 | O | | T | T | | | | | |
| 22 | | | | | T | | T | | |
| 23 | | | | | T | | O | | |
| 24 | | Q | | Q | | | | | T |
| 25 | T | T | | | | Q | | | |
| 26 | | | X | O | X | | | | Q |
| 27 | Q | Q | | | | | O | | |
| 28 | | | | | | X | | T | X |
| 29 | | | | | | | | | |
| 30 | X | X | | | C | | | Q | |
| 31 | | | C | T | | | | T | |

| Date | Aries | Taurus | Gemini | Cancer | Leo | Virgo | Libra | Scorpio | Sagittarius | Capricorn | Aquarius | Pisces |
|---|---|---|---|---|---|---|---|---|---|---|---|---|
| 1 | | U | | f | u | f | | F | | f | u | f |
| 2 | | U | | f | u | f | | F | | f | u | f |
| 3 | f | | U | | f | u | f | | F | | f | u |
| 4 | f | | U | | f | u | f | | F | | f | u |
| 5 | u | f | | U | | f | u | f | | F | | f |
| 6 | u | f | | U | | f | u | f | | F | | f |
| 7 | f | u | f | | U | | f | u | f | | | F |
| 8 | f | u | f | | U | | f | u | f | | F | |
| 9 | f | u | f | | U | | f | u | f | | F | |
| 10 | | f | u | f | | U | | f | u | f | | F |
| 11 | | f | u | f | | U | | f | u | f | | F |
| 12 | | f | u | f | | U | | f | u | f | | F |
| 13 | F | | f | u | f | | U | | f | u | f | |
| 14 | F | | f | u | f | | U | | f | u | f | |
| 15 | | F | | f | u | f | | U | | f | u | f |
| 16 | | F | | f | u | f | | U | | f | u | f |
| 17 | f | | F | | f | u | f | | U | | f | u |
| 18 | f | | F | | f | u | f | | U | | f | u |
| 19 | u | f | | F | | f | u | f | | U | | f |
| 20 | u | f | | F | | f | u | f | | U | | f |
| 21 | f | u | f | | F | | f | u | f | | U | |
| 22 | f | u | f | | F | | f | u | f | | U | |
| 23 | | f | u | f | | F | | f | u | f | | U |
| 24 | | f | u | f | | F | | f | u | f | | U |
| 25 | U | | f | u | f | | F | | f | u | f | |
| 26 | U | | f | u | f | | F | | f | u | f | |
| 27 | | U | | f | u | f | | F | | f | u | f |
| 28 | | U | | f | u | f | | F | | f | u | f |
| 29 | | U | | f | u | f | | F | | f | u | f |
| 30 | f | | U | | f | u | f | | F | | f | u |
| 31 | f | | U | | f | u | f | | F | | f | u |

# February Moon Table

| Date | Sign | Element | Nature | Phase |
|---|---|---|---|---|
| 1 Fri | Capricorn | Earth | Semi-fruitful | 4th |
| 2 Sat | Capricorn | Earth | Semi-fruitful | 4th |
| 3 Sun 8:03 am | Aquarius | Air | Barren | 4th |
| 4 Mon | Aquarius | Air | Barren | New 4:04 pm |
| 5 Tue 9:02 pm | Pisces | Water | Fruitful | 1st |
| 6 Wed | Pisces | Water | Fruitful | 1st |
| 7 Thu | Pisces | Water | Fruitful | 1st |
| 8 Fri 9:34 am | Aries | Fire | Barren | 1st |
| 9 Sat | Aries | Fire | Barren | 1st |
| 10 Sun 8:28 pm | Taurus | Earth | Semi-fruitful | 1st |
| 11 Mon | Taurus | Earth | Semi-fruitful | 1st |
| 12 Tue | Taurus | Earth | Semi-fruitful | 2nd 5:26 pm |
| 13 Wed 4:32 am | Gemini | Air | Barren | 2nd |
| 14 Thu | Gemini | Air | Barren | 2nd |
| 15 Fri 9:03 am | Cancer | Water | Fruitful | 2nd |
| 16 Sat | Cancer | Water | Fruitful | 2nd |
| 17 Sun 10:21 am | Leo | Fire | Barren | 2nd |
| 18 Mon | Leo | Fire | Barren | 2nd |
| 19 Tue 9:47 am | Virgo | Earth | Barren | Full 10:54 am |
| 20 Wed | Virgo | Earth | Barren | 3rd |
| 21 Thu 9:17 am | Libra | Air | Semi-fruitful | 3rd |
| 22 Fri | Libra | Air | Semi-fruitful | 3rd |
| 23 Sat 10:56 am | Scorpio | Water | Fruitful | 3rd |
| 24 Sun | Scorpio | Water | Fruitful | 3rd |
| 25 Mon 4:19 pm | Sagittarius | Fire | Barren | 3rd |
| 26 Tue | Sagittarius | Fire | Barren | 4th 6:28 am |
| 27 Wed | Sagittarius | Fire | Barren | 4th |
| 28 Thu 1:48 am | Capricorn | Earth | Semi-fruitful | 4th |

# February Aspectarian/Favorable & Unfavorable Days

| Date | Sun | Mercury | Venus | Mars | Jupiter | Saturn | Uranus | Neptune | Pluto |
|---|---|---|---|---|---|---|---|---|---|
| 1 | | | | | | | | | |
| 2 | | | Q | | | C | | X | C |
| 3 | | | | | | | Q | | |
| 4 | C | | | | X | | | | |
| 5 | | C | | X | | | X | | |
| 6 | | | X | | | | | | |
| 7 | | | | | Q | X | | C | X |
| 8 | | | Q | | | | | | |
| 9 | | | | | T | Q | | | |
| 10 | X | X | | C | | | | C | Q |
| 11 | | | T | | | | | | |
| 12 | Q | | | | | T | | X | T |
| 13 | | Q | | | | | | | |
| 14 | | | | O | | | | Q | |
| 15 | T | | | X | | | X | | |
| 16 | | T | O | | | O | | T | O |
| 17 | | | Q | | | | Q | | |
| 18 | | | | | T | | | | |
| 19 | O | | | T | | | T | | |
| 20 | | O | T | | Q | T | | O | T |
| 21 | | | | | | | | | |
| 22 | | | Q | | X | Q | | | Q |
| 23 | T | | | O | | | O | | |
| 24 | | | | | | X | | T | |
| 25 | | T | X | | | | | | X |
| 26 | Q | | | | | | | Q | |
| 27 | | Q | | | C | | | | |
| 28 | X | | | T | | | T | | |
| | | | | | | | | | |

| Date | Aries | Taurus | Gemini | Cancer | Leo | Virgo | Libra | Scorpio | Sagittarius | Capricorn | Aquarius | Pisces |
|---|---|---|---|---|---|---|---|---|---|---|---|---|
| 1 | u | f | | U | | f | u | f | | F | | f |
| 2 | u | f | | U | | f | u | f | | F | | f |
| 3 | u | f | | U | | f | u | f | | F | | f |
| 4 | f | u | f | | U | | f | u | f | | F | |
| 5 | f | u | f | | U | | f | u | f | | F | |
| 6 | | f | u | f | | U | | f | u | f | | F |
| 7 | | f | u | f | | U | | f | u | f | | F |
| 8 | | f | u | f | | U | | f | u | f | | F |
| 9 | F | | f | u | f | | U | | f | u | f | |
| 10 | F | | f | u | f | | U | | f | u | f | |
| 11 | | F | | f | u | f | | U | | f | u | f |
| 12 | | F | | f | u | f | | U | | f | u | f |
| 13 | | F | | f | u | f | | U | | f | u | f |
| 14 | f | | F | | f | u | f | | U | | f | u |
| 15 | f | | F | | f | u | f | | U | | f | u |
| 16 | u | f | | F | | f | u | f | | U | | f |
| 17 | u | f | | F | | f | u | f | | U | | f |
| 18 | f | u | f | | F | | f | u | f | | U | |
| 19 | f | u | f | | F | | f | u | f | | U | |
| 20 | | f | u | f | | F | | f | u | f | | U |
| 21 | | f | u | f | | F | | f | u | f | | U |
| 22 | U | | f | u | f | | F | | f | u | f | |
| 23 | U | | f | u | f | | F | | f | u | f | |
| 24 | | U | | f | u | f | | F | | f | u | f |
| 25 | | U | | f | u | f | | F | | f | u | f |
| 26 | f | | U | | f | u | f | | F | | f | u |
| 27 | f | | U | | f | u | f | | F | | f | u |
| 28 | u | f | | U | | f | u | f | | F | | f |
| | | | | | | | | | | | | |

139

# March Moon Table

| Date | Sign | Element | Nature | Phase |
|---|---|---|---|---|
| 1 Fri | Capricorn | Earth | Semi-fruitful | 4th |
| 2 Sat 2:06 pm | Aquarius | Air | Barren | 4th |
| 3 Sun | Aquarius | Air | Barren | 4th |
| 4 Mon | Aquarius | Air | Barren | 4th |
| 5 Tue 3:11 am | Pisces | Water | Fruitful | 4th |
| 6 Wed | Pisces | Water | Fruitful | New 11:04 am |
| 7 Thu 3:27 pm | Aries | Fire | Barren | 1st |
| 8 Fri | Aries | Fire | Barren | 1st |
| 9 Sat | Aries | Fire | Barren | 1st |
| 10 Sun 3:10 am | Taurus | Earth | Semi-fruitful | 1st |
| 11 Mon | Taurus | Earth | Semi-fruitful | 1st |
| 12 Tue 11:48 am | Gemini | Air | Barren | 1st |
| 13 Wed | Gemini | Air | Barren | 1st |
| 14 Thu 5:49 pm | Cancer | Water | Fruitful | 2nd 6:27 am |
| 15 Fri | Cancer | Water | Fruitful | 2nd |
| 16 Sat 8:57 pm | Leo | Fire | Barren | 2nd |
| 17 Sun | Leo | Fire | Barren | 2nd |
| 18 Mon 9:41 pm | Virgo | Earth | Barren | 2nd |
| 19 Tue | Virgo | Earth | Barren | 2nd |
| 20 Wed 9:28 pm | Libra | Air | Semi-fruitful | Full 9:43 pm |
| 21 Thu | Libra | Air | Semi-fruitful | 3rd |
| 22 Fri 10:16 pm | Scorpio | Water | Fruitful | 3rd |
| 23 Sat | Scorpio | Water | Fruitful | 3rd |
| 24 Sun | Scorpio | Water | Fruitful | 3rd |
| 25 Mon 2:06 am | Sagittarius | Fire | Barren | 3rd |
| 26 Tue | Sagittarius | Fire | Barren | 3rd |
| 27 Wed 10:07 am | Capricorn | Earth | Semi-fruitful | 3rd |
| 28 Thu | Capricorn | Earth | Semi-fruitful | 4th 12:10 am |
| 29 Fri 9:46 pm | Aquarius | Air | Barren | 4th |
| 30 Sat | Aquarius | Air | Barren | 4th |
| 31 Sun | Aquarius | Air | Barren | 4th |

# March Aspectarian/Favorable & Unfavorable Days

| Date | Sun | Mercury | Venus | Mars | Jupiter | Saturn | Uranus | Neptune | Pluto |
|---|---|---|---|---|---|---|---|---|---|
| 1 | | | | | | C | | X | C |
| 2 | | X | C | | | | Q | | |
| 3 | | | | Q | | | | | |
| 4 | | | | | X | | | | |
| 5 | | | | | | | X | | |
| 6 | C | | | X | | X | | C | |
| 7 | | C | | | Q | | | | X |
| 8 | | | X | | | | | | |
| 9 | | | | | T | Q | | | Q |
| 10 | | | | | | | C | | |
| 11 | X | | Q | C | | T | | X | T |
| 12 | | X | | | | | | | |
| 13 | | | T | | | | | Q | |
| 14 | Q | Q | | | O | | X | | |
| 15 | | | | | | | T | | |
| 16 | T | T | | X | | O | Q | | O |
| 17 | | | | | | | | | |
| 18 | | | O | Q | T | | T | | |
| 19 | | | | | | | | | |
| 20 | O | O | | T | Q | T | | O | T |
| 21 | | | | | | | | | |
| 22 | | | T | | X | Q | O | | Q |
| 23 | | | | | | | | | |
| 24 | | T | Q | O | | X | | T | X |
| 25 | T | | | | | | | | |
| 26 | | Q | | | C | | | Q | |
| 27 | | | X | | | | T | | |
| 28 | Q | X | | | | | | X | |
| 29 | | | | T | | C | | | C |
| 30 | X | | | | | | Q | | |
| 31 | | | | | X | | | | |

| Date | Aries | Taurus | Gemini | Cancer | Leo | Virgo | Libra | Scorpio | Sagittarius | Capricorn | Aquarius | Pisces |
|---|---|---|---|---|---|---|---|---|---|---|---|---|
| 1 | u | f | | U | | f | u | f | | F | | f |
| 2 | u | f | | U | | f | u | f | | F | | f |
| 3 | f | u | f | | U | | f | u | f | | F | |
| 4 | f | u | f | | U | | f | u | f | | F | |
| 5 | f | u | f | | U | | f | u | f | | F | |
| 6 | | f | u | f | | U | | f | u | f | | F |
| 7 | | f | u | f | | U | | f | u | f | | F |
| 8 | F | | f | u | f | | U | | f | u | f | |
| 9 | F | | f | u | f | | U | | f | u | f | |
| 10 | | F | | f | u | f | | U | | f | u | f |
| 11 | | F | | f | u | f | | U | | f | u | f |
| 12 | | F | | f | u | f | | U | | f | u | f |
| 13 | f | | F | | f | u | f | | U | | f | u |
| 14 | f | | F | | f | u | f | | U | | f | u |
| 15 | u | f | | F | | f | u | f | | U | | f |
| 16 | u | f | | F | | f | u | f | | U | | f |
| 17 | f | u | f | | F | | f | u | f | | U | |
| 18 | f | u | f | | F | | f | u | f | | U | |
| 19 | | f | u | f | | F | | f | u | f | | U |
| 20 | | f | u | f | | F | | f | u | f | | U |
| 21 | U | | f | u | f | | F | | f | u | f | |
| 22 | U | | f | u | f | | F | | f | u | f | |
| 23 | | U | | f | u | f | | F | | f | u | f |
| 24 | | U | | f | u | f | | F | | f | u | f |
| 25 | f | | U | | f | u | f | | F | | f | u |
| 26 | f | | U | | f | u | f | | F | | f | u |
| 27 | f | | U | | f | u | f | | F | | f | u |
| 28 | u | f | | U | | f | u | f | | F | | f |
| 29 | u | f | | U | | f | u | f | | F | | f |
| 30 | f | u | f | | U | | f | u | f | | F | |
| 31 | f | u | f | | U | | f | u | f | | F | |

# April Moon Table

| Date | Sign | Element | Nature | Phase |
|------|------|---------|--------|-------|
| 1 Mon 10:48 am | Pisces | Water | Fruitful | 4th |
| 2 Tue | Pisces | Water | Fruitful | 4th |
| 3 Wed 10:56 pm | Aries | Fire | Barren | 4th |
| 4 Thu | Aries | Fire | Barren | 4th |
| 5 Fri | Aries | Fire | Barren | New 4:50 am |
| 6 Sat 9:06 am | Taurus | Earth | Semi-fruitful | 1st |
| 7 Sun | Taurus | Earth | Semi-fruitful | 1st |
| 8 Mon 5:15 pm | Gemini | Air | Barren | 1st |
| 9 Tue | Gemini | Air | Barren | 1st |
| 10 Wed 11:31 pm | Cancer | Water | Fruitful | 1st |
| 11 Thu | Cancer | Water | Fruitful | 1st |
| 12 Fri | Cancer | Water | Fruitful | 2nd 3:06 pm |
| 13 Sat 3:50 am | Leo | Fire | Barren | 2nd |
| 14 Sun | Leo | Fire | Barren | 2nd |
| 15 Mon 6:14 am | Virgo | Earth | Barren | 2nd |
| 16 Tue | Virgo | Earth | Barren | 2nd |
| 17 Wed 7:22 am | Libra | Air | Semi-fruitful | 2nd |
| 18 Thu | Libra | Air | Semi-fruitful | 2nd |
| 19 Fri 8:41 am | Scorpio | Water | Fruitful | Full 7:12 am |
| 20 Sat | Scorpio | Water | Fruitful | 3rd |
| 21 Sun 11:59 am | Sagittarius | Fire | Barren | 3rd |
| 22 Mon | Sagittarius | Fire | Barren | 3rd |
| 23 Tue 6:50 pm | Capricorn | Earth | Semi-fruitful | 3rd |
| 24 Wed | Capricorn | Earth | Semi-fruitful | 3rd |
| 25 Thu | Capricorn | Earth | Semi-fruitful | 3rd |
| 26 Fri 5:27 am | Aquarius | Air | Barren | 4th 6:18 pm |
| 27 Sat | Aquarius | Air | Barren | 4th |
| 28 Sun 6:11 pm | Pisces | Water | Fruitful | 4th |
| 29 Mon | Pisces | Water | Fruitful | 4th |
| 30 Tue | Pisces | Water | Fruitful | 4th |

# April Aspectarian/Favorable & Unfavorable Days

| Date | Sun | Mercury | Venus | Mars | Jupiter | Saturn | Uranus | Neptune | Pluto |
|---|---|---|---|---|---|---|---|---|---|
| 1 | | | | Q | | | X | | |
| 2 | | C | C | | | | | C | |
| 3 | | | | | Q | X | | | X |
| 4 | | | | X | | | | | |
| 5 | C | | | | | T | Q | | Q |
| 6 | | | | | | | C | | |
| 7 | | | X | | | T | | X | |
| 8 | | X | | | | | | | T |
| 9 | | | | C | | | | | |
| 10 | X | Q | Q | | O | | | Q | |
| 11 | | | | | | | X | | |
| 12 | Q | T | T | | | O | | T | O |
| 13 | | | | X | | | Q | | |
| 14 | T | | | | T | | | | |
| 15 | | | | | Q | | T | | |
| 16 | | | | | Q | T | | O | T |
| 17 | | O | O | | | | | | |
| 18 | | | | T | X | Q | | | Q |
| 19 | O | | | | | | | O | |
| 20 | | | | | | X | | T | |
| 21 | | T | T | | | | | | X |
| 22 | | | | O | | | | Q | |
| 23 | | | | | C | | T | | |
| 24 | T | Q | Q | | | | | | |
| 25 | | | | | | C | | X | C |
| 26 | Q | | X | | | | | Q | |
| 27 | | X | | T | | | | | |
| 28 | | | | | X | | | | |
| 29 | X | | | | | | X | | |
| 30 | | | | Q | Q | X | | C | X |

| Date | Aries | Taurus | Gemini | Cancer | Leo | Virgo | Libra | Scorpio | Sagittarius | Capricorn | Aquarius | Pisces |
|---|---|---|---|---|---|---|---|---|---|---|---|---|
| 1 | f | u | f | | U | | f | u | f | | F | |
| 2 | | f | u | f | | U | | f | u | f | | F |
| 3 | | f | u | f | | U | | f | u | f | | F |
| 4 | F | | f | u | f | | U | | f | u | f | |
| 5 | F | | f | u | f | | U | | f | u | f | |
| 6 | F | | f | u | f | | U | | f | u | f | |
| 7 | | F | | f | u | f | | U | | f | u | f |
| 8 | | F | | f | u | f | | U | | f | u | f |
| 9 | f | | F | | f | u | f | | U | | f | u |
| 10 | f | | F | | f | u | f | | U | | f | u |
| 11 | u | f | | F | | f | u | f | | U | | f |
| 12 | u | f | | F | | f | u | f | | U | | f |
| 13 | u | f | | F | | f | u | f | | U | | f |
| 14 | f | u | f | | F | | f | u | f | | U | |
| 15 | f | u | f | | F | | f | u | f | | U | |
| 16 | | f | u | f | | F | | f | u | f | | U |
| 17 | | f | u | f | | F | | f | u | f | | U |
| 18 | U | | f | u | f | | F | | f | u | f | |
| 19 | U | | f | u | f | | F | | f | u | f | |
| 20 | | U | | f | u | f | | F | | f | u | f |
| 21 | | U | | f | u | f | | F | | f | u | f |
| 22 | f | | U | | f | u | f | | F | | f | u |
| 23 | f | | U | | f | u | f | | F | | f | u |
| 24 | u | f | | U | | f | u | f | | F | | f |
| 25 | u | f | | U | | f | u | f | | F | | f |
| 26 | u | f | | U | | f | u | f | | F | | f |
| 27 | f | u | f | | U | | f | u | f | | F | |
| 28 | f | u | f | | U | | f | u | f | | F | |
| 29 | | f | u | f | | U | | f | u | f | | F |
| 30 | | f | u | f | | U | | f | u | f | | F |

# May Moon Table

| Date | Sign | Element | Nature | Phase |
|------|------|---------|--------|-------|
| 1 Wed 6:24 am | Aries | Fire | Barren | 4th |
| 2 Thu | Aries | Fire | Barren | 4th |
| 3 Fri 4:18 pm | Taurus | Earth | Semi-fruitful | 4th |
| 4 Sat | Taurus | Earth | Semi-fruitful | New 6:45 pm |
| 5 Sun 11:40 pm | Gemini | Air | Barren | 1st |
| 6 Mon | Gemini | Air | Barren | 1st |
| 7 Tue | Gemini | Air | Barren | 1st |
| 8 Wed 5:06 am | Cancer | Water | Fruitful | 1st |
| 9 Thu | Cancer | Water | Fruitful | 1st |
| 10 Fri 9:14 am | Leo | Fire | Barren | 1st |
| 11 Sat | Leo | Fire | Barren | 2nd 9:12 pm |
| 12 Sun 12:22 pm | Virgo | Earth | Barren | 2nd |
| 13 Mon | Virgo | Earth | Barren | 2nd |
| 14 Tue 2:51 pm | Libra | Air | Semi-fruitful | 2nd |
| 15 Wed | Libra | Air | Semi-fruitful | 2nd |
| 16 Thu 5:26 pm | Scorpio | Water | Fruitful | 2nd |
| 17 Fri | Scorpio | Water | Fruitful | 2nd |
| 18 Sat 9:21 pm | Sagittarius | Fire | Barren | Full 5:11 pm |
| 19 Sun | Sagittarius | Fire | Barren | 3rd |
| 20 Mon | Sagittarius | Fire | Barren | 3rd |
| 21 Tue 3:56 am | Capricorn | Earth | Semi-fruitful | 3rd |
| 22 Wed | Capricorn | Earth | Semi-fruitful | 3rd |
| 23 Thu 1:49 pm | Aquarius | Air | Barren | 3rd |
| 24 Fri | Aquarius | Air | Barren | 3rd |
| 25 Sat | Aquarius | Air | Barren | 3rd |
| 26 Sun 2:08 am | Pisces | Water | Fruitful | 4th 12:34 pm |
| 27 Mon | Pisces | Water | Fruitful | 4th |
| 28 Tue 2:32 pm | Aries | Fire | Barren | 4th |
| 29 Wed | Aries | Fire | Barren | 4th |
| 30 Thu | Aries | Fire | Barren | 4th |
| 31 Fri 12:43 am | Taurus | Earth | Semi-fruitful | 4th |

# May Aspectarian/Favorable & Unfavorable Days

| Date | Sun | Mercury | Venus | Mars | Jupiter | Saturn | Uranus | Neptune | Pluto |
|---|---|---|---|---|---|---|---|---|---|
| 1 | | | | | | | | | |
| 2 | | | C | | | Q | | | |
| 3 | | C | | X | T | | C | | Q |
| 4 | C | | | | | | | | |
| 5 | | | | | | T | | X | T |
| 6 | | | | | | | | | |
| 7 | | | X | C | O | | | Q | |
| 8 | | X | | | | | X | | |
| 9 | X | | Q | | | O | | T | O |
| 10 | | Q | | | | | Q | | |
| 11 | Q | | | | | | | | |
| 12 | | | T | X | T | | T | | |
| 13 | | T | | | | T | | O | |
| 14 | T | | | Q | Q | | | | T |
| 15 | | | | | | | | | |
| 16 | | | O | T | X | Q | | | Q |
| 17 | | | | | | | | O | |
| 18 | O | O | | | | X | | T | X |
| 19 | | | | | | | | | |
| 20 | | | | C | | | | Q | |
| 21 | | | T | O | | | T | | |
| 22 | | | | | | C | | X | C |
| 23 | T | | | | | | Q | | |
| 24 | | T | Q | | | | | | |
| 25 | | | | | X | | | | |
| 26 | Q | | | T | | | X | | |
| 27 | | Q | X | | Q | X | | C | |
| 28 | | | | | | | | | X |
| 29 | X | | | Q | | | | | |
| 30 | | X | | | T | Q | | | Q |
| 31 | | | | X | | | C | | |

| Date | Aries | Taurus | Gemini | Cancer | Leo | Virgo | Libra | Scorpio | Sagittarius | Capricorn | Aquarius | Pisces |
|---|---|---|---|---|---|---|---|---|---|---|---|---|
| 1 | | f | u | f | | U | | f | u | f | | F |
| 2 | F | | f | u | f | | U | | f | u | f | |
| 3 | F | | f | u | f | | U | | f | u | f | |
| 4 | | F | | f | u | f | | U | | f | u | f |
| 5 | | F | | f | u | f | | U | | f | u | f |
| 6 | f | | F | | f | u | f | | U | | f | u |
| 7 | f | | F | | f | u | f | | U | | f | u |
| 8 | f | | F | | f | u | f | | U | | f | u |
| 9 | u | f | | F | | f | u | f | | U | | f |
| 10 | u | f | | F | | f | u | f | | U | | f |
| 11 | f | u | f | | F | | f | u | f | | U | |
| 12 | f | u | f | | F | | f | u | f | | U | |
| 13 | | f | u | f | | F | | f | u | f | | U |
| 14 | | f | u | f | | F | | f | u | f | | U |
| 15 | U | | f | u | f | | F | | f | u | f | |
| 16 | U | | f | u | f | | F | | f | u | f | |
| 17 | | U | | f | u | f | | F | | f | u | f |
| 18 | | U | | f | u | f | | F | | f | u | f |
| 19 | f | | U | | f | u | f | | F | | f | u |
| 20 | f | | U | | f | u | f | | F | | f | u |
| 21 | f | | U | | f | u | f | | F | | f | u |
| 22 | u | f | | U | | f | u | f | | F | | f |
| 23 | u | f | | U | | f | u | f | | F | | f |
| 24 | f | u | f | | U | | f | u | f | | F | |
| 25 | f | u | f | | U | | f | u | f | | F | |
| 26 | | f | u | f | | U | | f | u | f | | F |
| 27 | | f | u | f | | U | | f | u | f | | F |
| 28 | | f | u | f | | U | | f | u | f | | F |
| 29 | F | | f | u | f | | U | | f | u | f | |
| 30 | F | | f | u | f | | U | | f | u | f | |
| 31 | | F | | f | u | f | | U | | f | u | f |

# June Moon Table

| Date | Sign | Element | Nature | Phase |
|------|------|---------|--------|-------|
| 1 Sat | Taurus | Earth | Semi-fruitful | 4th |
| 2 Sun 7:48 am | Gemini | Air | Barren | 4th |
| 3 Mon | Gemini | Air | Barren | New 6:02 am |
| 4 Tue 12:17 pm | Cancer | Water | Fruitful | 1st |
| 5 Wed | Cancer | Water | Fruitful | 1st |
| 6 Thu 3:16 pm | Leo | Fire | Barren | 1st |
| 7 Fri | Leo | Fire | Barren | 1st |
| 8 Sat 5:45 pm | Virgo | Earth | Barren | 1st |
| 9 Sun | Virgo | Earth | Barren | 1st |
| 10 Mon 8:29 pm | Libra | Air | Semi-fruitful | 2nd 1:59 am |
| 11 Tue | Libra | Air | Semi-fruitful | 2nd |
| 12 Wed | Libra | Air | Semi-fruitful | 2nd |
| 13 Thu 12:02 am | Scorpio | Water | Fruitful | 2nd |
| 14 Fri | Scorpio | Water | Fruitful | 2nd |
| 15 Sat 5:03 am | Sagittarius | Fire | Barren | 2nd |
| 16 Sun | Sagittarius | Fire | Barren | 2nd |
| 17 Mon 12:13 pm | Capricorn | Earth | Semi-fruitful | Full 4:31 am |
| 18 Tue | Capricorn | Earth | Semi-fruitful | 3rd |
| 19 Wed 10:01 pm | Aquarius | Air | Barren | 3rd |
| 20 Thu | Aquarius | Air | Barren | 3rd |
| 21 Fri | Aquarius | Air | Barren | 3rd |
| 22 Sat 10:01 am | Pisces | Water | Fruitful | 3rd |
| 23 Sun | Pisces | Water | Fruitful | 3rd |
| 24 Mon 10:38 pm | Aries | Fire | Barren | 3rd |
| 25 Tue | Aries | Fire | Barren | 4th 5:46 am |
| 26 Wed | Aries | Fire | Barren | 4th |
| 27 Thu 9:32 am | Taurus | Earth | Semi-fruitful | 4th |
| 28 Fri | Taurus | Earth | Semi-fruitful | 4th |
| 29 Sat 5:09 pm | Gemini | Air | Barren | 4th |
| 30 Sun | Gemini | Air | Barren | 4th |

# June Aspectarian/Favorable & Unfavorable Days

| Date | Sun | Mercury | Venus | Mars | Jupiter | Saturn | Uranus | Neptune | Pluto |
|---|---|---|---|---|---|---|---|---|---|
| 1 | | | C | | | T | | X | T |
| 2 | | | | | | | | | |
| 3 | C | | | | O | | | Q | |
| 4 | | C | | | | | X | | |
| 5 | | | | C | | O | | T | |
| 6 | | | X | | | | Q | | O |
| 7 | X | | | | | | | | |
| 8 | | | Q | | T | | | | |
| 9 | | X | | X | | | T | | |
| 10 | Q | | | | Q | T | | O | T |
| 11 | | Q | T | | | | | | |
| 12 | T | | | Q | X | Q | | | Q |
| 13 | | | | | | | O | | |
| 14 | | T | | T | | X | | T | X |
| 15 | | | O | | | | | | |
| 16 | | | | | C | | | Q | |
| 17 | O | | | | | | T | | |
| 18 | | | | | | C | | X | |
| 19 | | O | | O | | | | | C |
| 20 | | | | | | | Q | | |
| 21 | | | T | | X | | | | |
| 22 | T | | | | | | X | | |
| 23 | | | Q | | Q | X | | C | |
| 24 | | T | | T | | | | | X |
| 25 | Q | | | | | | | | |
| 26 | | | X | | T | Q | | | Q |
| 27 | X | Q | | Q | | | C | | |
| 28 | | | | | | T | | X | |
| 29 | | X | | X | | | | | T |
| 30 | | | | | O | | | | |

| Date | Aries | Taurus | Gemini | Cancer | Leo | Virgo | Libra | Scorpio | Sagittarius | Capricorn | Aquarius | Pisces |
|---|---|---|---|---|---|---|---|---|---|---|---|---|
| 1 | | F | | f | u | f | | U | | f | u | f |
| 2 | | F | | f | u | f | | U | | f | u | f |
| 3 | f | | F | | f | u | f | | U | | f | u |
| 4 | f | | F | | f | u | f | | U | | f | u |
| 5 | u | f | | F | | f | u | f | | U | | f |
| 6 | u | f | | F | | f | u | f | | U | | f |
| 7 | f | u | f | | F | | f | u | f | | U | |
| 8 | f | u | f | | F | | f | u | f | | U | |
| 9 | | f | u | f | | F | | f | u | f | | U |
| 10 | | f | u | f | | F | | f | u | f | | U |
| 11 | U | | f | u | f | | F | | f | u | f | |
| 12 | U | | f | u | f | | F | | f | u | f | |
| 13 | | U | | f | u | f | | F | | f | u | f |
| 14 | | U | | f | u | f | | F | | f | u | f |
| 15 | | U | | f | u | f | | F | | f | u | f |
| 16 | f | | U | | f | u | f | | F | | f | u |
| 17 | f | | U | | f | u | f | | F | | f | u |
| 18 | u | f | | U | | f | u | f | | F | | f |
| 19 | u | f | | U | | f | u | f | | F | | f |
| 20 | f | u | f | | U | | f | u | f | | F | |
| 21 | f | u | f | | U | | f | u | f | | F | |
| 22 | f | u | f | | U | | f | u | f | | F | |
| 23 | | f | u | f | | U | | f | u | f | | F |
| 24 | | f | u | f | | U | | f | u | f | | F |
| 25 | F | | f | u | f | | U | | f | u | f | |
| 26 | F | | f | u | f | | U | | f | u | f | |
| 27 | F | | f | u | f | | U | | f | u | f | |
| 28 | | F | | f | u | f | | U | | f | u | f |
| 29 | | F | | f | u | f | | U | | f | u | f |
| 30 | f | | F | | f | u | f | | U | | f | u |

# July Moon Table

| Date | Sign | Element | Nature | Phase |
|------|------|---------|--------|-------|
| 1 Mon 9:24 pm | Cancer | Water | Fruitful | 4th |
| 2 Tue | Cancer | Water | Fruitful | New 3:16 pm |
| 3 Wed 11:19 pm | Leo | Fire | Barren | 1st |
| 4 Thu | Leo | Fire | Barren | 1st |
| 5 Fri | Leo | Fire | Barren | 1st |
| 6 Sat 12:25 am | Virgo | Earth | Barren | 1st |
| 7 Sun | Virgo | Earth | Barren | 1st |
| 8 Mon 2:07 am | Libra | Air | Semi-fruitful | 1st |
| 9 Tue | Libra | Air | Semi-fruitful | 2nd 6:55 am |
| 10 Wed 5:29 am | Scorpio | Water | Fruitful | 2nd |
| 11 Thu | Scorpio | Water | Fruitful | 2nd |
| 12 Fri 11:05 am | Sagittarius | Fire | Barren | 2nd |
| 13 Sat | Sagittarius | Fire | Barren | 2nd |
| 14 Sun 7:05 pm | Capricorn | Earth | Semi-fruitful | 2nd |
| 15 Mon | Capricorn | Earth | Semi-fruitful | 2nd |
| 16 Tue | Capricorn | Earth | Semi-fruitful | Full 5:38 pm |
| 17 Wed 5:19 am | Aquarius | Air | Barren | 3rd |
| 18 Thu | Aquarius | Air | Barren | 3rd |
| 19 Fri 5:19 pm | Pisces | Water | Fruitful | 3rd |
| 20 Sat | Pisces | Water | Fruitful | 3rd |
| 21 Sun | Pisces | Water | Fruitful | 3rd |
| 22 Mon 6:02 am | Aries | Fire | Barren | 3rd |
| 23 Tue | Aries | Fire | Barren | 3rd |
| 24 Wed 5:42 pm | Taurus | Earth | Semi-fruitful | 4th 9:18 pm |
| 25 Thu | Taurus | Earth | Semi-fruitful | 4th |
| 26 Fri | Taurus | Earth | Semi-fruitful | 4th |
| 27 Sat 2:29 am | Gemini | Air | Barren | 4th |
| 28 Sun | Gemini | Air | Barren | 4th |
| 29 Mon 7:31 am | Cancer | Water | Fruitful | 4th |
| 30 Tue | Cancer | Water | Fruitful | 4th |
| 31 Wed 9:18 am | Leo | Fire | Barren | New 11:12 pm |

# July Aspectarian/Favorable & Unfavorable Days

| Date | Sun | Mercury | Venus | Mars | Jupiter | Saturn | Uranus | Neptune | Pluto |
|------|-----|---------|-------|------|---------|--------|--------|---------|-------|
| 1 | | | C | | | | | Q | |
| 2 | C | | | | | | X | | |
| 3 | | | | | | O | | T | O |
| 4 | | C | | C | | | Q | | |
| 5 | | | | | T | | | | |
| 6 | | | X | | | | T | | |
| 7 | X | | | | Q | T | | O | T |
| 8 | | X | Q | X | | | | | |
| 9 | Q | | | | X | Q | | | Q |
| 10 | | Q | T | Q | | | O | | |
| 11 | T | | | | | X | | T | X |
| 12 | | T | | | | | | | |
| 13 | | | | T | C | | | Q | |
| 14 | | | | | | | | | |
| 15 | | | | | | | T | | |
| 16 | O | | O | | | C | | X | C |
| 17 | | O | | | | | Q | | |
| 18 | | | | O | X | | | | |
| 19 | | | | | | | | | |
| 20 | | | | | | | X | | |
| 21 | | | T | | Q | X | | C | X |
| 22 | T | T | | | | | | | |
| 23 | | | | T | T | Q | | | |
| 24 | Q | Q | Q | | | | | | Q |
| 25 | | | | Q | | | C | | |
| 26 | | X | | | | T | | X | T |
| 27 | X | | X | | | | | | |
| 28 | | | | X | O | | | Q | |
| 29 | | | | | | | X | | |
| 30 | | C | | | | O | | T | O |
| 31 | C | | C | | | | | Q | |

| Date | Aries | Taurus | Gemini | Cancer | Leo | Virgo | Libra | Scorpio | Sagittarius | Capricorn | Aquarius | Pisces |
|------|-------|--------|--------|--------|-----|-------|-------|---------|-------------|-----------|----------|--------|
| 1 | f | | F | | f | u | f | | U | | f | u |
| 2 | u | f | | F | | f | u | f | | U | | f |
| 3 | u | f | | F | | f | u | f | | U | | f |
| 4 | f | u | f | | F | | f | u | f | | U | |
| 5 | f | u | f | | F | | f | u | f | | U | |
| 6 | | f | u | f | | F | | f | u | f | | U |
| 7 | | f | u | f | | F | | f | u | f | | U |
| 8 | U | | f | u | f | | F | | f | u | f | |
| 9 | U | | f | u | f | | F | | f | u | f | |
| 10 | U | | f | u | f | | F | | f | u | f | |
| 11 | | U | | f | u | f | | F | | f | u | f |
| 12 | | U | | f | u | f | | F | | f | u | f |
| 13 | f | | U | | f | u | f | | F | | f | u |
| 14 | f | | U | | f | u | f | | F | | f | u |
| 15 | u | f | | U | | f | u | f | | F | | f |
| 16 | u | f | | U | | f | u | f | | F | | f |
| 17 | u | f | | U | | f | u | f | | F | | f |
| 18 | f | u | f | | U | | f | u | f | | F | |
| 19 | f | u | f | | U | | f | u | f | | F | |
| 20 | | f | u | f | | U | | f | u | f | | F |
| 21 | | f | u | f | | U | | f | u | f | | F |
| 22 | | f | u | f | | U | | f | u | f | | F |
| 23 | F | | f | u | f | | U | | f | u | f | |
| 24 | F | | f | u | f | | U | | f | u | f | |
| 25 | | F | | f | u | f | | U | | f | u | f |
| 26 | | F | | f | u | f | | U | | f | u | f |
| 27 | f | | F | | f | u | f | | U | | f | u |
| 28 | f | | F | | f | u | f | | U | | f | u |
| 29 | f | | F | | f | u | f | | U | | f | u |
| 30 | u | f | | F | | f | u | f | | U | | f |
| 31 | u | f | | F | | f | u | f | | U | | f |

## August Moon Table

| Date | Sign | Element | Nature | Phase |
|------|------|---------|--------|-------|
| 1 Thu | Leo | Fire | Barren | 1st |
| 2 Fri 9:20 am | Virgo | Earth | Barren | 1st |
| 3 Sat | Virgo | Earth | Barren | 1st |
| 4 Sun 9:30 am | Libra | Air | Semi-fruitful | 1st |
| 5 Mon | Libra | Air | Semi-fruitful | 1st |
| 6 Tue 11:31 am | Scorpio | Water | Fruitful | 1st |
| 7 Wed | Scorpio | Water | Fruitful | 2nd 1:31 pm |
| 8 Thu 4:35 pm | Sagittarius | Fire | Barren | 2nd |
| 9 Fri | Sagittarius | Fire | Barren | 2nd |
| 10 Sat | Sagittarius | Fire | Barren | 2nd |
| 11 Sun 12:50 am | Capricorn | Earth | Semi-fruitful | 2nd |
| 12 Mon | Capricorn | Earth | Semi-fruitful | 2nd |
| 13 Tue 11:35 am | Aquarius | Air | Barren | 2nd |
| 14 Wed | Aquarius | Air | Barren | 2nd |
| 15 Thu 11:49 pm | Pisces | Water | Fruitful | Full 8:29 am |
| 16 Fri | Pisces | Water | Fruitful | 3rd |
| 17 Sat | Pisces | Water | Fruitful | 3rd |
| 18 Sun 12:33 pm | Aries | Fire | Barren | 3rd |
| 19 Mon | Aries | Fire | Barren | 3rd |
| 20 Tue | Aries | Fire | Barren | 3rd |
| 21 Wed 12:37 am | Taurus | Earth | Semi-fruitful | 3rd |
| 22 Thu | Taurus | Earth | Semi-fruitful | 3rd |
| 23 Fri 10:34 am | Gemini | Air | Barren | 4th 10:56 am |
| 24 Sat | Gemini | Air | Barren | 4th |
| 25 Sun 5:05 pm | Cancer | Water | Fruitful | 4th |
| 26 Mon | Cancer | Water | Fruitful | 4th |
| 27 Tue 7:53 pm | Leo | Fire | Barren | 4th |
| 28 Wed | Leo | Fire | Barren | 4th |
| 29 Thu 7:57 pm | Virgo | Earth | Barren | 4th |
| 30 Fri | Virgo | Earth | Barren | New 6:37 am |
| 31 Sat 7:08 pm | Libra | Air | Semi-fruitful | 1st |

# August Aspectarian/Favorable & Unfavorable Days

| Date | Sun | Mercury | Venus | Mars | Jupiter | Saturn | Uranus | Neptune | Pluto |
|------|-----|---------|-------|------|---------|--------|--------|---------|-------|
| 1 | | | | C | T | | | | |
| 2 | | | | | | | T | | |
| 3 | | | | | Q | T | | O | T |
| 4 | | X | | | | | | | |
| 5 | X | | X | X | X | Q | | | Q |
| 6 | | Q | | | | | O | | |
| 7 | Q | | Q | | | X | | T | |
| 8 | | T | | Q | | | | | X |
| 9 | | | T | | C | | | | |
| 10 | T | | | T | | | | Q | |
| 11 | | | | | | | T | | |
| 12 | | | | | | C | | X | C |
| 13 | | O | | | | | | | |
| 14 | | | | | X | | Q | | |
| 15 | O | | O | O | | | | | |
| 16 | | | | | | | | X | |
| 17 | | | | | Q | X | | C | X |
| 18 | | | | | | | | | |
| 19 | | T | | | T | Q | | | |
| 20 | T | | | | | | | | Q |
| 21 | | | T | T | | | C | | |
| 22 | | Q | | | | T | | X | T |
| 23 | Q | | Q | Q | | | | | |
| 24 | | | | | O | | | Q | |
| 25 | X | X | | | | | | | |
| 26 | | | X | X | | O | X | T | |
| 27 | | | | | | | | | O |
| 28 | | | | | T | | Q | | |
| 29 | | C | | | | | | | |
| 30 | C | | C | C | Q | T | T | O | |
| 31 | | | | | | | | | T |

| Date | Aries | Taurus | Gemini | Cancer | Leo | Virgo | Libra | Scorpio | Sagittarius | Capricorn | Aquarius | Pisces |
|------|-------|--------|--------|--------|-----|-------|-------|---------|-------------|-----------|----------|--------|
| 1 | f | u | f | | F | | f | u | f | | U | |
| 2 | f | u | f | | F | | f | u | f | | U | |
| 3 | | f | u | f | | F | | f | u | f | | U |
| 4 | | f | u | f | | F | | f | u | f | | U |
| 5 | U | | f | u | f | | F | | f | u | f | |
| 6 | U | | f | u | f | | F | | f | u | f | |
| 7 | | U | | f | u | f | | F | | f | u | f |
| 8 | | U | | f | u | f | | F | | f | u | f |
| 9 | f | | U | | f | u | f | | F | | f | u |
| 10 | f | | U | | f | u | f | | F | | f | u |
| 11 | u | f | | U | | f | u | f | | F | | f |
| 12 | u | f | | U | | f | u | f | | F | | f |
| 13 | u | f | | U | | f | u | f | | F | | f |
| 14 | f | u | f | | U | | f | u | f | | F | |
| 15 | f | u | f | | U | | f | u | f | | F | |
| 16 | | f | u | f | | U | | f | u | f | | F |
| 17 | | f | u | f | | U | | f | u | f | | F |
| 18 | | f | u | f | | U | | f | u | f | | F |
| 19 | F | | f | u | f | | U | | f | u | f | |
| 20 | F | | f | u | f | | U | | f | u | f | |
| 21 | | F | | f | u | f | | U | | f | u | f |
| 22 | | F | | f | u | f | | U | | f | u | f |
| 23 | | F | | f | u | f | | U | | f | u | f |
| 24 | f | | F | | f | u | f | | U | | f | u |
| 25 | f | | F | | f | u | f | | U | | f | u |
| 26 | u | f | | F | | f | u | f | | U | | f |
| 27 | u | f | | F | | f | u | f | | U | | f |
| 28 | f | u | f | | F | | f | u | f | | U | |
| 29 | f | u | f | | F | | f | u | f | | U | |
| 30 | | f | u | f | | F | | f | u | f | | U |
| 31 | | f | u | f | | F | | f | u | f | | U |

## September Moon Table

| Date | Sign | Element | Nature | Phase |
|------|------|---------|--------|-------|
| 1 Sun | Libra | Air | Semi-fruitful | 1st |
| 2 Mon 7:35 pm | Scorpio | Water | Fruitful | 1st |
| 3 Tue | Scorpio | Water | Fruitful | 1st |
| 4 Wed 11:08 pm | Sagittarius | Fire | Barren | 1st |
| 5 Thu | Sagittarius | Fire | Barren | 2nd 11:10 pm |
| 6 Fri | Sagittarius | Fire | Barren | 2nd |
| 7 Sat 6:37 am | Capricorn | Earth | Semi-fruitful | 2nd |
| 8 Sun | Capricorn | Earth | Semi-fruitful | 2nd |
| 9 Mon 5:24 pm | Aquarius | Air | Barren | 2nd |
| 10 Tue | Aquarius | Air | Barren | 2nd |
| 11 Wed | Aquarius | Air | Barren | 2nd |
| 12 Thu 5:52 am | Pisces | Water | Fruitful | 2nd |
| 13 Fri | Pisces | Water | Fruitful | 2nd |
| 14 Sat 6:32 pm | Aries | Fire | Barren | Full 12:33 am |
| 15 Sun | Aries | Fire | Barren | 3rd |
| 16 Mon | Aries | Fire | Barren | 3rd |
| 17 Tue 6:31 am | Taurus | Earth | Semi-fruitful | 3rd |
| 18 Wed | Taurus | Earth | Semi-fruitful | 3rd |
| 19 Thu 4:58 pm | Gemini | Air | Barren | 3rd |
| 20 Fri | Gemini | Air | Barren | 3rd |
| 21 Sat | Gemini | Air | Barren | 4th 10:41 pm |
| 22 Sun 12:50 am | Cancer | Water | Fruitful | 4th |
| 23 Mon | Cancer | Water | Fruitful | 4th |
| 24 Tue 5:19 am | Leo | Fire | Barren | 4th |
| 25 Wed | Leo | Fire | Barren | 4th |
| 26 Thu 6:37 am | Virgo | Earth | Barren | 4th |
| 27 Fri | Virgo | Earth | Barren | 4th |
| 28 Sat 6:03 am | Libra | Air | Semi-fruitful | New 2:26 pm |
| 29 Sun | Libra | Air | Semi-fruitful | 1st |
| 30 Mon 5:42 am | Scorpio | Water | Fruitful | 1st |

# September Aspectarian/Favorable & Unfavorable Days

| Date | Sun | Mercury | Venus | Mars | Jupiter | Saturn | Uranus | Neptune | Pluto |
|---|---|---|---|---|---|---|---|---|---|
| 1 | | | | | X | Q | | | |
| 2 | | | | | | | | | Q |
| 3 | X | X | | X | | X | O | | |
| 4 | | | X | | | | | T | X |
| 5 | Q | | | Q | | | | | |
| 6 | | Q | Q | | C | | | Q | |
| 7 | | | | | | | T | | |
| 8 | T | T | | T | | C | | X | C |
| 9 | | | T | | | | | | |
| 10 | | | | | | | Q | | |
| 11 | | | | | X | | | | |
| 12 | | | | | | | X | | |
| 13 | | | | O | Q | X | | C | X |
| 14 | O | O | O | | | | | | |
| 15 | | | | | | Q | | | |
| 16 | | | | | T | | | | Q |
| 17 | | | | | | | C | | |
| 18 | | | | T | | T | | X | T |
| 19 | T | | | | | | | | |
| 20 | | T | T | | | | | | |
| 21 | Q | | | Q | O | | | Q | |
| 22 | | | Q | | | | X | | |
| 23 | | Q | | X | | O | | T | O |
| 24 | X | | | | | | Q | | |
| 25 | | X | X | | T | | | | |
| 26 | | | | | | | T | | |
| 27 | | | C | Q | T | | | O | T |
| 28 | C | | | | | | | | |
| 29 | | C | C | | X | Q | | | Q |
| 30 | | | | | | | O | | |

| Date | Aries | Taurus | Gemini | Cancer | Leo | Virgo | Libra | Scorpio | Sagittarius | Capricorn | Aquarius | Pisces |
|---|---|---|---|---|---|---|---|---|---|---|---|---|
| 1 | U | | f | u | f | | F | | f | u | f | |
| 2 | U | | f | u | f | | F | | f | u | f | |
| 3 | | U | | f | u | f | | F | | f | u | f |
| 4 | | U | | f | u | f | | F | | f | u | f |
| 5 | f | | U | | f | u | f | | F | | f | u |
| 6 | f | | U | | f | u | f | | F | | f | u |
| 7 | f | | U | | f | u | f | | F | | f | u |
| 8 | u | f | | U | | f | u | f | | F | | f |
| 9 | u | f | | U | | f | u | f | | F | | f |
| 10 | f | u | f | | U | | f | u | f | | F | |
| 11 | f | u | f | | U | | f | u | f | | F | |
| 12 | f | u | f | | U | | f | u | f | | F | |
| 13 | | f | u | f | | U | | f | u | f | | F |
| 14 | | f | u | f | | U | | f | u | f | | F |
| 15 | F | | f | u | f | | U | | f | u | f | |
| 16 | F | | f | u | f | | U | | f | u | f | |
| 17 | F | | f | u | f | | U | | f | u | f | |
| 18 | | F | | f | u | f | | U | | f | u | f |
| 19 | | F | | f | u | f | | U | | f | u | f |
| 20 | f | | F | | f | u | f | | U | | f | u |
| 21 | f | | F | | f | u | f | | U | | f | u |
| 22 | u | f | | F | | f | u | f | | U | | f |
| 23 | u | f | | F | | f | u | f | | U | | f |
| 24 | u | f | | F | | f | u | f | | U | | f |
| 25 | f | u | f | | F | | f | u | f | | U | |
| 26 | f | u | f | | F | | f | u | f | | U | |
| 27 | | f | u | f | | F | | f | u | f | | U |
| 28 | | f | u | f | | F | | f | u | f | | U |
| 29 | U | | f | u | f | | F | | f | u | f | |
| 30 | U | | f | u | f | | F | | f | u | f | |

## October Moon Table

| Date | Sign | Element | Nature | Phase |
|------|------|---------|--------|-------|
| 1 Tue | Scorpio | Water | Fruitful | 1st |
| 2 Wed 7:44 am | Sagittarius | Fire | Barren | 1st |
| 3 Thu | Sagittarius | Fire | Barren | 1st |
| 4 Fri 1:43 pm | Capricorn | Earth | Semi-fruitful | 1st |
| 5 Sat | Capricorn | Earth | Semi-fruitful | 2nd 12:47 pm |
| 6 Sun 11:42 pm | Aquarius | Air | Barren | 2nd |
| 7 Mon | Aquarius | Air | Barren | 2nd |
| 8 Tue | Aquarius | Air | Barren | 2nd |
| 9 Wed 12:05 pm | Pisces | Water | Fruitful | 2nd |
| 10 Thu | Pisces | Water | Fruitful | 2nd |
| 11 Fri | Pisces | Water | Fruitful | 2nd |
| 12 Sat 12:46 am | Aries | Fire | Barren | 2nd |
| 13 Sun | Aries | Fire | Barren | Full 5:08 pm |
| 14 Mon 12:24 pm | Taurus | Earth | Semi-fruitful | 3rd |
| 15 Tue | Taurus | Earth | Semi-fruitful | 3rd |
| 16 Wed 10:30 pm | Gemini | Air | Barren | 3rd |
| 17 Thu | Gemini | Air | Barren | 3rd |
| 18 Fri | Gemini | Air | Barren | 3rd |
| 19 Sat 6:43 am | Cancer | Water | Fruitful | 3rd |
| 20 Sun | Cancer | Water | Fruitful | 3rd |
| 21 Mon 12:29 pm | Leo | Fire | Barren | 4th 8:39 am |
| 22 Tue | Leo | Fire | Barren | 4th |
| 23 Wed 3:29 pm | Virgo | Earth | Barren | 4th |
| 24 Thu | Virgo | Earth | Barren | 4th |
| 25 Fri 4:20 pm | Libra | Air | Semi-fruitful | 4th |
| 26 Sat | Libra | Air | Semi-fruitful | 4th |
| 27 Sun 4:29 pm | Scorpio | Water | Fruitful | New 11:39 pm |
| 28 Mon | Scorpio | Water | Fruitful | 1st |
| 29 Tue 5:58 pm | Sagittarius | Fire | Barren | 1st |
| 30 Wed | Sagittarius | Fire | Barren | 1st |
| 31 Thu 10:38 pm | Capricorn | Earth | Semi-fruitful | 1st |

# October Aspectarian/Favorable & Unfavorable Days

| Date | Sun | Mercury | Venus | Mars | Jupiter | Saturn | Uranus | Neptune | Pluto |
|---|---|---|---|---|---|---|---|---|---|
| 1 | | | | | | X | | T | X |
| 2 | | | X | | | | | | |
| 3 | X | | | | C | | | Q | |
| 4 | | X | X | Q | | | | | |
| 5 | Q | | | | | C | T | X | |
| 6 | | | Q | | | | | | C |
| 7 | | Q | | T | | | | Q | |
| 8 | T | | | | X | | | | |
| 9 | | | T | | | | | X | |
| 10 | | T | | | | X | | C | |
| 11 | | | | | Q | | | | X |
| 12 | | | | O | | | | | |
| 13 | O | | | | T | Q | | | Q |
| 14 | | | | | | | | C | |
| 15 | | O | O | | | T | | X | |
| 16 | | | | | | | | | T |
| 17 | | | | T | | | | | |
| 18 | T | | | | O | | | Q | |
| 19 | | | | | | | | X | |
| 20 | | T | T | Q | O | | | T | O |
| 21 | Q | | | | | | | Q | |
| 22 | | | Q | X | | | | | |
| 23 | X | Q | | | T | | T | | |
| 24 | | | | | T | | O | | |
| 25 | | X | X | | Q | | | | T |
| 26 | | | | C | | Q | | | |
| 27 | C | | | | X | | O | | Q |
| 28 | | | | | | X | | T | |
| 29 | | C | C | | | | | | X |
| 30 | | | | | | | | Q | |
| 31 | | | | X | C | | | | |

| Date | Aries | Taurus | Gemini | Cancer | Leo | Virgo | Libra | Scorpio | Sagittarius | Capricorn | Aquarius | Pisces |
|---|---|---|---|---|---|---|---|---|---|---|---|---|
| 1 | | U | | f | u | f | | F | | f | u | f |
| 2 | | U | | f | u | f | | F | | f | u | f |
| 3 | f | | U | | f | u | f | | F | | f | u |
| 4 | f | | U | | f | u | f | | F | | f | u |
| 5 | u | f | | U | | f | u | f | | F | | f |
| 6 | u | f | | U | | f | u | f | | F | | f |
| 7 | f | u | f | | U | | f | u | f | | F | |
| 8 | f | u | f | | U | | f | u | f | | F | |
| 9 | f | u | f | | U | | f | u | f | | F | |
| 10 | | f | u | f | | U | | f | u | f | | F |
| 11 | | f | u | f | | U | | f | u | f | | F |
| 12 | F | | f | u | f | | U | | f | u | f | |
| 13 | F | | f | u | f | | U | | f | u | f | |
| 14 | F | | f | u | f | | U | | f | u | f | |
| 15 | | F | | f | u | f | | U | | f | u | f |
| 16 | | F | | f | u | f | | U | | f | u | f |
| 17 | f | | F | | f | u | f | | U | | f | u |
| 18 | f | | F | | f | u | f | | U | | f | u |
| 19 | f | | F | | f | u | f | | U | | f | u |
| 20 | u | f | | F | | f | u | f | | U | | f |
| 21 | u | f | | F | | f | u | f | | U | | f |
| 22 | f | u | f | | F | | f | u | f | | U | |
| 23 | f | u | f | | F | | f | u | f | | U | |
| 24 | | f | u | f | | F | | f | u | f | | U |
| 25 | | f | u | f | | F | | f | u | f | | U |
| 26 | U | | f | u | f | | F | | f | u | f | |
| 27 | U | | f | u | f | | F | | f | u | f | |
| 28 | | U | | f | u | f | | F | | f | u | f |
| 29 | | U | | f | u | f | | F | | f | u | f |
| 30 | f | | U | | f | u | f | | F | | f | u |
| 31 | f | | U | | f | u | f | | F | | f | u |

## November Moon Table

| Date | Sign | Element | Nature | Phase |
|---|---|---|---|---|
| 1 Fri | Capricorn | Earth | Semi-fruitful | 1st |
| 2 Sat | Capricorn | Earth | Semi-fruitful | 1st |
| 3 Sun 6:19 am | Aquarius | Air | Barren | 1st |
| 4 Mon | Aquarius | Air | Barren | 2nd 5:23 am |
| 5 Tue 6:08 pm | Pisces | Water | Fruitful | 2nd |
| 6 Wed | Pisces | Water | Fruitful | 2nd |
| 7 Thu | Pisces | Water | Fruitful | 2nd |
| 8 Fri 6:49 am | Aries | Fire | Barren | 2nd |
| 9 Sat | Aries | Fire | Barren | 2nd |
| 10 Sun 6:18 pm | Taurus | Earth | Semi-fruitful | 2nd |
| 11 Mon | Taurus | Earth | Semi-fruitful | 2nd |
| 12 Tue | Taurus | Earth | Semi-fruitful | Full 8:34 am |
| 13 Wed 3:46 am | Gemini | Air | Barren | 3rd |
| 14 Thu | Gemini | Air | Barren | 3rd |
| 15 Fri 11:15 am | Cancer | Water | Fruitful | 3rd |
| 16 Sat | Cancer | Water | Fruitful | 3rd |
| 17 Sun 4:57 pm | Leo | Fire | Barren | 3rd |
| 18 Mon | Leo | Fire | Barren | 3rd |
| 19 Tue 8:54 pm | Virgo | Earth | Barren | 4th 4:11 pm |
| 20 Wed | Virgo | Earth | Barren | 4th |
| 21 Thu 11:20 pm | Libra | Air | Semi-fruitful | 4th |
| 22 Fri | Libra | Air | Semi-fruitful | 4th |
| 23 Sat | Libra | Air | Semi-fruitful | 4th |
| 24 Sun 12:58 am | Scorpio | Water | Fruitful | 4th |
| 25 Mon | Scorpio | Water | Fruitful | 4th |
| 26 Tue 3:11 am | Sagittarius | Fire | Barren | New 10:06 am |
| 27 Wed | Sagittarius | Fire | Barren | 1st |
| 28 Thu 7:33 am | Capricorn | Earth | Semi-fruitful | 1st |
| 29 Fri | Capricorn | Earth | Semi-fruitful | 1st |
| 30 Sat 3:13 pm | Aquarius | Air | Barren | 1st |

# November Aspectarian/Favorable & Unfavorable Days

| Date | Sun | Mercury | Venus | Mars | Jupiter | Saturn | Uranus | Neptune | Pluto |
|---|---|---|---|---|---|---|---|---|---|
| 1 | X | | | | | | T | | |
| 2 | | | Q | | | C | | X | C |
| 3 | | X | X | | | | Q | | |
| 4 | Q | | | T | | | | | |
| 5 | | Q | | | X | | | | |
| 6 | T | | Q | | | | X | | |
| 7 | | T | | | Q | X | | C | X |
| 8 | | | | | | | | | |
| 9 | | | T | | | | Q | | |
| 10 | | | | O | T | | | | Q |
| 11 | | | | | | | C | | |
| 12 | O | O | | | | T | | X | T |
| 13 | | | | | | | | | |
| 14 | | | O | | | | | Q | |
| 15 | | | | T | O | | X | | |
| 16 | | T | | | | O | | T | |
| 17 | T | | | Q | | | Q | | O |
| 18 | | Q | | | | | | | |
| 19 | Q | | T | X | T | | | | |
| 20 | | X | | | | | T | O | |
| 21 | X | | Q | | Q | T | | | T |
| 22 | | | | | | | | | |
| 23 | | X | | | X | Q | | | Q |
| 24 | | C | | C | | | O | | |
| 25 | | | | | | X | | T | X |
| 26 | C | | | | | | | | |
| 27 | | | | | | | | Q | |
| 28 | | C | | X | C | | T | | |
| 29 | | X | | | | C | | X | C |
| 30 | | | | | | | Q | | |

| Date | Aries | Taurus | Gemini | Cancer | Leo | Virgo | Libra | Scorpio | Sagittarius | Capricorn | Aquarius | Pisces |
|---|---|---|---|---|---|---|---|---|---|---|---|---|
| 1 | u | f | | U | | f | u | f | | F | | f |
| 2 | u | f | | U | | f | u | f | | F | | f |
| 3 | u | f | | U | | f | u | f | | F | | f |
| 4 | f | u | f | | U | | f | u | f | | F | |
| 5 | f | u | f | | U | | f | u | f | | F | |
| 6 | | f | u | f | | U | | f | u | f | | F |
| 7 | | f | u | f | | U | | f | u | f | | F |
| 8 | | f | u | f | | U | | f | u | f | | F |
| 9 | F | | f | u | f | | U | | f | u | f | |
| 10 | F | | f | u | f | | U | | f | u | f | |
| 11 | | F | | f | u | f | | U | | f | u | f |
| 12 | | F | | f | u | f | | U | | f | u | f |
| 13 | | F | | f | u | f | | U | | f | u | f |
| 14 | f | | F | | f | u | f | | U | | f | u |
| 15 | f | | F | | f | u | f | | U | | f | u |
| 16 | u | f | | F | | f | u | f | | U | | f |
| 17 | u | f | | F | | f | u | f | | U | | f |
| 18 | f | u | f | | F | | f | u | f | | U | |
| 19 | f | u | f | | F | | f | u | f | | U | |
| 20 | | f | u | f | | F | | f | u | f | | U |
| 21 | | f | u | f | | F | | f | u | f | | U |
| 22 | U | | f | u | f | | F | | f | u | f | |
| 23 | U | | f | u | f | | F | | f | u | f | |
| 24 | | U | | f | u | f | | F | | f | u | f |
| 25 | | U | | f | u | f | | F | | f | u | f |
| 26 | | U | | f | u | f | | F | | f | u | f |
| 27 | f | | U | | f | u | f | | F | | f | u |
| 28 | f | | U | | f | u | f | | F | | f | u |
| 29 | u | f | | U | | f | u | f | | F | | f |
| 30 | u | f | | U | | f | u | f | | F | | f |

## December Moon Table

| Date | Sign | Element | Nature | Phase |
|------|------|---------|--------|-------|
| 1 Sun | Aquarius | Air | Barren | 1st |
| 2 Mon | Aquarius | Air | Barren | 1st |
| 3 Tue 2:11 am | Pisces | Water | Fruitful | 1st |
| 4 Wed | Pisces | Water | Fruitful | 2nd 1:58 am |
| 5 Thu 2:44 pm | Aries | Fire | Barren | 2nd |
| 6 Fri | Aries | Fire | Barren | 2nd |
| 7 Sat | Aries | Fire | Barren | 2nd |
| 8 Sun 2:29 am | Taurus | Earth | Semi-fruitful | 2nd |
| 9 Mon | Taurus | Earth | Semi-fruitful | 2nd |
| 10 Tue 11:47 am | Gemini | Air | Barren | 2nd |
| 11 Wed | Gemini | Air | Barren | 2nd |
| 12 Thu 6:23 pm | Cancer | Water | Fruitful | Full 12:12 am |
| 13 Fri | Cancer | Water | Fruitful | 3rd |
| 14 Sat 10:56 pm | Leo | Fire | Barren | 3rd |
| 15 Sun | Leo | Fire | Barren | 3rd |
| 16 Mon | Leo | Fire | Barren | 3rd |
| 17 Tue 2:16 am | Virgo | Earth | Barren | 3rd |
| 18 Wed | Virgo | Earth | Barren | 4th 11:57 pm |
| 19 Thu 5:04 am | Libra | Air | Semi-fruitful | 4th |
| 20 Fri | Libra | Air | Semi-fruitful | 4th |
| 21 Sat 7:57 am | Scorpio | Water | Fruitful | 4th |
| 22 Sun | Scorpio | Water | Fruitful | 4th |
| 23 Mon 11:34 am | Sagittarius | Fire | Barren | 4th |
| 24 Tue | Sagittarius | Fire | Barren | 4th |
| 25 Wed 4:45 pm | Capricorn | Earth | Semi-fruitful | 4th |
| 26 Thu | Capricorn | Earth | Semi-fruitful | New 12:13 am |
| 27 Fri | Capricorn | Earth | Semi-fruitful | 1st |
| 28 Sat 12:21 am | Aquarius | Air | Barren | 1st |
| 29 Sun | Aquarius | Air | Barren | 1st |
| 30 Mon 10:41 am | Pisces | Water | Fruitful | 1st |
| 31 Mon | Scorpio | Water | Fruitful | 4th |

# December Aspectarian/Favorable & Unfavorable Days

| Date | Sun | Mercury | Venus | Mars | Jupiter | Saturn | Uranus | Neptune | Pluto |
|------|-----|---------|-------|------|---------|--------|--------|---------|-------|
| 1 | X | | Q | | | | | | |
| 2 | | Q | | | | | | | |
| 3 | | | X | T | X | | X | | |
| 4 | Q | | | | | X | | C | X |
| 5 | | T | | | Q | | | | |
| 6 | T | | Q | | | | | | |
| 7 | | | | | | Q | | | Q |
| 8 | | | | | T | | C | | |
| 9 | | | T | O | | T | | X | T |
| 10 | | O | | | | | | | |
| 11 | | | | | | | | Q | |
| 12 | O | | | | O | | X | | |
| 13 | | | T | | | | | T | |
| 14 | | | O | | | O | | | O |
| 15 | | T | | | | | Q | | |
| 16 | T | | Q | | | | | | |
| 17 | | | | | T | | T | | |
| 18 | Q | Q | | X | | T | | O | T |
| 19 | | | T | | Q | | | | |
| 20 | | X | | | | Q | | | Q |
| 21 | X | | Q | | X | | O | | |
| 22 | | | C | | X | | | T | X |
| 23 | | | X | | | | | | |
| 24 | | | | | | | | Q | |
| 25 | | C | | | | | T | | |
| 26 | C | | | | C | | | X | |
| 27 | | | X | | C | | | | C |
| 28 | | C | | | | Q | | | |
| 29 | | | | | | | | | |
| 30 | | X | | Q | X | | X | | |
| 31 | X | | | | | | | C | |

| Date | Aries | Taurus | Gemini | Cancer | Leo | Virgo | Libra | Scorpio | Sagittarius | Capricorn | Aquarius | Pisces |
|------|-------|--------|--------|--------|-----|-------|-------|---------|-------------|-----------|----------|--------|
| 1 | f | u | f | | U | | f | u | f | | F | |
| 2 | f | u | f | | U | | f | u | f | | F | |
| 3 | | f | u | f | | U | | f | u | f | | F |
| 4 | | f | u | f | | U | | f | u | f | | F |
| 5 | | f | u | f | | U | | f | u | f | | F |
| 6 | F | | f | u | f | | U | | f | u | f | |
| 7 | F | | f | u | f | | U | | f | u | f | |
| 8 | | F | | f | u | f | | U | | f | u | f |
| 9 | | F | | f | u | f | | U | | f | u | f |
| 10 | | F | | f | u | f | | U | | f | u | f |
| 11 | f | | F | | f | u | f | | U | | f | u |
| 12 | f | | F | | f | u | f | | U | | f | u |
| 13 | u | f | | F | | f | u | f | | U | | f |
| 14 | u | f | | F | | f | u | f | | U | | f |
| 15 | f | u | f | | F | | f | u | f | | U | |
| 16 | f | u | f | | F | | f | u | f | | U | |
| 17 | | f | u | f | | F | | f | u | f | | U |
| 18 | | f | u | f | | F | | f | u | f | | U |
| 19 | | f | u | f | | F | | f | u | f | | U |
| 20 | U | | f | u | f | | F | | f | u | f | |
| 21 | U | | f | u | f | | F | | f | u | f | |
| 22 | | U | | f | u | f | | F | | f | u | f |
| 23 | | U | | f | u | f | | F | | f | u | f |
| 24 | f | | U | | f | u | f | | F | | f | u |
| 25 | f | | U | | f | u | f | | F | | f | u |
| 26 | u | f | | U | | f | u | f | | F | | f |
| 27 | u | f | | U | | f | u | f | | F | | f |
| 28 | f | u | f | | U | | f | u | f | | F | |
| 29 | f | u | f | | U | | f | u | f | | F | |
| 30 | f | u | f | | U | | f | u | f | | F | |
| 31 | | f | u | f | | U | | f | u | f | | F |

# 2019 Retrograde Planets

| Planet | Begin | Eastern | Pacific | End | Eastern | Pacific |
|--------|-------|---------|---------|-----|---------|---------|
| Uranus | 8/7/18 | 12:48 pm | **9:48 am** | 1/6/19 | 3:27 pm | **12:27 pm** |
| Mercury | 3/5 | 1:19 pm | **10:19 am** | 3/28 | 9:59 am | **6:59 am** |
| Jupiter | 4/10 | 1:01 pm | **10:01 am** | 8/11 | 9:37 am | **6:37 am** |
| Pluto | 4/24 | 2:48 pm | **11:48 am** | 10/2 | | **11:39 pm** |
| Pluto | 4/24 | 2:48 pm | **11:48 am** | 10/3 | 2:39 am | |
| Saturn | 4/29 | 8:54 pm | **5:54 pm** | 9/18 | 4:47 am | **1:47 am** |
| Neptune | 6/21 | 10:36 am | **7:36 am** | 11/27 | 7:32 am | **4:32 am** |
| Mercury | 7/7 | 7:14 pm | **4:14 pm** | 7/31 | 11:58 pm | **8:58 pm** |
| Uranus | 8/11 | 10:27 pm | **7:27 pm** | 1/10/20 | 8:49 pm | **5:49 pm** |
| Mercury | 10/31 | 11:41 am | **8:41 am** | 11/20 | 2:12 pm | **11:12 am** |

Eastern Time in plain type, **Pacific Time in bold type**

| | Dec 18 | Jan 19 | Feb | Mar | Apr | May | Jun | Jul | Aug | Sep | Oct | Nov | Dec | Jan 20 |
|---|---|---|---|---|---|---|---|---|---|---|---|---|---|---|
| ☿ | | | | ▓ | | | | ▓ | | | | ▓ | | |
| ♃ | | | | | ▓ | ▓ | ▓ | | | | | | | |
| ♀ | | | | | | | | | | | | | | |
| ♄ | | | | | ▓ | ▓ | ▓ | ▓ | ▓ | | | | | |
| ♇ | | | | | ▓ | ▓ | ▓ | ▓ | ▓ | ▓ | | | | |
| ♆ | | | | | | | ▓ | ▓ | ▓ | ▓ | ▓ | | | |
| ♅ | ▓ | | | | | | | | ▓ | ▓ | ▓ | ▓ | | |
| ♂ | | | | | | | | | | | | | | |

# Egg-Setting Dates

| To Have Eggs by this Date | Sign | Qtr. | Date to Set Eggs |
|---|---|---|---|
| Jan 9, 2:44 pm–Jan 12, 3:18 am | Pisces | 1st | Dec 19, 2018 |
| Jan 14, 1:31 pm–Jan 16, 8:00 pm | Taurus | 2nd | Dec 24, 2018 |
| Jan 18, 10:44 pm–Jan 20, 10:54 pm | Cancer | 2nd | Dec 28, 2018 |
| Feb 5, 9:02 pm–Feb 8, 9:34 am | Pisces | 1st | Jan 15, 2019 |
| Feb 10, 8:28 pm–Feb 13, 4:32 am | Taurus | 1st | Jan 20 |
| Feb 15, 9:03 am–Feb 17, 10:21 am | Cancer | 2nd | Jan 25 |
| Mar 6, 11:04 am–Mar 7, 3:27 pm | Pisces | 1st | Feb 13 |
| Mar 10, 3:10 am–Mar 12, 11:48 am | Taurus | 1st | Feb 17 |
| Mar 14, 5:49 pm–Mar 16, 8:57 pm | Cancer | 2nd | Feb 21 |
| Mar 20, 9:28 pm–Mar 20, 9:43 pm | Libra | 2nd | Feb 27 |
| Apr 6, 9:06 am–Apr 8, 5:15 pm | Taurus | 1st | Mar 16 |
| Apr 10, 11:31 pm–Apr 13, 3:50 am | Cancer | 1st | Mar 20 |
| Apr 17, 7:22 am–Apr 19, 7:12 am | Libra | 2nd | Mar 27 |
| May 4, 6:45 pm–May 5, 11:40 pm | Taurus | 1st | Apr 13 |
| May 8, 5:06 am–May 10, 9:14 am | Cancer | 1st | Apr 17 |
| May 14, 2:51 pm–May 16, 5:26 pm | Libra | 2nd | Apr 23 |
| Jun 4, 12:17 pm–Jun 6, 3:16 pm | Cancer | 1st | May 14 |
| Jun 10, 8:29 pm–Jun 13, 12:02 am | Libra | 2nd | May 20 |
| Jul 2, 3:16 pm–Jul 3, 11:19 pm | Cancer | 1st | Jun 11 |
| Jul 8, 2:07 am–Jul 10, 5:29 am | Libra | 1st | Jun 17 |
| Aug 4, 9:30 am–Aug 6, 11:31 am | Libra | 1st | Jul 14 |
| Aug 31, 7:08 pm–Sep 2, 7:35 pm | Libra | 1st | Aug 10 |
| Sep 12, 5:52 am–Sep 14, 12:33 am | Pisces | 2nd | Aug 22 |
| Sep 28, 2:26 pm–Sep 30, 5:42 am | Libra | 1st | Sep 07 |
| Oct 9, 12:05 pm–Oct 12, 12:46 am | Pisces | 2nd | Sep 18 |
| Nov 5, 6:08 pm–Nov 8, 6:49 am | Pisces | 2nd | Oct 15 |
| Nov 10, 6:18 pm–Nov 12, 8:34 am | Taurus | 2nd | Oct 20 |
| Dec 3, 2:11 am–Dec 5, 2:44 pm | Pisces | 1st | Nov 12 |
| Dec 8, 2:29 am–Dec 10, 11:47 am | Taurus | 2nd | Nov 17 |

# Dates to Hunt and Fish

| Date | Quarter | Sign |
|------|---------|------|
| Jan 9, 2:44 pm–Jan 12, 3:18 am | 1st | Pisces |
| Jan 18, 10:44 pm–Jan 20, 10:54 pm | 2nd | Cancer |
| Jan 27, 2:31 am–Jan 29, 9:33 am | 3rd | Scorpio |
| Feb 5, 9:02 pm–Feb 8, 9:34 am | 1st | Pisces |
| Feb 15, 9:03 pm–Feb 17, 10:21 am | 2nd | Cancer |
| Feb 23, 10:56 am–Feb 25, 4:19 pm | 3rd | Scorpio |
| Feb 25, 4:19 pm–Feb 28, 1:48 am | 3rd | Sagittarius |
| Mar 5, 3:11 am–Mar 7, 3:27 pm | 4th | Pisces |
| Mar 14, 5:49 pm–Mar 16, 8:57 pm | 2nd | Cancer |
| Mar 22, 10:16 pm–Mar 25, 2:06 am | 3rd | Scorpio |
| Mar 25, 2:06 am–Mar 27, 10:07 am | 3rd | Sagittarius |
| Apr 1, 10:48 am–Apr 3, 10:56 pm | 4th | Pisces |
| Apr 10, 11:31 pm–Apr 13, 3:50 am | 1st | Cancer |
| Apr 19, 8:41 am–Apr 21, 11:59 am | 3rd | Scorpio |
| Apr 21, 11:59 am–Apr 23, 6:50 pm | 3rd | Sagittarius |
| Apr 28, 6:11 pm–May 1, 6:24 am | 4th | Pisces |
| May 8, 5:06 am–May 10, 9:14 am | 1st | Cancer |
| May 16, 5:26 pm–May 18, 9:21 pm | 2nd | Scorpio |
| May 18, 9:21 pm–May 21, 3:56 am | 3rd | Sagittarius |
| May 26, 2:08 am–May 28, 2:32 pm | 3rd | Pisces |
| Jun 4, 12:17 pm–Jun 6, 3:16 pm | 1st | Cancer |
| Jun 13, 12:02 am–Jun 15, 5:03 am | 2nd | Scorpio |
| Jun 15, 5:03 am–Jun 17, 12:13 pm | 2nd | Sagittarius |
| Jun 22, 10:01 am–Jun 24, 10:38 pm | 3rd | Pisces |
| Jun 24, 10:38 pm–Jun 27, 9:32 am | 3rd | Aries |
| Jul 1, 9:24 pm–Jul 3, 11:19 pm | 4th | Cancer |
| Jul 10, 5:29 am–Jul 12, 11:05 am | 2nd | Scorpio |
| Jul 12, 11:05 am–Jul 14, 7:05 pm | 2nd | Sagittarius |
| Jul 19, 5:19 pm–Jul 22, 6:02 am | 3rd | Pisces |
| Jul 22, 6:02 am–Jul 24, 5:42 pm | 3rd | Aries |
| Jul 29, 7:31 am–Jul 31, 9:18 am | 4th | Cancer |
| Aug 6, 11:31 am–Aug 8, 4:35 pm | 1st | Scorpio |
| Aug 8, 4:35 pm–Aug 11, 12:50 am | 2nd | Sagittarius |
| Aug 15, 11:49 pm–Aug 18, 12:33 pm | 3rd | Pisces |
| Aug 18, 12:33 pm–Aug 21, 12:37 am | 3rd | Aries |
| Aug 25, 5:05 pm–Aug 27, 7:53 pm | 4th | Cancer |
| Sep 2, 7:35 pm–Sep 4, 11:08 pm | 1st | Scorpio |
| Sep 12, 5:52 am–Sep 14, 6:32 pm | 2nd | Pisces |
| Sep 14, 6:32 pm–Sep 17, 6:31 am | 3rd | Aries |
| Sep 22, 12:50 am–Sep 24, 5:19 am | 4th | Cancer |
| Sep 30, 5:42 am–Oct 2, 7:44 am | 1st | Scorpio |
| Oct 9, 12:05 pm–Oct 12, 12:46 am | 2nd | Pisces |
| Oct 12, 12:46 am–Oct 14, 12:24 pm | 2nd | Aries |
| Oct 19, 6:43 am–Oct 21, 12:29 pm | 3rd | Cancer |
| Oct 27, 4:29 pm–Oct 29, 5:58 pm | 4th | Scorpio |
| Nov 5, 6:08 pm–Nov 8, 6:49 am | 2nd | Pisces |
| Nov 8, 6:49 am–Nov 10, 6:18 pm | 2nd | Aries |
| Nov 15, 11:15 am–Nov 17, 4:57 pm | 3rd | Cancer |
| Nov 24, 12:58 am–Nov 26, 3:11 am | 4th | Scorpio |
| Dec 3, 2:11 am–Dec 5, 2:44 pm | 1st | Pisces |
| Dec 5, 2:44 pm–Dec 8, 2:29 am | 2nd | Aries |
| Dec 12, 6:23 pm–Dec 14, 10:56 pm | 3rd | Cancer |
| Dec 21, 7:57 am–Dec 23, 11:34 am | 4th | Scorpio |

# Dates to Destroy Weeds and Pests

| Date | Sign | Qtr. |
|------|------|------|
| Jan 21 12:16 am–Jan 22 10:22 pm | Leo | 3rd |
| Jan 22 10:22 pm–Jan 24 11:02 pm | Virgo | 3rd |
| Jan 29 9:33 am–Jan 31 7:47 pm | Sagittarius | 4th |
| Feb 3 8:03 am–Feb 4 4:04 pm | Aquarius | 4th |
| Feb 19 10:54 am–Feb 21 9:17 am | Virgo | 3rd |
| Feb 25 4:19 pm–Feb 26 6:28 am | Sagittarius | 3rd |
| Feb 26 6:28 am–Feb 28 1:48 am | Sagittarius | 4th |
| Mar 2 2:06 pm–Mar 5 3:11 am | Aquarius | 4th |
| Mar 25 2:06 am–Mar 27 10:07 am | Sagittarius | 3rd |
| Mar 29 9:46 pm–Apr 1 10:48 am | Aquarius | 4th |
| Apr 3 10:56 pm–Apr 5 4:50 am | Aries | 4th |
| Apr 21 11:59 am–Apr 23 6:50 pm | Sagittarius | 3rd |
| Apr 26 5:27 am–Apr 26 6:18 pm | Aquarius | 3rd |
| Apr 26 6:18 pm–Apr 28 6:11 pm | Aquarius | 4th |
| May 1 6:24 am–May 3 4:18 pm | Aries | 4th |
| May 18 9:21 am–May 21 3:56 am | Sagittarius | 3rd |
| May 23 1:49 pm–May 26 2:08 am | Aquarius | 3rd |
| May 28 2:32 pm–May 31 12:43 am | Aries | 4th |
| Jun 2 7:48 am–Jun 3 6:02 am | Gemini | 4th |
| Jun 17 4:31 am–Jun 17 12:13 pm | Sagittarius | 3rd |
| Jun 19 10:01 pm–Jun 22 10:01 am | Aquarius | 3rd |
| Jun 24 10:38 pm–Jun 25 5:46 am | Aries | 3rd |
| Jun 25 5:46 am–Jun 27 9:32 am | Aries | 4th |
| Jun 29 5:09 pm–Jul 1 9:24 pm | Gemini | 4th |
| Jul 17 5:19 am–Jul 24 5:42 pm | Aquarius | 3rd |
| Jul 22 6:02 am–Jul 24 5:42 pm | Aries | 3rd |
| Jul 27 2:29 am–Jul 29 7:31 am | Gemini | 4th |
| Jul 31 9:18 am–Jul 31 11:12 pm | Leo | 4th |
| Aug 15 8:29 am–Aug 15 11:49 pm | Aquarius | 3rd |
| Aug 18 12:33 pm–Aug 21 12:37 am | Aries | 3rd |
| Aug 23 10:34 am–Aug 23 10:56 am | Gemini | 3rd |
| Aug 23 10:56 am–Aug 25 5:05 pm | Gemini | 4th |
| Aug 27 7:53 pm–Aug 29 7:57 pm | Leo | 4th |
| Aug 29 7:57 pm–Aug 30 6:37 am | Virgo | 4th |
| Sep 14 6:32 pm–Sep 17 6:31 am | Aries | 3rd |
| Sep 19 4:58 pm–Sep 21 10:41 pm | Gemini | 3rd |
| Sep 21 10:41 pm–Sep 22 12:50 am | Gemini | 4th |
| Sep 24 5:19 am–Sep 26 6:37 am | Leo | 4th |
| Sep 26 6:37 am–Sep 28 6:03 am | Virgo | 4th |
| Oct 13 5:08 pm–Oct 14 12:24 pm | Aries | 3rd |
| Oct 16 10:30 pm–Oct 19 6:43 am | Gemini | 3rd |
| Oct 21 12:29 pm–Oct 23 3:29 pm | Leo | 4th |
| Oct 23 3:29 pm–Oct 25 4:20 pm | Virgo | 4th |
| Nov 13 3:46 am–Nov 15 11:15 am | Gemini | 3rd |
| Nov 17 4:57 pm–Nov 19 4:11 pm | Leo | 3rd |
| Nov 19 4:11 pm–Nov 19 8:54 pm | Leo | 4th |
| Nov 19 8:54 pm–Nov 21 11:20 pm | Virgo | 4th |
| Nov 26 3:11 am–Nov 26 10:06 am | Sagittarius | 4th |
| Dec 12 12:12 am–Dec 12 6:23 pm | Gemini | 3rd |
| Dec 14 10:56 pm–Dec 17 2:16 am | Leo | 3rd |
| Dec 17 2:16 am–Dec 18 11:57 pm | Virgo | 3rd |
| Dec 18 11:57 pm–Dec 19 5:04 am | Virgo | 4th |
| Dec 23 11:34 am–Dec 25 4:45 pm | Sagittarius | 4th |

# Time Zone Map

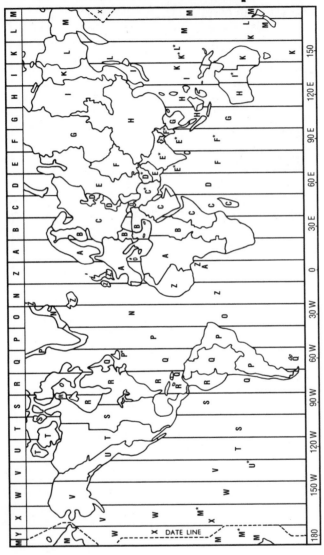

# Time Zone Conversions

(R)  EST—Used in book
(S)  CST—Subtract 1 hour
(T)  MST—Subtract 2 hours
(U)  PST—Subtract 3 hours
(V)  Subtract 4 hours
(V*) Subtract 4½ hours
(U*) Subtract 3½ hours
(W)  Subtract 5 hours
(X)  Subtract 6 hours
(Y)  Subtract 7 hours
(Q)  Add 1 hour
(P)  Add 2 hours
(P*) Add 2½ hours
(O)  Add 3 hours
(N)  Add 4 hours
(Z)  Add 5 hours
(A)  Add 6 hours
(B)  Add 7 hours
(C)  Add 8 hours
(C*) Add 8½ hours

(D)  Add 9 hours
(D*) Add 9½ hours
(E)  Add 10 hours
(E*) Add 10½ hours
(F)  Add 11 hours
(F*) Add 11½ hours
(G)  Add 12 hours
(H)  Add 13 hours
(I)  Add 14 hours
(I*) Add 14½ hours
(K)  Add 15 hours
(K*) Add 15½ hours
(L)  Add 16 hours
(L*) Add 16½ hours
(M)  Add 17 hours
(M*) Add 18 hours
(P*) Add 2½ hours

---

**Important!**

All times given in the *Moon Sign Book* are set in Eastern Time.
The conversions shown here are for standard times only.
Use the time zone conversions map and table to calculate
the difference in your time zone. You must make the adjust-
ment for your time zone and adjust for Daylight Saving Time
where applicable.

# Weather, Economic
# & Lunar Forecasts

2018 © evgeny atamanenko Image from BigStockPhoto.com

# Forecasting the Weather

*by Kris Brandt Riske*

Astrometeorology—astrological weather forecasting—reveals seasonal and weekly weather trends based on the cardinal ingresses (Summer and Winter Solstices, and Spring and Autumn Equinoxes) and the four monthly lunar phases. The planetary alignments and the longitudes and latitudes they influence have the strongest effect, but the zodiacal signs are also involved in creating weather conditions.

The components of a thunderstorm, for example, are heat, wind, and electricity. A Mars-Jupiter configuration generates the necessary heat and Mercury adds wind and electricity. A severe thunderstorm, and those that produce tornados, usually involve Mercury, Mars, Uranus, or Neptune. The zodiacal signs add their energy to the planetary mix to increase or decrease the chance for weather phenomena and their severity.

In general, the fire signs (Aries, Leo, Sagittarius) indicate heat and dryness, both of which peak when Mars, the planet with a similar nature, is in these signs. Water signs (Cancer, Scorpio, Pisces) are conducive to precipitation, and air signs (Gemini, Libra, Aquarius) are conducive to cool temperatures and wind. Earth signs (Taurus, Virgo, Capricorn) vary from wet to dry, heat to cold. The signs and their prevailing weather conditions are listed here:

Aries: Heat, dry, wind
Taurus: Moderate temperatures, precipitation
Gemini: Cool temperatures, wind, dry
Cancer: Cold, steady precipitation
Leo: Heat, dry, lightning
Virgo: Cold, dry, windy
Libra: Cool, windy, fair
Scorpio: Extreme temperatures, abundant precipitation
Sagittarius: Warm, fair, moderate wind
Capricorn: Cold, wet, damp
Aquarius: Cold, dry, high pressure, lightning
Pisces: Wet, cool, low pressure

Take note of the Moon's sign at each lunar phase. It reveals the prevailing weather conditions for the next six to seven days. The same is true of Mercury and Venus. These two influential weather planets transit the entire zodiac each year, unless retrograde patterns add their influence.

## Planetary Influences

People relied on astrology to forecast weather for thousands of years. They were able to predict drought, floods, and temperature variations through interpreting planetary alignments. In recent years there has been a renewed interest in astrometeorology.

A weather forecast can be composed for any date—tomorrow, next week, or a thousand years in the future. According to astrometeorology, each planet governs certain weather phenomena. When certain planets are aligned with other planets, weather—precipitation, cloudy or clear skies, tornados, hurricanes, and other conditions—are generated.

### Sun and Moon

The Sun governs the constitution of the weather and, like the Moon, it serves as a trigger for other planetary configurations that result in weather events. When the Sun is prominent in a cardinal ingress or lunar phase chart, the area is often warm and sunny. The Moon can bring or withhold moisture, depending upon its sign placement.

### Mercury

Mercury is also a triggering planet, but its main influence is wind direction and velocity. In its stationary periods, Mercury reflects high winds, and its influence is always prominent in major weather events, such as hurricanes and tornadoes, when it tends to lower the temperature.

### Venus

Venus governs moisture, clouds, and humidity. It brings warming trends that produce sunny, pleasant weather if in positive aspect to other planets. In some signs—Libra, Virgo, Gemini, Sagittarius—Venus is drier. It is at its wettest when placed in Cancer, Scorpio, Pisces, or Taurus.

### Mars

Mars is associated with heat, drought, and wind, and can raise the temperature to record-setting levels when in a fire sign (Aries, Leo, Sagittarius). Mars is also the planet that provides the spark that generates thunderstorms and is prominent in tornado and hurricane configurations.

## Jupiter

Jupiter, a fair-weather planet, tends toward higher temperatures when in Aries, Leo, or Sagittarius. It is associated with high-pressure systems and is a contributing factor at times to dryness. Storms are often amplified by Jupiter.

## Saturn

Saturn is associated with low-pressure systems, cloudy to overcast skies, and excessive precipitation. Temperatures drop when Saturn is involved. Major winter storms always have a strong Saturn influence, as do storms that produce a slow, steady downpour for hours or days.

## Uranus

Like Jupiter, Uranus indicates high-pressure systems. It reflects descending cold air and, when prominent, is responsible for a jet stream that extends far south. Uranus can bring drought in winter, and it is involved in thunderstorms, tornados, and hurricanes.

## Neptune

Neptune is the wettest planet. It signals low-pressure systems and is dominant when hurricanes are in the forecast. When Neptune is strongly placed, flood danger is high. It's often associated with winter thaws. Temperatures, humidity, and cloudiness increase where Neptune influences weather.

## Pluto

Pluto is associated with weather extremes, as well as unseasonably warm temperatures and drought. It reflects the high winds involved in major hurricanes, storms, and tornados.

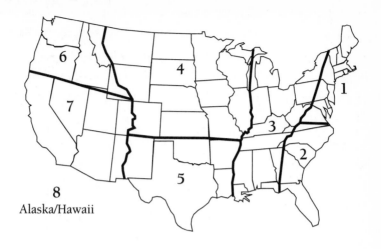

# Weather Forecast for 2019

*by Kris Brandt Riske*

## Winter

Temperatures in zone 1 will range from seasonal to above this winter, along with a higher percentage of cloudy days and precipitation seasonal to above. Zone 2 will be much the same, although not as warm as in zone 1. Warmer temperatures will also be the norm in zone 3, where precipitation levels will be seasonal to below. Zone 3 will, however, experience some days of strong thunderstorms, as well as stormy conditions descending from Canada into southern parts of the zone.

Temperatures in zones 4 and 5 will range from seasonal to above, but these zones are also likely to experience periods of significant cold as a result of high pressure systems. Winter storms entering from Canada will travel a path from eastern Montana southeast to Texas, and others will find their way from Idaho and Montana southeast to New Mexico and Texas. Precipitation in these zones will range from seasonal to above.

Although coastal areas in zones 6 and 7 will see precipitation, other parts of these zones are likely to be more dry than wet, except for the far eastern areas of these zones. Temperatures in these zones will range from seasonal to above, with an above average number of windy days.

In zone 8, winter temperatures in Alaska will range from seasonal to below with precipitation the same. Hawaii will be warm and mostly fair to partly cloudy with precipitation ranging from seasonal to below.

## 4th Quarter Moon, December 29, 2018–January 4, 2019

**Zone 1:** Partly cloudy to cloudy and windy skies accompany seasonal temperatures and precipitation south, possibly locally heavy.

**Zone 2:** Northern areas see precipitation, some abundant, central and southern areas see scattered precipitation, skies are partly cloudy to cloudy, and temperatures are seasonal.

**Zone 3:** Temperatures are seasonal to below, skies are variably cloudy, and much of the zone sees precipitation, some possibly abundant.

**Zone 4:** Much of the zone is windy with precipitation, skies are partly cloudy to cloudy, and temperatures are seasonal.

**Zone 5:** Central and eastern parts of the zone see precipitation, temperatures are seasonal, and the zone is variably cloudy.

**Zone 6:** Seasonal temperatures accompany fair to partly cloudy skies.

**Zone 7:** Central and eastern areas have a chance for precipitation, skies are partly cloudy to cloudy, and temperatures are seasonal.

**Zone 8:** Alaska is seasonal with partly cloudy to cloudy skies and abundant precipitation east. Hawaii is windy, skies are fair, and temperatures are seasonal to above.

## New Moon, January 5–13

**Zone 1:** The zone is overcast with precipitation and temperatures below seasonal.

**Zone 2:** Northern areas are cloudy with precipitation, central and southern areas are fair to partly cloudy and windy with potential for strong thunderstorms.

**Zone 3:** The zone is windy and variably cloudy with showers and thunderstorms, and temperatures are seasonal to below.

**Zone 4:** Western areas are mostly fair, the Plains see storms with high winds, eastern areas are fair to partly cloudy, and temperatures are seasonal to below

**Zone 5:** Western areas are mostly fair and windy, central parts of the zone are partly cloudy to cloudy with scattered precipitation, eastern areas are partly cloudy with a chance for precipitation, and temperatures are seasonal to below.

**Zone 6:** The zone is windy as a front moves across, bringing precipitation, some locally heavy, and temperatures seasonal to below.

**Zone 7:** Western areas are windy and variably cloudy, central and eastern areas see more cloudiness with precipitation, and temperatures are seasonal to below.

**Zone 8:** Central and western parts of Alaska see precipitation, skies are variably cloudy, and temperatures are seasonal to below. Much of Hawaii sees precipitation and cloudy skies with temperatures ranging from seasonal to below.

### 2nd Quarter Moon, January 14–20

**Zone 1:** Skies are partly cloudy to cloudy, the zone sees scattered precipitation later in the week, northern areas are windy, and temperatures are seasonal to below.

**Zone 2:** Fair to partly cloudy skies accompany scattered precipitation central and south with temperatures seasonal to above.

**Zone 3:** Eastern areas are windy, western parts of the zone see locally heavy precipitation, skies are partly cloudy to cloudy but fair to partly cloudy east; temperatures are seasonal.

**Zone 4:** Western and central parts of the zone are cloudy and stormy as a front moves from the northwest across the Plains, bringing abundant precipitation east later in the week;

temperatures are seasonal to below and conditions are windy.

**Zone 5:** The zone is windy, variably cloudy, and stormy as a front advances, bringing abundant precipitation; temperatures are seasonal to below, and eastern and central areas are stormy.

**Zone 6:** Temperatures range from seasonal to below, skies are cloudy east and stormy, precipitation develops across the zone as the week unfolds, and windy conditions prevail.

**Zone 7:** Skies are partly cloudy to cloudy and windy, eastern areas are overcast with heavy precipitation and stormy conditions, and temperatures are seasonal to below.

**Zone 8:** Central and eastern parts of Alaska see precipitation, skies are partly cloudy to cloudy, temperatures are seasonal, and western areas are windy with precipitation later in the week. Hawaii is fair to partly cloudy with temperatures seasonal to above.

### Full Moon, January 21–26

**Zone 1:** The zone is stormy, cold, and icy with abundant precipitation and overcast skies.

**Zone 2:** Much of the zone is cold and windy and cloudy with abundant precipitation and high winds; central and southern areas have tornado potential.

**Zone 3:** Skies are partly cloudy to cloudy and windy with precipitation, temperatures are seasonal to below, and sleet is possible in the east.

**Zone 4:** Western areas are mostly fair and seasonal, eastern areas are overcast and stormy with high winds and temperatures seasonal to below.

**Zone 5:** Skies are fair to partly cloudy west and central, eastern areas see precipitation with abundant downfall with possible strong thunderstorms with tornados, and temperatures seasonal to below.

**Zone 6:** Precipitation in the west moves into central parts of the zone, eastern areas are mostly fair to partly cloudy, and temperatures are seasonal to below.

**Zone 7:** Skies are variably cloudy, precipitation north coast moves into central mountains, and temperatures are seasonal but warmer in the east.

**Zone 8:** Alaska is variably cloudy and seasonal with precipitation west; temperatures are colder later in the week. Hawaii is partly cloudy and seasonal with scattered precipitation.

### 4th Quarter Moon, January 27–February 3

**Zone 1:** The zone is windy with precipitation north, partly cloudy to cloudy skies, and temperatures seasonal to above.

**Zone 2:** Variable cloud and windy conditions accompany precipitation north and temperatures seasonal to below.

**Zone 3:** Precipitation west moves into central parts of the zone with increasing cloudiness, central and eastern areas are very windy, skies are partly cloudy to cloudy, and temperatures are seasonal to below.

**Zone 4:** Much of the zone is windy with precipitation and possible strong thunderstorms central and east, skies are variably cloudy, and temperatures are seasonal.

**Zone 5:** Western areas are mostly fair and seasonal, central parts of the zone see scattered precipitation, eastern areas are cloudy with precipitation, some abundant, and temperatures are seasonal to above.

**Zone 6:** Skies are fair to partly cloudy, eastern areas are windy, and temperatures are seasonal to above.

**Zone 7:** The zone is fair to partly cloudy and seasonal with a chance for precipitation east.

**Zone 8:** Western and central Alaska are cloudy and stormy, and temperatures are seasonal to below. Hawaii is mostly cloudy and windy with temperatures seasonal to below, and central and eastern areas are stormy.

### New Moon, February 4–11

**Zone 1:** High winds accompany stormy conditions across much of the zone, especially south, with abundant precipitation and temperatures seasonal to below.

**Zone 2:** Northern areas are stormy with abundant precipitation, the zone is windy, temperatures are seasonal to below, and central and southern areas see scattered precipitation under partly cloudy to cloudy skies.

**Zone 3:** Western parts of the zone are overcast with precipitation, some abundant, eastern areas see precipitation, skies are partly cloudy to cloudy, and temperatures are seasonal to below.

**Zone 4:** Much of the zone is cloudy and windy with precipitation and temperatures seasonal to below.

**Zone 5:** Skies are variably cloudy and windy and the zone sees precipitation, some abundant, and temperatures seasonal to below.

**Zone 6:** The zone is windy and seasonal with partly cloudy to cloudy skies and precipitation east.

**Zone 7:** Northern coastal areas see locally heavy precipitation under cloudy skies, central parts of the zone are partly cloudy with scattered precipitation, eastern areas are windy, and temperatures are seasonal to above.

**Zone 8:** Alaska is windy and stormy central, cloudy west with scattered precipitation, and fair to partly cloudy east; temperatures are seasonal. Hawaii is fair to partly cloudy and windy with storms in central areas.

## 2nd Quarter Moon, February 12–18

**Zone 1:** Northern areas see precipitation, southern areas see scattered precipitation, skies are partly cloudy to cloudy, and temperatures are seasonal to below.

**Zone 2:** The zone is partly cloudy and seasonal with a chance for scattered precipitation.

**Zone 3:** Western and central parts of the zone could see strong thunderstorms with tornado potential, eastern areas see scattered precipitation, and temperatures are seasonal but colder west.

**Zone 4:** Western areas are overcast with precipitation, some locally heavy, that moves into central parts of the zone with increasing cloudiness, becoming windy and stormy; strong thunderstorms with tornado potential are possible.

**Zone 5:** Precipitation and windy conditions move across the zone with potential for strong thunderstorms with tornados east; temperatures are seasonal.

**Zone 6:** Much of the zone is windy with variably cloudiness, precipitation east, and temperatures seasonal to below.

**Zone 7:** Western and central parts of the zone see scattered precipitation, eastern areas are cloudy with precipitation, and temperatures are seasonal.

**Zone 8:** Alaska is seasonal and mostly fair with more cloudiness and precipitation east later in the week. Hawaii is fair to partly cloudy and seasonal.

### Full Moon, February 19–25

**Zone 1:** The zone is windy, skies are fair to partly cloudy with scattered precipitation, and temperatures are seasonal.

**Zone 2:** Northern areas are fair to partly cloudy, central and southern parts of the zone see more cloudiness along with potential for strong thunderstorms and tornados, and temperatures are seasonal to above.

**Zone 3:** Stormy conditions include possible strong thunderstorms with tornado and hail potential across much of the zone under variably cloudy skies, and abundant precipitation in some locations; temperatures are seasonal.

**Zone 4:** Much of the zone sees precipitation, some locally heavy west and central, skies are overcast, central and eastern areas experience high winds, and temperatures are seasonal to below.

**Zone 5:** Very windy conditions accompany precipitation, some abundant, across much of the zone, skies are overcast, and temperatures are seasonal to below.

**Zone 6:** The zone is fair to partly cloudy and windy with a chance for precipitation west.

**Zone 7:** Temperatures range from seasonal to above, skies are windy and variably cloudy, and western areas have a chance for precipitation.

**Zone 8:** Western and central parts of Alaska are windy, eastern areas see precipitation, skies are variably cloudy, and temperatures are seasonal. Hawaii is fair to partly cloudy and seasonal.

## 4th Quarter Moon, February 26–March 5

**Zone 1:** Precipitation across the zone could be abundant, causing flooding, skies are cloudy and windy, and temperatures are below seasonal.

**Zone 2:** Northern areas are cold and cloudy with precipitation, central and southern parts of the zone are fair to partly cloudy and windy with scattered precipitation.

**Zone 3:** The zone is partly cloudy with scattered precipitation under variably cloudy skies, eastern areas see more cloudiness with a chance for precipitation, and temperatures are seasonal.

**Zone 4:** Temperatures are seasonal to below and the zone is variably cloudy and windy with precipitation in central areas.

**Zone 5:** The zone is variably cloudy with precipitation east, strong thunderstorms with tornado potential, western areas are windy and stormy, and temperatures are seasonal.

**Zone 6:** Precipitation in western parts of the zone moves into central areas; skies are variably cloudy and windy and temperatures below seasonal.

**Zone 7:** Northern coastal areas see precipitation, skies are partly cloudy to cloudy, eastern areas are windy with precipitation, and temperatures are seasonal to above.

**Zone 8:** Alaska is variably cloudy and windy with precipitation west and central and temperatures seasonal to below. Much of Hawaii is windy with precipitation, some abundant, and temperatures seasonal to below.

## New Moon, March 6–13

**Zone 1:** The zone is fair to partly cloudy with temperatures seasonal to below.

**Zone 2:** Seasonal temperatures accompany fair to partly cloudy skies with more cloudiness south and precipitation later in the week.

**Zone 3:** Western areas are windy with scattered precipitation, central parts of the zone could see abundant downfall, eastern areas see scattered precipitation, skies are variably cloudy, and temperatures are seasonal.

**Zone 4:** Western and central areas are stormy with locally heavy precipitation, eastern areas see scattered showers, skies are variably cloudy, and temperatures are seasonal.

**Zone 5:** Temperatures are seasonal to above, central and eastern areas see precipitation, and skies are variably cloudy.

**Zone 6:** Much of the zone is windy and cloudy with precipitation and temperatures seasonal to below.

**Zone 7:** Temperatures are seasonal to above and much of the zone is cloudy with scattered precipitation.

**Zone 8:** Eastern areas of Alaska are cloudy and windy with precipitation, central and western parts of the zone are fair to partly cloudy with a chance for precipitation, and temperatures are seasonal. Hawaii is windy, fair to partly cloudy, and seasonal.

## 2nd Quarter Moon, March 14–19

**Zone 1:** The zone sees locally heavy precipitation under cloudy skies and seasonal temperatures.

**Zone 2:** Northern areas are cloudy with scattered precipitation, central and southern parts of the zone are windy and seasonal with fair to partly cloudy skies.

**Zone 3:** Western and central parts of the zone are windy with variably cloudy skies and potential for strong thunderstorms, eastern areas see precipitation, some locally heavy, and temperatures are seasonal.

**Zone 4:** Precipitation west moves into central parts of the zone, with variably cloudy and windy skies, strong thunderstorms, and seasonal temperatures.

**Zone 5:** The zone is windy and variably cloudy, with precipitation west and central and temperatures seasonal to below.

**Zone 6:** Much of the zone sees precipitation, central areas are stormy with locally heavy downfall, western areas are windy, skies are partly cloudy to cloudy, and temperatures are seasonal to below.

**Zone 7:** Eastern areas are windy, the zone is partly cloudy to cloudy, with scattered precipitation and seasonal temperatures.

**Zone 8:** Alaska is mostly fair to partly cloudy and seasonal, with scattered precipitation east and central. Hawaii sees locally heavy precipitation central and east and seasonal temperatures under variably cloudy and windy skies.

## Spring

Zones 1 and 2 have an increased probability of strong thunderstorms with tornado potential this spring, along with temperatures that are seasonal to below. Cloudiness will be more prevalent in zone 1 than in zone 2, which is likely to see less precipitation than zone 1. Zone 3 will be mostly seasonal, although precipitation is likely to be below the norm during.

As is usually true, storms will traverse zones 4 and 5, entering the continental United States in mid-Montana and traveling southeast to west Texas, and also from the Dakotas southeast to Louisiana. Some of these storms will have very high winds and precipitation, as well as temperatures seasonal to below. Strong thunderstorms with tornado potential are most likely from the Dakotas south to Texas.

Temperatures in zones 6 and 7 will range from seasonal to above and precipitation well below seasonal. High-pressure systems will elevate temperatures in the western parts of these zones, while the eastern areas of zone 7 have a chance for more precipitation.

In zone 8, Alaska will be seasonal in both precipitation and temperatures, but with western parts of the state seeing abundant downfall. Western and central Hawaii will see precipitation levels ranging from seasonal to above, the state will be windy, and temperatures seasonal to above.

### Full Moon, March 20–27

**Zone 1:** Much of the zone sees precipitation under windy, variably cloudy skies, and temperatures are seasonal to below.

**Zone 2:** The zone is stormy with strong thunderstorms with tornado potential, and temperatures seasonal to below.

**Zone 3:** Stormy conditions with high winds accompany overcast skies, temperatures seasonal to below, and strong thunderstorms with tornado potential.

**Zone 4:** Western areas are windy with precipitation, increasing cloudiness central and east accompanies strong thunderstorms with tornado potential, and temperatures are seasonal to below.

**Zone 5:** Skies are variably cloudy and windy and the zone sees precipitation with temperatures seasonal to below.

**Zone 6:** Western and central parts of the zone are cloudy with precipitation and temperatures are seasonal to above but cooler east.

**Zone 7:** Skies are partly cloudy to cloudy with precipitation west and central and temperatures seasonal to above.

**Zone 8:** Alaska is windy and seasonal with precipitation central and east. Hawaii is windy with precipitation east and temperatures seasonal to above.

### 4th Quarter Moon, March 28–April 4

**Zone 1:** The zone is partly cloudy to cloudy with scattered precipitation, windy north, and seasonal temperatures.

**Zone 2:** Central and southern areas see locally heavy precipitation under variably cloudy and windy skies, strong thunderstorms with tornado potential, and temperatures seasonal to below.

**Zone 3:** The zone is windy and cloudy with locally heavy precipitation east and strong thunderstorms with tornado potential, stormy conditions, and seasonal temperatures.

**Zone 4:** Conditions are windy with partly cloudy to cloudy skies, locally heavy precipitation east, and temperatures seasonal to below.

**Zone 5:** Western and central skies are fair to partly cloudy and windy with increasing cloudiness, eastern areas see precipitation, and temperatures are seasonal to below.

**Zone 6:** Western parts of the zone are fair to partly cloudy with precipitation, central and eastern areas have a chance for showers, and temperatures are seasonal.

**Zone 7:** The zone is partly cloudy to cloudy with precipitation, some locally heavy in northern coastal areas, and temperatures are seasonal.

**Zone 8:** Alaska is windy east and cloudy with scattered precipitation, western and central skies are fair to partly cloudy, and temperatures are seasonal. Hawaii is partly cloudy with scattered showers and temperatures seasonal to above.

### New Moon, April 5–11

**Zone 1:** The zone sees precipitation, abundant in northern areas, skies are partly cloudy to cloudy and windy, and temperatures are seasonal to below.

**Zone 2:** Northern areas are cloudy with precipitation, central and southern areas are partly cloudy to cloudy and windy with precipitation, including strong thunderstorms with tornado potential, and temperatures are seasonal to above.

**Zone 3:** Skies are variably cloudy with precipitation, some locally heavy, central and east; strong thunderstorms with tornado potential are possible.

**Zone 4:** Western areas are cloudy with scattered showers, central and eastern parts of the zone are windy and partly cloudy to

cloudy with a chance for showers, and temperatures are seasonal to below.

**Zone 5:** Temperatures are seasonal to below, skies are partly cloudy to cloudy, and central areas see strong thunderstorms with tornado potential.

**Zone 6:** Much of the zone is cloudy with precipitation and temperatures are seasonal to below.

**Zone 7:** Skies are variably cloudy and windy with precipitation west and central, eastern areas are windy, and temperatures are seasonal to above.

**Zone 8:** Alaska is windy with precipitation west and central, some locally heavy, and temperatures are seasonal to below. Hawaii is windy with seasonal to below temperatures and precipitation across much of the state under variable clouds.

### 2nd Quarter Moon, April 12–18

**Zone 1:** Northern areas are windy and partly cloudy to cloudy with potential for thunderstorms, southern areas see precipitation, and temperatures are seasonal.

**Zone 2:** Much of the zone sees precipitation under variable cloudiness with seasonal temperatures.

**Zone 3:** Temperatures are seasonal, skies are variably cloudy, and the zone sees scattered precipitation.

**Zone 4:** Western areas see precipitation, central and eastern areas see scattered showers, skies are variably cloudy, and temperatures are seasonal.

**Zone 5:** Skies are partly cloudy to cloudy, temperatures are seasonal, and the zone sees strong thunderstorms with tornado potential.

**Zone 6:** Western areas are windy with scattered showers, central and eastern parts of the zone see more precipitation and cloudiness, and temperatures are seasonal.

**Zone 7:** Western and central parts of the one are windy and partly cloudy to cloudy, eastern areas see more cloudiness, and temperatures are seasonal to above.

**Zone 8:** Alaska is fair to partly cloudy, windy, and seasonal. Hawaii is windy, fair to partly cloudy, and seasonal to above.

### Full Moon, April 19–25

**Zone 1:** Temperatures range from seasonal to below and the zone is stormy and variably cloudy with thunderstorms with tornado potential.

**Zone 2:** The zone is variably cloudy, temperatures are seasonal to below, and northern areas have a chance for precipitation.

**Zone 3:** Western and central areas are windy with precipitation, including thunderstorms with tornado potential, skies are partly cloudy to cloudy, and temperatures are seasonal to below.

**Zone 4:** Much of the zone sees precipitation under variably cloudy and windy skies, and temperatures are seasonal to above.

**Zone 5:** Western areas see precipitation, central and eastern areas are windy, skies are partly cloudy to cloudy, and temperatures are seasonal to above.

**Zone 6:** Skies are partly cloudy to cloudy and windy, central and eastern areas see precipitation, and temperatures are seasonal.

**Zone 7:** Northern coastal parts of the zone are cloudy with precipitation, central and eastern areas are fair to partly cloudy with showers east, and temperatures are seasonal.

**Zone 8:** Alaska is fair to partly cloudy central and west, cloudy east with precipitation, and temperatures seasonal to below. Hawaii sees showers under partly cloudy to cloudy skies with seasonal temperatures.

### 4th Quarter Moon, April 26–May 3

**Zone 1:** The zone is stormy, cloudy, and windy with temperatures seasonal to below.

**Zone 2:** Central and southern areas are windy with thunderstorms with tornado potential and temperatures seasonal to below, and northern areas see precipitation.

**Zone 3:** Eastern areas are overcast, western and central parts of the zone are partly cloudy to cloudy, and much of the zone sees precipitation with thunderstorms with tornado potential in some locations; temperatures are seasonal to below.

**Zone 4:** Central and eastern areas are partly cloudy to cloudy with precipitation, western areas see thunderstorms with tornado potential, and temperatures are seasonal to above.

**Zone 5:** The zone is partly cloudy to cloudy and seasonal with scattered thunderstorms.

**Zone 6:** Skies are partly cloudy to cloudy and windy with showers, especially east, which is stormy with locally heavy downfall; temperatures are seasonal to below.

**Zone 7:** Northern coastal areas are stormy with high winds, and much of the zone is windy with precipitation, some locally heavy, variable cloudiness, and temperatures seasonal to above.

**Zone 8:** Alaska is partly cloudy to cloudy with scattered showers and temperatures seasonal to above.

### New Moon, May 4–10

**Zone 1:** Skies are windy and partly cloudy to cloudy with showers and strong thunderstorms; temperatures are seasonal to above.

**Zone 2:** Much of the zone sees thunderstorms, some with high winds and tornado potential, precipitation is locally heavy, and temperatures range from seasonal to below as a front moves through.

**Zone 3:** Western areas are overcast and stormy with abundant precipitation, central and eastern areas are partly cloudy to cloudy, temperatures are seasonal to below, and much of the zone sees severe thunderstorms with high winds and tornado potential.

**Zone 4:** Skies are fair to partly cloudy west, central and eastern areas are cloudy with precipitation, eastern areas could see high winds with locally heavy precipitation from strong thunderstorms with tornado potential, and temperatures are seasonal to below.

**Zone 5:** Western and central areas are mostly fair, eastern areas are windy and cloudy with abundant precipitation later in the week along with strong thunderstorms with tornado potential, and temperatures are seasonal to below.

**Zone 6:** Locally heavy precipitation and thunderstorms west could result in flooding, central and eastern areas see precipitation and thunderstorms, skies are variably cloudy, and temperatures are seasonal to above.

**Zone 7:** Western and central parts of the zone are windy with variable cloudiness and precipitation later in the week, eastern areas are fair, and temperatures are seasonal to above.

**Zone 8:** Alaska is mostly fair to partly cloudy and seasonal, with precipitation west. Temperatures in Hawaii are seasonal and skies are fair to partly cloudy.

## 2nd Quarter Moon, May 11–17

**Zone 1:** Precipitation across the zone is accompanied by windy conditions, variable clouds and seasonal temperatures; southern areas could see locally heavy downfall.

**Zone 2:** Skies are partly cloudy to cloudy and the zone is humid with temperatures ranging from seasonal to above with locally heavy precipitation throughout the zone.

**Zone 3:** Temperatures are seasonal to below and skies are cloudy, bringing precipitation across the zone and locally heavy downfall east.

**Zone 4:** The zone is windy and seasonal with scattered precipitation from partly cloudy to cloudy skies; eastern areas see more cloudiness and precipitation.

**Zone 5:** Skies are fair to partly cloudy and windy, and temperatures are seasonal.

**Zone 6:** Much of the zone sees precipitation, some locally heavy, and skies are variably cloudy.

**Zone 7:** The zone is windy with precipitation west and central under variably cloudy skies, eastern areas are partly cloudy and windy, and temperatures are seasonal.

**Zone 8:** Alaska is fair to partly cloudy, windy, and seasonal with scattered precipitation. Hawaii is windy, western and central areas see scattered precipitation, and temperatures are seasonal to above.

## Full Moon, May 18–25

**Zone 1:** Skies are partly cloudy to cloudy and windy, temperatures range from seasonal to below, and northern areas see precipitation.

**Zone 2:** Much of the zone is cloudy with precipitation, wind, and temperatures seasonal to below.

**Zone 3:** Skies are partly cloudy to cloudy with more cloudiness east with precipitation, some locally heavy; temperatures are seasonal.

**Zone 4:** Western parts of the zone are windy as a front moves across, bringing wind and scattered precipitation to eastern areas; skies are partly cloudy to cloudy and temperatures are seasonal.

**Zone 5:** The zone is windy, partly cloudy to cloudy, and seasonal with scattered precipitation.

**Zone 6:** Seasonal temperatures accompany partly cloudy to cloudy skies and scattered showers central and east later in the week with potential for locally heavy downfall.

**Zone 7:** Western and central parts of the zone see locally heavy precipitation under partly cloudy to cloudy skies with seasonal temperatures; eastern areas are mostly fair.

**Zone 8:** Western and central parts of Alaska see precipitation under partly cloudy to cloudy skies, eastern areas are windy and mostly fair, and temperatures are seasonal. Much of Hawaii sees showers under variably cloudy skies with seasonal temperatures.

### 4th Quarter Moon, May 26–June 2

**Zone 1:** Skies are windy and partly cloudy to cloudy with precipitation north and scattered showers south, and temperatures seasonal to below.

**Zone 2:** The zone is seasonal and fair to partly cloudy with scattered precipitation central and south.

**Zone 3:** Much of the zone sees precipitation, strong thunderstorms with tornado potential west and central, humidity, variably cloudy skies, and seasonal temperatures.

**Zone 4:** Precipitation across the zone is locally heavy central and east, with strong thunderstorms with tornado potential central and east; humidity accompanies temperatures seasonal to above.

**Zone 5:** Strong thunderstorms with tornado potential are possible under variably cloudy skies and temperatures seasonal to above.

**Zone 6:** Eastern areas are very windy, central and eastern areas see precipitation and partly cloudy to cloudy skies, with heaviest downfall east; temperatures are seasonal.

**Zone 7:** Western and central areas are fair to partly cloudy, eastern areas are windy with more cloudiness and precipitation, and temperatures are seasonal to above.

**Zone 8:** Eastern Alaska sees locally heavy precipitation, skies are variably cloudy, and central areas are windy. Central and eastern areas of Hawaii see precipitation, and the state is windy, partly cloudy to cloudy, and seasonal.

## New Moon, June 3–9

**Zone 1:** The zone is windy with precipitation, seasonal to above, and variably cloudy; strong thunderstorms with tornado potential are possible in the south.

**Zone 2:** Precipitation across the zone accompanies humidity and partly cloudy to cloudy skies; temperatures are seasonal.

**Zone 3:** Western and central areas are windy and fair to partly cloudy, eastern areas see locally heavy precipitation under windy, cloudy skies; temperatures are seasonal.

**Zone 4:** Skies are partly cloudy to cloudy, central parts of the zone see scattered precipitation, strong thunderstorms with tornado potential are possible central and east, and temperatures are seasonal to above.

**Zone 5:** Skies are fair to partly cloudy with more cloudiness east, where strong thunderstorms with tornado potential bring locally heavy precipitation; conditions are humid and temperatures are seasonal.

**Zone 6:** Western and central areas see precipitation and wind under variable clouds, eastern areas see more cloudiness and wind along with locally heavy downfall, and temperatures are seasonal to below.

**Zone 7:** Skies are partly cloudy to cloudy and windy west and central, eastern areas see more cloudiness and scattered precipitation, and temperatures are seasonal to above.

**Zone 8:** Alaska is partly cloudy to cloudy, western areas see precipitation, and temperatures are seasonal. Hawaii is fair to partly cloudy and windy with temperatures seasonal to above.

## 2nd Quarter Moon, June 10–16

**Zone 1:** Temperatures seasonal to below accompany cloudy, windy skies and precipitation.

**Zone 2:** Northern areas are windy with precipitation and cloudy skies, central and southern areas are fair to partly cloudy, and temperatures are seasonal to above.

**Zone 3:** Western areas see locally heavy precipitation, western and central areas see strong thunderstorms with tornado potential, skies are variably cloudy, and the zone is humid with temperatures seasonal to above.

**Zone 4:** Western areas see precipitation and cloudy skies move into central parts of the zone, eastern areas are windy with locally heavy downfall from thunderstorms, temperatures range from seasonal to above, and much of the zone is stormy.

**Zone 5:** Much of the zone is stormy with heavy precipitation and thunderstorms with tornado potential, and temperatures are seasonal to above.

**Zone 6:** Seasonal temperatures accompany precipitation in much of the zone under partly cloudy to cloudy and windy skies.

**Zone 7:** Western and central parts of the zone see precipitation under variable clouds, eastern areas are windy with showers and thunderstorms, and temperatures are seasonal.

**Zone 8:** Alaska is seasonal, central and eastern areas are variably cloudy and windy with precipitation, western areas are fair to partly cloudy, and temperatures are seasonal. Much of Hawaii is partly cloudy to cloudy, windy, and seasonal with showers and thunderstorms.

### Full Moon, June 17–24

**Zone 1:** The zone is humid and seasonal with variably cloudy skies and showers and thunderstorms.

**Zone 2:** Scattered showers and thunderstorms accompany variably cloudy skies with temperatures seasonal to above.

**Zone 3:** The zone is partly cloudy to cloudy and humid with scattered precipitation and temperatures seasonal to above.

**Zone 4:** Western and central parts of the zone are cloudy and humid with precipitation that moves east; temperatures are seasonal to above.

**Zone 5:** The zone is windy with precipitation as a front advances, bringing precipitation and cloudy skies, along with thunderstorms with tornado potential; humidity accompanies temperatures seasonal to above.

**Zone 6:** Skies are fair to partly cloudy and the zone is seasonal and windy with thunderstorms east.

**Zone 7:** Temperatures range from seasonal to above, skies are mostly fair, and eastern areas are partly cloudy.

**Zone 8:** Eastern and central parts of Alaska see precipitation, some locally heavy, temperatures are seasonal, and skies are variably cloudy. Hawaii is mostly fair and seasonal.

## Summer

Abundant precipitation that could trigger flooding will be the norm in zone 1 this summer, along with humidity and elevated temperatures. Although zone 2 will see less precipitation, levels will range from seasonal to above in northern areas; precipitation in central and southern parts of zone 2 will be below seasonal. Zone 3 will be much the same with high-pressure systems elevating temperatures in western parts of the zone, as well as eastern parts of zone 4.

Zones 4 and 5 will see increased cloudiness, temperatures, and wind, but despite a higher range of humidity, precipitation will be below seasonal. Central parts of these zones, however, will have a better chance for precipitation.

Zones 6 and 7, especially the eastern areas of these zones, will experience excessively high heat under high-pressure systems. Precipitation is likely to be seasonal to below even though skies will tend to be partly cloudy.

In zone 8, central Alaska will see above average precipitation and temperatures. The remainder of the state will be more seasonal with a tendency toward dryness in eastern areas. In Hawaii, humidity will mix with higher temperatures and precipitation, as well as partly cloudy to cloudy and windy skies.

**4th Quarter Moon, June 25–July 1**

**Zone 1:** The zone is windy and variably cloudy with thunderstorms and locally heavy downfall north; temperatures are seasonal to above.

**Zone 2:** Temperatures seasonal to above accompany humidity, windy conditions, variably cloudy skies, thunderstorms, and locally heavy precipitation south.

**Zone 3:** The zone is variably cloudy with thunderstorms and showers and temperatures seasonal to above.

**Zone 4:** Skies are fair to partly cloudy with thunderstorms, locally heavy precipitation east, humidity, and temperatures seasonal to above.

**Zone 5:** Temperatures ranging from seasonal to above trigger scattered thunderstorms under partly cloudy to cloudy skies.

**Zone 6:** Skies are variably cloudy, temperatures are seasonal to above, and the zone sees scattered showers and thunderstorms.

**Zone 7:** The zone is windy with temperatures ranging from seasonal to above, scattered thunderstorms west and central, showers and thunderstorms east, and humidity east.

**Zone 8:** Western and central Alaska see precipitation, eastern skies are windy, and temperatures are seasonal. Much of Hawaii sees showers and scattered thunderstorms under variably cloudy skies with humidity and temperatures seasonal to above.

## New Moon, July 2–8

**Zone 1:** The zone is windy and humid with showers and thunderstorms and temperatures ranging from seasonal to above.

**Zone 2:** Windy and humid conditions accompany thunderstorms with tornado potential and locally heavy downfall central and south; temperatures range from seasonal to above.

**Zone 3:** The zone sees strong thunderstorms with tornado potential, variably cloudy skies, humidity, and temperatures seasonal to above.

**Zone 4:** Skies are cloudy and stormy, the zone sees strong thunderstorms with tornado potential, high winds, and temperatures ranging from seasonal to above.

**Zone 5:** Much of the zone is cloudy with showers and scattered thunderstorms and temperatures ranging from seasonal to above.

**Zone 6:** Precipitation in western areas moves into central and eastern parts of the zone under variably cloudy skies with seasonal temperatures.

**Zone 7:** Western and central parts of the zone see showers, skies are partly cloudy to cloudy, and temperatures are seasonal to above.

**Zone 8:** Western and central Alaska see scattered precipitation, skies are mostly fair to partly cloudy, and temperatures are seasonal. Western parts of Hawaii see showers, skies are fair to partly cloudy, and temperatures are seasonal.

## 2nd Quarter Moon, July 9–15

**Zone 1:** Much of the zone is stormy, windy, and humid with scattered thunderstorms and temperatures seasonal to above.

**Zone 2:** Variably cloudy skies bring showers across the zone with locally heavy precipitation north; high winds and strong thunderstorms with tornado potential are possible.

**Zone 3:** Eastern areas are cloudy with locally heavy precipitation, central areas are partly cloudy to cloudy with showers, western and central parts of the zone see showers and thunderstorms, temperatures are seasonal to above, and conditions are windy.

**Zone 4:** Western parts of the zone see scattered showers, with central and eastern areas seeing more cloudiness and precipitation, including locally heavy downfall; temperatures are seasonal.

**Zone 5:** The zone is variably cloudy with thunderstorms with tornado potential central and east, some areas see locally heavy downfall, and temperatures range from seasonal to above.

**Zone 6:** Skies are variably cloudy, temperatures are seasonal to above, and much of the zone sees scattered showers.

**Zone 7:** Temperatures are seasonal to above under variably cloudy skies, western and central areas see precipitation and locally heavy downfall, and eastern areas see scattered thunderstorms.

**Zone 8:** Western and central Alaska are cloudy and stormy with abundant precipitation, eastern areas are windy and partly cloudy to cloudy; temperatures are seasonal. Western and central areas of Hawaii see strong thunderstorms, and the state is windy with seasonal temperatures.

### Full Moon, July 16–23

**Zone 1:** The zone is windy, skies are partly cloudy to cloudy, and conditions are humid with temperatures ranging from seasonal to above.

**Zone 2:** Temperatures range from seasonal to above, skies are windy and partly cloudy to cloudy, and the zone sees scattered thunderstorms with tornado potential.

**Zone 3:** The zone sees scattered showers and thunderstorms, temperatures are seasonal to above, and conditions are windy and humid; a tropical storm is possible in the Gulf.

**Zone 4:** Skies are partly cloudy to cloudy, temperatures are seasonal to below, eastern areas see more cloudiness, and the zone is windy with precipitation, some locally heavy that could trigger flooding.

**Zone 5:** Precipitation across the zone is heaviest east with flood potential, skies are variably cloudy, temperatures are seasonal, and some areas see scattered thunderstorms.

**Zone 6:** The zone is variably cloudy and seasonal with scattered showers and thunderstorms.

**Zone 7:** Temperatures range from seasonal to above, skies are windy and variably cloudy, and much of the zone sees showers and thunderstorms.

**Zone 8:** Central and eastern Alaska are stormy and the state is partly cloudy to cloudy with temperatures ranging from seasonal to below. Hawaii is partly cloudy to cloudy with precipitation east, some locally heavy, and temperatures seasonal to below.

### 4th Quarter Moon, July 24–30

**Zone 1:** The zone is mostly cloudy, humid, windy, and seasonal with showers and thunderstorms.

**Zone 2:** Scattered showers accompany mostly partly cloudy skies, humidity, and temperatures seasonal to above.

**Zone 3:** Temperatures are seasonal to above, skies are partly cloudy to cloudy, western and central areas see showers, and eastern parts of the zone see scattered thunderstorms.

**Zone 4:** Much of the zone sees precipitation, showers and thunderstorms, under partly cloudy to cloudy skies, and temperatures and humidity seasonal to above.

**Zone 5:** Skies are partly cloudy to cloudy, temperatures seasonal to above, and the zone sees showers and thunderstorms.

**Zone 6:** Western skies are cloudy, central and eastern areas are partly cloudy to cloudy and windy, and the zone is windy with temperatures seasonal to above.

**Zone 7:** Much of the zone sees precipitation with thunderstorms in eastern areas, skies are variably cloudy, and temperatures are seasonal to above.

**Zone 8:** Central and western Alaska see precipitation, some locally heavy with flood potential, skies are windy and partly cloudy to cloudy, and temperatures are seasonal. Hawaii is windy with temperatures seasonal to above and showers and thunderstorms.

### New Moon, July 31–August 6

**Zone 1:** The zone is windy with strong thunderstorms south, showers north, partly cloudy to cloudy skies, and temperatures ranging from seasonal to above.

**Zone 2:** Northern areas are cloudy, central and southern areas are windy with strong thunderstorms, skies are variably cloudy, and temperatures are seasonal to above.

**Zone 3:** The zone is fair to partly cloudy and windy with more cloudiness and thunderstorms east; temperatures are seasonal to above.

**Zone 4:** Windy conditions accompany scattered showers and thunderstorms, skies are variably cloudy but mostly fair east, and temperatures are seasonal.

**Zone 5:** Skies are partly cloudy to cloudy with more cloudiness central and east along with locally heavy precipitation from thunderstorms and possible flooding; conditions are humid and temperatures seasonal to above.

**Zone 6:** Skies are fair to partly cloudy, eastern areas see scattered precipitation, and conditions are windy with temperatures seasonal to above.

**Zone 7:** Eastern areas see showers and thunderstorms, skies are partly cloudy to cloudy, temperatures are seasonal to above, and western and central parts of the zone have a chance for precipitation.

**Zone 8:** Central Alaska is windy with thunderstorms, eastern areas see precipitation, skies are partly cloudy to cloudy, and temperatures are seasonal. Hawaii is windy with variably cloudy skies, thunderstorms in central areas, and seasonal temperatures.

## 2nd Quarter Moon, August 7–14

**Zone 1:** The zone sees precipitation, along with windy conditions, showers and thunderstorms, partly cloudy to cloudy skies, variable cloudiness, and temperatures seasonal to above.

**Zone 2:** Temperatures range from seasonal to above, the zone sees showers and thunderstorms, and skies are partly cloudy to cloudy.

**Zone 3:** The zone is humid with temperatures seasonal to above, precipitation is heaviest east with showers and thunderstorms across the zone.

**Zone 4:** Skies are partly cloudy to cloudy and windy with locally heavy precipitation west, scattered precipitation central, scattered thunderstorms east with locally heavy downfall and flood potential.

**Zone 5:** Temperatures range from seasonal to above, skies are windy and partly cloudy to cloudy with more cloudiness east, and western and central areas see scattered thunderstorms.

**Zone 6:** The zone is fair to partly cloudy but overcast east with scattered precipitation, temperatures are seasonal to above, and skies are windy.

**Zone 7:** The zone is windy with temperatures seasonal to above and skies are partly cloudy with scattered showers; eastern areas see more cloudiness, humidity, and scattered thunderstorms.

**Zone 8:** Alaska is windy with locally heavy precipitation central and east, variable cloudiness, and seasonal temperatures. Hawaii is seasonal to above with scattered thunderstorms.

## Full Moon, August 15–22

**Zone 1:** The zone sees abundant precipitation, possibly from a tropical storm or hurricane, variably cloudy skies, windy conditions, and seasonal temperatures.

**Zone 2:** Northern areas see abundant precipitation, possibly from a tropical storm or hurricane, partly cloudy to cloudy skies, and high humidity accompanying temperatures seasonal to above.

**Zone 3:** The zone is partly cloudy to cloudy, with more cloudiness and locally heavy precipitation east, with scattered thunderstorms and possibly a tropical storm or hurricane, and temperatures seasonal to above.

**Zone 4:** Skies are partly cloudy to cloudy with precipitation central and east along with scattered thunderstorms and temperatures seasonal to above.

**Zone 5:** Western areas see scattered precipitation, precipitation in central areas moves into eastern parts of the zone with thunderstorms, conditions are windy, skies are partly cloudy to cloudy, and temperatures are seasonal to above.

**Zone 6:** Scattered thunderstorms accompany windy conditions and variably cloudy skies, along with temperatures seasonal to above.

**Zone 7:** Temperatures are seasonal to above, western and central areas see scattered thunderstorms, eastern areas have a chance for precipitation, and skies are partly cloudy to cloudy.

**Zone 8:** Alaska is windy with scattered precipitation, variably cloudy skies, and temperatures ranging from seasonal to above. Hawaii is partly cloudy to cloudy and seasonal with scattered thunderstorms.

### 4th Quarter Moon, August 23–29

**Zone 1:** The zone sees scattered thunderstorms, humidity, seasonal temperatures, and partly cloudy to cloudy skies, with locally heavy downfall north.

**Zone 2:** Northern areas see scattered precipitation, central and southern areas are stormy with strong thunderstorms with high winds and tornado potential; temperatures are seasonal to above.

**Zone 3:** Much of the zone is cloudy with thunderstorms, western and central parts of the zone are stormy with a possible tropical storm or hurricane in the Gulf, temperatures range from seasonal to above, eastern areas are partly cloudy with scattered thunderstorms.

**Zone 4:** Temperatures range from seasonal to above under variably cloudy skies with more cloudiness east and showers and thunderstorms.

**Zone 5:** Temperatures are seasonal to above, central and western parts of the zone see scattered showers and thunderstorms, and skies are fair to partly cloudy.

**Zone 6:** Western and central skies are cloudy with precipitation, eastern areas are mostly fair, and temperatures range from seasonal to above.

**Zone 7:** Scattered showers and thunderstorms in western and central areas accompany partly cloudy to cloudy skies with locally heavy precipitation central; temperatures are seasonal to above.

**Zone 8:** Central and eastern Alaska see precipitation under partly cloudy to cloudy skies and windy skies and temperatures are seasonal. Hawaii is seasonal and partly cloudy to cloudy with scattered showers and thunderstorms.

### New Moon, August 30–September 4

**Zone 1:** The zone is windy with temperatures ranging seasonal to above, showers and thunderstorms, and partly cloudy to cloudy skies.

**Zone 2:** Much of the zone is cloudy with showers and temperatures are seasonal.

**Zone 3:** Skies are windy and partly cloudy to cloudy, eastern areas see thunderstorms, temperatures are seasonal.

**Zone 4:** Much of the zone sees showers and thunderstorms under partly cloudy to cloudy skies and temperatures are seasonal.

**Zone 5:** Western and central areas are variably cloudy with thunderstorms and showers, eastern skies are mostly fair with scattered precipitation, and temperatures are seasonal to above.

**Zone 6:** Precipitation across the zone is locally heavy west and central, central areas are windy, skies are variably cloudy, and temperatures are seasonal.

**Zone 7:** Abundant precipitation is possible west and central, eastern areas see scattered showers and thunderstorms with locally heavy downfall, skies are partly cloudy to cloudy, and temperatures are seasonal.

**Zone 8:** Central and eastern Alaska are cloudy with abundant precipitation, western areas are mostly fair, and temperatures are seasonal. Hawaiian skies are variably cloudy, temperatures are seasonal, and central and eastern parts of the state see showers.

## 2nd Quarter Moon, September 5–13

**Zone 1:** Showers and thunderstorms bring locally heavy precipitation, temperatures are seasonal, and skies are partly cloudy to cloudy.

**Zone 2:** Much of the zone sees precipitation, including thunderstorms central and south, under partly cloudy to cloudy and windy skies; temperatures are seasonal.

**Zone 3:** Locally heavy precipitation from showers and thunderstorms west moves into central and eastern areas under partly cloudy to cloudy skies and temperatures ranging from seasonal to below.

**Zone 4:** The zone is cloudy with locally heavy precipitation west, showers and strong thunderstorms with tornado potential, windy skies, and seasonal temperatures.

**Zone 5:** The zone is windy and partly cloudy to cloudy with thunderstorms and showers, some yielding locally heavy precipitation west; temperatures are seasonal to above.

**Zone 6:** Temperatures ranging from seasonal to below accompany fair to partly cloudy skies.

**Zone 7:** Temperatures are seasonal to above, skies are fair to partly cloudy west and central and cloudy east, and central and eastern areas have a chance for showers and thunderstorms.

**Zone 8:** Precipitation in western areas of Alaksa moves into central areas with locally heavy downfall; temperatures are seasonal and skies are partly cloudy to cloudy. Hawaii is seasonal and fair to partly cloudy with scattered showers.

**Full Moon, September 14–20**

**Zone 1:** The zone is windy with showers and thunderstorms, along with locally heavy precipitation, mostly cloudy skies, and temperatures ranging from seasonal to above.

**Zone 2:** Northern and central areas see scattered precipitation, temperatures are seasonal, and skies are mostly partly cloudy with more cloudiness north.

**Zone 3:** Precipitation is locally heavy west and scattered central and east, temperatures are seasonal, and skies are partly cloudy to cloudy.

**Zone 4:** Partly cloudy to cloudy skies bring showers and thunderstorms, with locally heavy precipitation central from strong thunderstorms with possible tornados; temperatures are seasonal to above.

**Zone 5:** Precipitation in western parts of the zone moves across the zone with showers and thunderstorms, which are locally heavy in central areas; conditions are windy and temperatures range from seasonal to above.

**Zone 6:** The zone is windy with scattered showers and thunderstorms, and temperatures are seasonal.

**Zone 7:** Variably cloudy skies accompany thunderstorms and showers across the zone, some bringing locally heavy precipitation; conditions are windy and temperatures range from seasonal to above.

**Zone 8:** Precipitation in western areas of Alaska moves into central and eastern parts of the state; skies are partly cloudy to cloudy and temperatures are seasonal. Eastern areas of Hawaii see showers, the state is mostly fair to partly cloudy, and temperatures are seasonal.

2018 © Wollwerth Imagery Image from BigStockPhoto.com

## Autumn

Temperatures in zone 1 will be seasonal to above and precipitation will be seasonal to below. Zone 2 will be much the same, with sunny skies and minimal precipitation. Zone 3 will be windy with temperatures seasonal to above and high-pressure systems that minimize precipitation.

Eastern parts of zones 4 and 5 will also experience high-pressure systems, elevating temperatures and restricting precipitation. The central and western parts of zones 4 and 5, however, will see precipitation levels from seasonal to above along with increased cloudiness and low-pressure systems.

Zones 6 and 7 will be windy with temperatures seasonal to above, and western parts of these zones will see precipitation levels seasonal to above, along with higher temperatures.

In zone 8, Alaska will be windy and seasonal, with a tendency toward dryness. Eastern areas have a better chance for seasonal precipitation. Precipitation in Hawaii will be seasonal to below and temperatures seasonal to above.

**4th Quarter Moon, September 21–27**

**Zone 1:** Partly cloudy to cloudy skies bring precipitation, which is abundant south along with more cloudiness and temperatures seasonal to below.

**Zone 2:** Northern areas see locally heavy precipitation, temperatures range from seasonal to below, skies are mostly cloudy, and strong thunderstorms with tornado potential are possible central and south.

**Zone 3:** Much of the zone sees showers and thunderstorms, some strong, downfall is locally heavy east, and the zone is cloudy and seasonal.

**Zone 4:** The zone is windy and seasonal with variable clouds and much of the zone sees showers and thunderstorms, some strong.

**Zone 5:** Skies are windy and partly cloudy to cloudy, bringing precipitation to much of the zone, along with wind, humidity, and seasonal temperatures, and strong thunderstorms with tornado potential are possible east.

**Zone 6:** Precipitation in western areas moves into central parts of the zone, which is mostly cloudy and windy with seasonal temperatures.

**Zone 7:** Western and central areas see showers, scattered thunderstorms are possible in eastern areas, and the zone is windy and partly cloudy to cloudy.

**Zone 8:** Alaska is partly cloudy to cloudy and seasonal with scattered precipitation and heavy downfall in eastern areas with flood potential. Hawaii is fair to partly cloudy and seasonal with scattered showers.

**New Moon, September 28–October 4**

**Zone 1:** Temperatures range from seasonal to below under fair to partly cloudy skies.

**Zone 2:** Skies are partly cloudy to cloudy and windy with scattered showers and thunderstorms, locally heavy precipitation north, and seasonal temperatures.

**Zone 3:** The zone is windy with thunderstorms, some strong, partly cloudy to cloudy skies, and temperature ranging from seasonal to above.

**Zone 4:** Windy conditions accompany temperatures ranging from seasonal to above; strong thunderstorms with tornado potential are possible in central areas, eastern areas see showers, and skies are partly cloudy to cloudy.

**Zone 5:** The zone is seasonal and windy under fair to partly cloudy skies.

**Zone 6:** Much of the zone sees precipitation and partly cloudy to cloudy skies, and temperatures are seasonal to below.

**Zone 7:** Abundant precipitation is possible in central areas, western parts of the zone see scattered precipitation, skies are partly cloudy to cloudy, and temperatures are seasonal.

**Zone 8:** Much of Alaska is windy with temperatures ranging from seasonal to below and scattered precipitation and skies are partly cloudy to cloudy. Hawaii is variably cloudy with seasonal temperatures, central and western areas see thunderstorms and showers, some producing locally heavy downfall.

## 2nd Quarter Moon, October 5–12

**Zone 1:** The zone is cloudy with precipitation and temperatures ranging from seasonal to below.

**Zone 2:** Skies are variably cloudy and windy, temperatures are seasonal, and the zone sees scattered thunderstorms.

**Zone 3:** Much of the zone sees precipitation and scattered thunderstorms under variably cloudy skies with seasonal temperatures.

**Zone 4:** Temperatures are seasonal, skies are partly cloudy to cloudy, western and eastern parts of the zone see showers and thunderstorms, and heavy precipitation in central areas could bring flooding.

**Zone 5:** Skies are partly cloudy to cloudy, much of the zone sees strong thunderstorms with tornado potential and locally heavy precipitation, and temperatures are seasonal.

**Zone 6:** Central and eastern parts of the zone are cloudy with locally heavy precipitation, temperatures are mostly seasonal, and western areas are fair to partly cloudy.

**Zone 7:** Skies are partly cloudy to cloudy with precipitation across much of the zone and seasonal temperatures.

**Zone 8:** Much of Alaska is windy and stormy and cloudy with temperatures seasonal to below. Hawaii is variably cloudy with seasonal temperatures and conditions in central areas stormy.

### Full Moon, October 13–20

**Zone 1:** Much of the zone sees precipitation as the week unfolds, skies are variably cloudy, and temperatures are seasonal.

**Zone 2:** Precipitation across the zone accompanies temperatures ranging from seasonal to below, conditions are windy with strong thunderstorms possible central and south, and skies are variably cloudy.

**Zone 3:** Skies are partly cloudy to cloudy, central and eastern areas see precipitation, possibly abundant, and temperatures are seasonal.

**Zone 4:** Precipitation in western areas moves into central parts of the zone with showers and thunderstorms, seasonal temperatures and partly cloudy to cloudy skies.

**Zone 5:** The zone is seasonal with variably cloudy skies and scattered precipitation.

**Zone 6:** Much of the zone sees showers under partly cloudy to cloudy skies and temperatures are seasonal.

**Zone 7:** Western and central areas see precipitation later in the week, the zone is windy and partly cloudy to cloudy, and temperatures are seasonal but warmer in eastern areas with scattered precipitation.

**Zone 8:** Alaska is windy and seasonal under partly cloudy to cloudy skies, and western and central parts of the state see precipitation. Hawaii is seasonal and fair to partly cloudy.

**4th Quarter Moon, October 21–26**

**Zone 1:** Much of the zone sees precipitation, along with seasonal temperatures and partly cloudy to cloudy skies.

**Zone 2:** Northern areas are windy, central and southern areas see precipitation, temperatures are seasonal, and skies are partly cloudy to cloudy.

**Zone 3:** Western and central areas see high winds and thunderstorms, central and eastern areas see showers and windy skies, skies are partly cloudy to cloudy, and temperatures are seasonal.

**Zone 4:** The zone is windy with scattered thunderstorms, skies are fair to partly cloudy, but western areas see more cloudiness, temperatures range from seasonal to above, and central parts of the zone see showers with more cloudiness.

**Zone 5:** Skies are fair to partly cloudy, temperatures are seasonal to above, and eastern areas see scattered thunderstorms and showers.

**Zone 6:** The zone is windy and seasonal with precipitation under partly cloudy to cloudy skies.

**Zone 7:** Western and central parts of the zone are windy with precipitation, eastern areas see scattered showers, skies are partly cloudy to cloudy, and temperatures are seasonal.

**Zone 8:** Alaska sees scattered precipitation, skies are variably cloudy, temperatures are seasonal, and western areas are windy. Hawaii is fair to partly cloudy and windy with temperatures ranging from seasonal to above.

**New Moon, October 27–November 3**

**Zone 1:** Temperatures range from seasonal to below and much of the zone is stormy, along with variably cloudy skies.

**Zone 2:** The zone is windy, temperatures are seasonal to above, conditions are humid or damp, and northern areas see more cloudiness.

**Zone 3:** Much of the zone is cloudy and windy, central and eastern areas see scattered precipitation later in the week, and temperatures are seasonal.

**Zone 4:** The zone is windy under partly cloudy to cloudy skies with scattered precipitation and temperatures ranging from seasonal to above.

**Zone 5:** Western areas see locally heavy precipitation, skies are variably cloudy, central and eastern areas see scattered precipitation, and temperatures are seasonal to above.

**Zone 6:** Western areas see showers, temperatures are seasonal to above, skies are partly cloudy to cloudy, and central areas are windy and stormy.

**Zone 7:** Central and western areas are very windy, eastern areas see precipitation, temperatures are seasonal, and skies are variably cloudy.

**Zone 8:** Eastern Alaska sees precipitation, western areas of Alaska are windy, temperatures are seasonal, and skies are variably cloudy. Hawaii sees scattered showers and thunderstorms under partly cloudy to cloudy skies, with temperatures ranging from seasonal to above.

### 2nd Quarter Moon, November 4–11

**Zone 1:** Temperatures are seasonal to below and skies are fair to partly cloudy with precipitation later in the week.

**Zone 2:** Skies are partly cloudy and windy, the zone sees scattered precipitation, and temperatures are seasonal to above.

**Zone 3:** Wind accompanies scattered showers and thunderstorms across much of the zone with some locally heavy precipitation, skies are variably cloudy and temperatures are seasonal to above.

**Zone 4:** Skies are partly cloudy to cloudy and windy with scattered showers and thunderstorms and temperatures seasonal to below.

**Zone 5:** The zone is windy with scattered showers and fair to partly cloudy skies west and central, while overcast skies east yield more precipitation; temperatures are seasonal to below.

**Zone 6:** Western areas see abundant precipitation with flood potential, central and eastern areas are stormy, temperatures are seasonal, and skies are variably cloudy.

**Zone 7:** Seasonal temperatures accompany abundant precipitation in northern coastal areas; south coastal, central and eastern parts of the zone are windy with precipitation.

**Zone 8:** Alaska is windy with scattered precipitation and temperatures seasonal to below. Hawaii is windy and seasonal with showers.

### Full Moon, November 12–18

**Zone 1:** The zone is partly cloudy to cloudy with precipitation, some locally heavy east; temperatures are seasonal.

**Zone 2:** Scattered showers and thunderstorms, some strong with tornado potential, central and south accompany variably cloudy skies, wind, and humidity; temperatures are seasonal to above.

**Zone 3:** Skies are variably cloudy and windy, temperatures are seasonal to below, and much of the zone sees precipitation, some locally heavy, along with strong thunderstorms with tornado potential west and central; temperatures are seasonal.

**Zone 4:** Western parts of the zone are windy and cloudy with precipitation, some locally heavy that could trigger flooding, eastern areas see precipitation later in the week, and temperatures are seasonal.

**Zone 5:** Skies are partly cloudy to cloudy and windy, temperatures are seasonal, and western areas see scattered thunderstorms.

**Zone 6:** Temperatures are seasonal, skies are windy and fair to partly cloudy and eastern areas see precipitation and more cloudiness.

**Zone 7:** The zone is windy and partly cloudy to cloudy with scattered precipitation.

**Zone 8:** Alaska is windy, partly cloudy to cloudy with scattered precipitation, and temperatures are seasonal to below. Hawaii is fair to partly cloudy and seasonal with scattered showers.

## 4th Quarter Moon, November 19–25

**Zone 1:** Northern areas are stormy, temperatures are seasonal to below, and skies are variably cloudy and windy.

**Zone 2:** The zone is windy with scattered precipitation, partly cloudy to cloudy, and seasonal.

**Zone 3:** Most of the zone is cloudy and windy with showers and thunderstorms with tornado potential; temperatures are seasonal.

**Zone 4:** Variably cloudy and windy skies and seasonal temperatures accompany thunderstorms with tornado potential west.

**Zone 5:** Skies are fair to partly cloudy with more cloudiness east and precipitation, western areas see precipitation later in the week, and temperatures are seasonal.

**Zone 6:** Much of the zone sees precipitation under variably cloudy skies with seasonal temperatures.

**Zone 7:** Precipitation across the zone is locally heavy east, skies are partly cloudy to cloudy and windy, and temperatures are seasonal.

**Zone 8:** Central and eastern areas of Alaska see precipitation, some locally heavy, skies are variably cloudy, and temperatures are seasonal. Central and eastern parts of Hawaii see showers, temperatures are seasonal, and the zone is variably cloudy and windy.

## New Moon, November 26–December 3

**Zone 1:** Temperatures are seasonal, skies are partly cloudy to cloudy, and northern areas see precipitation.

**Zone 2:** The zone is windy with strong thunderstorms with tornado potential central and south, skies are partly cloudy to cloudy, and temperatures are seasonal, and precipitation could be locally heavy, causing flooding.

**Zone 3:** Variably cloudy and windy skies accompany seasonal temperatures and thunderstorms with tornado potential central and east.

**Zone 4:** The zone sees scattered thunderstorms and showers, along with variably cloudy and windy skies, and seasonal temperatures.

**Zone 5:** Scattered thunderstorms and showers accompany windy and partly cloudy to cloudy skies and seasonal temperatures.

**Zone 6:** Much of the zone sees precipitation, temperatures are seasonal to above, and skies are windy and partly cloudy to cloudy.

**Zone 7:** Temperatures are seasonal to above, skies are partly cloudy to cloudy, and northern coastal and eastern areas see precipitation.

**Zone 8:** Alaska is windy and partly cloudy to cloudy with precipitation and seasonal temperatures. Hawaii is seasonal and partly cloudy to cloudy with showers and thunderstorms.

## 2nd Quarter Moon, December 4–11

**Zone 1:** Skies are windy and cloudy, temperatures seasonal to below, and the zone sees precipitation, some locally heavy.

**Zone 2:** Northern areas see precipitation, central and southern areas see scattered thunderstorms, skies are variably cloudy, and temperatures are seasonal.

**Zone 3:** Skies are fair to partly cloudy and windy, eastern areas see precipitation, temperatures are seasonal, and southern parts of the zone could see scattered thunderstorms.

**Zone 4:** Abundant precipitation with flooding is possible in western and central parts of the zone, temperatures are seasonal, skies are variably cloudy and windy, and eastern areas see scattered precipitation.

**Zone 5:** Locally heavy precipitation in western and central areas could trigger flooding, temperatures are seasonal to above, and skies are cloudy west and central, and fair to partly cloudy east.

**Zone 6:** The zone sees scattered precipitation under partly cloudy to cloudy skies, and temperatures are seasonal.

**Zone 7:** Precipitation west moves into central areas, eastern parts of the zone see scattered precipitation, temperatures are seasonal to below, and skies are variably cloudy.

**Zone 8:** Western and central Alaska are cloudy with abundant precipitation, eastern areas see scattered downfall, and temperatures are seasonal. Hawaii is fair to partly cloudy, windy, and seasonal.

### Full Moon, December 12–17
**Zone 1:** Partly cloudy and windy skies accompany seasonal temperatures and scattered precipitation.

**Zone 2:** Precipitation across the zone is abundant central and south with strong thunderstorms with tornado potential, skies are partly cloudy to cloudy, and flooding is possible.

**Zone 3:** Western skies are fair to partly cloudy, central and eastern areas are cloudy with precipitation, temperatures are seasonal, and the zone is windy.

**Zone 4:** Western and central areas are windy with precipitation, skies are partly cloudy to cloudy, and temperatures are seasonal.

**Zone 5:** Temperatures are seasonal, skies are partly cloudy to cloudy central and east, fair to partly cloudy west, and central and eastern areas see precipitation.

**Zone 6:** Seasonal temperatures accompany fair to partly cloudy and windy skies with scattered precipitation.

**Zone 7:** Much of the zone is windy with scattered precipitation, temperatures are seasonal to above, and skies are partly cloudy to cloudy.

**Zone 8:** Alaska is fair to partly cloudy, seasonal, and windy. Central and eastern Hawaii see scattered thunderstorms, skies are fair to partly cloudy, and temperatures seasonal to above.

### 4th Quarter Moon, December 18–25
**Zone 1:** Skies are fair to partly cloudy and temperatures are seasonal to below.

**Zone 2:** Temperatures are seasonal, skies partly cloudy to cloudy, and central and southern areas see scattered precipitation

**Zone 3:** Western and central areas are cloudy with abundant precipitation and flood potential, temperatures are seasonal to below, and eastern areas are windy with scattered precipitation.

**Zone 4:** Much of the zone sees precipitation under partly cloudy to cloudy and windy skies, locally heavy downfall with flood potential is possible, and temperatures are seasonal to below.

**Zone 5:** Skies are partly cloudy to cloudy and windy with thunderstorms central and east and temperatures seasonal to below.

**Zone 6:** Temperatures are seasonal to above and skies are windy and fair to partly cloudy.

**Zone 7:** The zone is windy, partly cloudy to cloudy and seasonal.

**Zone 8:** Alaska is windy, mostly fair, and seasonal. Hawaii is fair to partly cloudy with temperatures ranging from seasonal to above.

### New Moon, December 26–January 2, 2020

**Zone 1:** Northern areas are stormy, skies are partly cloudy to cloudy and windy, and temperatures are seasonal.

**Zone 2:** Northern areas see scattered precipitation, and the zone is windy, variably cloudy, and seasonal.

**Zone 3:** Seasonal temperatures accompany partly cloudy to cloudy and windy skies and precipitation across much of the zone.

**Zone 4:** Central and eastern areas see precipitation, some locally heavy, variably cloudiness, and seasonal temperatures.

**Zone 5:** Temperatures are seasonal, skies partly cloudy to cloudy with more cloudiness and precipitation, some locally heavy, east.

**Zone 6:** Western and central areas are windy, skies are partly cloudy to cloudy, temperatures are seasonal, and precipitation is scattered central and east.

**Zone 7:** The zone is mostly partly cloudy, windy west and central, cloudy east with precipitation, and temperatures are seasonal.

**Zone 8:** Alaska is windy west, skies are partly cloudy to cloudy, and temperatures are seasonal to below. Hawaii is partly cloudy to cloudy with scattered precipitation, and temperatures seasonal to below.

### About the Author

Kris Brandt Riske is the executive director and a professional member of the American Federation of Astrologers (AFA), the oldest US astrological organization, founded in 1938; and a member of the National Council for Geocosmic Research (NCGR). She has a master's degree in journalism and a certificate of achievement in weather forecasting from Penn State. Kris is the author of several books, including Llewellyn's Complete Book of Astrology: The Easy Way to Learn Astrology, Mapping Your Money, and Mapping Your Future. She is also the coauthor of Mapping Your Travels and Relocation and Astrometeorology: Planetary Powers in Weather Forecasting. Her newest book is Llewellyn's Complete Book of Predictive Astrology. She writes for astrology publications and contributes to the annual weather forecast for Llewellyn's Moon Sign Book. In addition to astrometeorology, she specializes in predictive astrology. Kris is an avid NASCAR fan, although she'd rather be a driver than a spectator. In 2011, she fulfilled her dream when she drove a stock car for twelve fast laps. She posts a weather forecast for each of the thirty-six race weekends (qualifying and race day) for NASCAR drivers and fans. Visit her at www.pitstopforecasting.com. Kris also enjoys gardening, reading, jazz, and her three cats.

# Economic Forecast for 2019

*by Christeen Skinner*

The year 2019 is exactly ninety years from the Wall Street Crash. The much-revered investor, W.D.Gann would no doubt have marked 2019 as being a potentially problematic year—using the simple premise that as ninety is a quarter of a circle, then a new phase—usually led by crisis—would occur. This ninety-year staging post may well bring global financial challenge.

In September 2019, not only will Uranus oppose the position of the Sun on one of the key 1929 dates, but the planetoid, Chiron, opposes the position held by the Moon in that same chart. Arguably as important is that Saturn will be at exactly the same declination as that planet held in 1929. That these three cosmic coincidences occur within days of the September equinox is just one notable feature of 2019: a year in which the position of the

Moon is set to mark clear turning points.

It is interesting to note that if we look back in history, using a unit of nintey years, three cycles back we come to 1659, (270 years before the crash on Wall Street) when the first hand-written check was drawn on a London bank. In 2019 we may well see the last of such transactions, as there is much to suggest that with the wheel having turned a full 360 years (degrees), that the world will enter a new era where financial transactions are concerned. Developments could yet take even the most confident of investors by surprise however.

In 2019, Uranus makes its final Taurus ingress. Though it visits that sign in 2018, geocentrically it retrogrades back into Aries before making a full Taurus entry in 2019. Uranus's last visit to Taurus was in the 1930s when over 7000 banks collapsed. Though history rarely repeats itself exactly, we should be prepared for major shake-ups within the banking sector and the emergence of entirely new ways of financial working. Uranus is, of course, the planet associated with technology and innovation. Though Bitcoin and its many competitors have been around for some years, their place within the financial sector will surely become more important in 2019.

Then too we must also take into consideration Chiron's move into Aries. Chiron, though often known as the "wounded healer" has an equally justified reputation as the "corrector," the "auditor" or "maverick." Chiron often holds a prominent position at times of market peak or trough: either marking a change in market sentiment. Chiron's move into Aries (the sign associated with Tarzan) could result in a few falls from the trees or financial misadventures that have global effect.

Markets are made up of people whose moods affect the direction of any given market. The future will be quite different. As the use of algorithms and robots increases, the markets, and the human emotions by which they are driven will play a decreasing role. The clash of sentiment versus totally non-emotional (even if man-made) mechanical behavior should result in a reduction in volatility whilst increasing the probability of a sudden crash through technical fault. 2019 could yet bring the last of the Moon-swings that have brought so much volatility in recent years.

By the end of 2019, Jupiter, the largest planet of our known solar system, joins Saturn and Pluto in Capricorn. Concentration of planetary activity in an area of the zodiac associated with major organizations and, specifically with banking, is indicative of major development in this sector. Leaving aside the Uranus in Taurus factor for the moment, the last time there was such a concentration was in the late thirteenth century: the period of the Lombard bankers whose control of lending is legendary.

With so many planets moving to one side of the Sun, we should anticipate some extraordinary solar behavior: possibly including an increase in coronal mass ejections (CMEs), which has the capacity to knock out satellite systems (and hence affect global trade) and is already acknowledged.

Though predicting such an event is not—at least at the time of writing—possible, we should all be aware of this possibility. In assessing this risk, it would be wise for everyone to ensure that they invest in friends and family who could offer support should such a crisis occur.

We should also note a marked decrease in sunspot activity, which is expected to reach a minimum in 2019. The combined effects will likely result in highly disturbed weather patterns leading to significant economic difficulty.

History shows direct correlation between maxima and minima positions of the Moon to Earth with life on Earth—and occasionally upheaval in the form of natural disaster. The Moon does not maintain an even distance from Earth, at times being over 50,000 km farther away than at others. The Moon will come close to

Earth on May 26, 2019. It is not abnormal for traders to respond to perigee (nearest to Earth) with frenetic activity that at times borders on panicked behavior. Any effect in May could be magnified in that Mars reaches extreme declination that month. As Mars is thought of as a planet of high energy, it is probable that this Mars position will coincide with extreme behavior and, where financial markets are concerned, considerable volatility.

Any overview of the year must also include mention of Saturn's long conjunction with the lunar south node through many months of 2019. Though this aspect occurs every few decades, the extra-ordinary duration of this aspect suggests a long and financially mournful period in 2019.

## First Quarter

A commonly used forecasting technique uses solstice and equinox charts to forecast the subsequent quarter. The Full Moon that precedes 2019 coincides with the winter solstice of 2018. In this chart, the Sun opposes the Moon across the Capricorn–Cancer axis. Of the twelve signs of the zodiac, four have particular strength: Aries, Cancer, Libra, and Capricorn. Each is said to mark the beginning of a new season so ushering in a fresh stage of the life cycle. Where the first degree of these signs is emphasized, developments are often dramatic. In this instance and with considerable emphasis on the sign of Capricorn, this first quarter of the year is marked by clear signs of business contraction. This possibility is much emphasized by the position of Saturn (the depressor) in Capricorn, which, at the 2018 winter solstice, is positioned half way between the Sun and Pluto. This planetary picture (a midpoint written in the form of Saturn=Sun/Pluto) suggests a cosmic "full stop" moment, as though a retailer announced "cash only, no credit given."

However, it is common for stocks—especially in the USA—to rise in the last week of the year, with much dependance on Mercury's position relative to the Sun. The close of 2018 should not disappoint in terms of short end-of-year rally. The end of year rising trend is unlikely to continue in January however. As early as the last quarter Moon on December 29, when Uranus is at a right angle with the lunar nodes, fault lines should be apparent—perhaps enough for some investors to take flight.

By the January 6 New Moon, Mercury will have made Capricorn ingress while the New Moon is on the Saturn–Pluto midpoint. This offers a twist on the aforementioned midpoint (this time Sun=Moon=Saturn/Pluto, an echo perhaps of the "cash only" phrase).

Even if a market high is reached in the early days of 2019, it is likely that there will be talk of constraint, and even, perhaps, another rate rise. Add this to the fault lines Uranus may have exposed, and it is probable that indices will have fallen by mid-month.

It should be remembered that many countries came into being while the Sun was moving through Capricorn (United Kingdom). These governments could be facing the high probability of tax revenues failing to cover costs. Echoes of the austerity measures put in place a decade earlier may be heard again but, this time, much louder. Many people are likely to experience a financial squeeze.

Mercury aligns with the south node at the January Full Moon. Though the Mercury–south node alignment does not always coincide with key turning points, as it coincides with a major lunation accenting the Aquarius/Leo axis, precious metals should reach a turning point. It may be that there is flight to gold-backed currencies mid-month. The challenge of bringing precious metals to the surface could be headline news around the twenty-first too. A cosmic signature that has in the past coincided with a mining disaster appears on that date and may be another factor affecting prices.

Of the precious metals, silver may be high profile in February.

Silver was first traded on the Chicago exchange in July 1933. That month Saturn was positioned mid-way through Aquarius: at exactly the position of the New Moon on February 4, 2019. Though it is essential to combine technical analysis with astro-information, it is likely that the price of silver on this date will have important resonance. It may be that this marks a key level.

Between the February New and Full Moons, Chiron moves from Pisces to Aries. Thanks to a retrograde period, Chiron last made this ingress twice: in 1968 and 1969. This year too, the ingress occurs more than once. In 1968, as Chiron moved to Aries, the Dow Jones index rose at the first entry into Aries but fell during Chiron's later Aries ingress. Though it is unwise to determine a trading strategy based solely on the position of one planet (or, in this case, planetoid), it would equally be wrong to ignore the correlation between ingress and index. There is much to suggest that indices will indeed rise during this quarter of the year, only to fall a few months later.

The Full Moon on February 19 coincides with the Sun's Pisces ingress. We thus have a sequence of Full Moons at zero degrees of signs (December 2018 at 0 Cancer, January at 0 Leo, and February now 0 Virgo). This fact too has relevance and is part of a recurrent cycle: the last such sequence occurring nineteen years earlier at the dawn of the millennium. A review of the S&P index for that period shows that although the S&P index rose from the December 1999 Full Moon to the end of that year, the January and February Full Moons (respectively 0 Leo and 0 Virgo) marked tops from which this index dropped.

The February Full Moon period does not appear promising for the British pound (sterling). A review of GBP–USD trading in 1999 reveals that at the 1999 January Full Moon a single pound bought $1.668. By the February New Moon, only $1.599. There was another decline between the February Full Moon and the March New Moon.

2018 © suthisa Image from BigStockPhoto.com

True, 2019 is markedly different in that these similar lunations occur within a few weeks of the planned withdrawal from the European Union. Few might expect the level to which the planets suggest sterling could fall however. For those interested, this might be the moment to buy this currency whose value should rise once Uranus is firmly established in Taurus.

A major rule in financial astrology is that when an ingress coincides with at least two major aspects, there is likely to be a change in trading attitude often leading to turning points.

March is special in that Mercury stations prior to turning retrograde but within minutes of moving into Aries. This factor alone suggests a precipice moment: a "so near, yet so far point." The fact that Uranus makes its final (as viewed from Earth) Taurus ingress just twenty-six hours later suggests that March 5 and 6 will see marked change in sentiment and hence in prices. Yet two factors are perhaps still not enough. Further confirmation that this will be critical comes from the New Moon on March 5 and the Sun's conjunction with Neptune. With so much concentrated activity around dates, which are themselves close to anniversaries of past trading challenges, it seems reasonable to expect a turning point.

A simple trading system involves purchase at the New Moon and sale at the Full Moon. This system has value—but only when those lunations coinciding with outer planet stations or outer planet ingress are not used. This would be one such occasion i.e., risk assessment suggests that this would not be the month to employ this strategy.

Mercury does not turn direct until March 28—some days after the Full Moon. It is a few weeks after that before it returns to the position held in early March. If markets do fall after March 6, it is quite possible that they will not recover until April.

Those born with the Sun in Pisces could find this retrograde period stressful. Note that not all retrograde Mercury periods are the same. This phase in its cycle generally gets a bad press. Yet the effect is not consistent. Mishap, miscommunication, and error appear more likely in some signs than others. As true, is that certain signs are more affected or afflicted than others through these periods. To the risk averse, this is not a good time to start a business or to sign important documents.

In the market place, and as Mercury retrogrades in Pisces, we might reasonably anticipate falls in pharmaceutical, oil, and media stocks, all of which are said to come under the Pisces heading.

The March Full Moon again comes at 0 degrees of a sign: this time Libra. What is especially interesting about this Full Moon is that the Moon also opposes (within a degree) Chiron. Chiron has a reputation for many things, one of which is auditor or corrector.

With the Cancer node at the midpoint of Venus and Jupiter in that chart and in Yod (Finger of God) formation, this could yet prove a critical date. True, this need not affect markets, though it is not dissimilar to planetary formations coinciding with "flash crashes." At the very least it is likely to affect values: leading many to question how money and goodwill or ethics can possibly work together.

## Second Quarter

As before, a review of the second quarter begins with study of the chart for the March Equinox. Since this coincides with the Full Moon in Libra, balance—which implies correction—is more likely than not.

A change of trend is indicated by Uranus's Taurus ingress. Though Uranus will have made Taurus ingress a year previously, its grand entrance comes in March 2019. Taurus is one of the Fixed signs, and Uranus has a reputation for making demands. Together Uranus in Taurus speaks of potential dictatorship and strict rules. This transit could also bring sudden changes in values (value being a keyword associated with Taurus).

Uranus's cycle is roughly eighty-four years. It last made Taurus ingress in 1934 and, thanks to a retrograde period as occurs in 2019, also did so in 1935. The latter occurred on March 28th 1935, the precise date on which Mercury stations in 2019. This date could yet prove a turning point as this station coincides with the last quarter Moon (often a signal for change of direction) while Venus and Uranus are in contra parallel. The potential for "flash crash" is noteworthy.

Following this event, and until April 16, market confusion is probable as Mercury, Venus, Mars, Jupiter, and Neptune holding positions in Mutable signs, offers curious planetary energy that, operating at the human level, could result in traders not knowing which way to turn.

Meanwhile, Pluto, in Capricorn, aligns with the south node. As a slow moving planet, and given that either mean or true node positions can be used, the effect of this transit lasts over a period of weeks. Isolating exact dates comes only when the movements of the faster moving planets are taken into consideration. What is fascinating on this occasion is that Pluto's conjunction with the south node in Cancer last took place in May 1935, drawing attention, again, to that earlier time.

History reveals that the Dow Jones Index fell sharply from the start of 1935 but reversed as Uranus moved into Taurus and gathered strength as Pluto aligned with the Cancer South Node. It is quite possible then that, should history repeat, then after April 16th, indices will make upward movement.

As mentioned earlier, Mars reaches maximum declination in May as the Moon reaches perigee. These factors suggest considerable volatility and, perhaps, panic. This could impact on the price of precious metals. Mars's opposition to Jupiter on May 5 could mean a turning point in this sector.

Meanwhile, major computer giants, many of whose charts have the exact degree of the Pluto-Node conjunction highlighted, could see their share price rise. The announcement of new revenue streams coming on line made as, Mercury, then in Taurus moves to conjoin Uranus, could see sharp movement here.

There is an old adage "sell in May and go away." A slight variation on this for 2019 would be to stay in the market until the New Moon on June 3 when both Mercury and Mars are out of bounds—beyond the Sun's reach in declination. As you might expect from a union between the planet of commerce (Mercury) and a force or energy (Mars), it is reasonable to expect that this will bring momentum and rising prices. It will surely also be an indicator of improved volume. The latter is essential for prices to rise: since volume implies activity.

Actually, that rising trend could continue through to the Full Moon on June 19. By his lunation, Mercury and Mars will be aligned with the lunar node in Cancer. This configuration may be of particular significance for the housing market: a strong possibility being an increased number of sales—but perhaps also an increase in the number of foreclosures. Yes, there are conflicting signals: on the one hand rising rates and prices will surely make for very real difficulties in cash flow for some people; others though may be in a position to drive up share prices.

Through these first two quarters of 2019, Jupiter's passage through Sagittarius should do much to offset calls for a further tightening of belts and even of austerity measures as indicated by the combined forces of Saturn and Pluto in Capricorn. Those who are able to move from one jurisdiction to another will surely make the most of the tax incentives to do so. Such moves may not be possible later in the year when Jupiter too moves into Capricorn.

## Third Quarter

With the high probability that severe weather patterns will affect growing cycles and bring disruption to travel arrangements, this three-month period could prove expensive.

In the southern hemisphere, drought may well prove a major issue, bringing some farmers to the brink of bankruptcy while also causing suffering to livestock. Elsewhere, monsoon rains and hurricanes threaten many livelihoods and contribute to major distribution crisis.

At the summer solstice—the chart used to assess this quarter of the year—Saturn conjoins the Moon's south node. Saturn's influence is likely to act as a depressor, resulting in indices moving to the downside: a possibility amplified by the Mercury-Mars conjunction whose influence on traders may be to send them running for cover. The mood for this quarter is likely to be sombre.

The solar eclipse of July 2 is at 10 degrees of Cancer: the degree in which Jupiter is said to be exalted. As Saturn opposes the eclipse, this is akin to a Jupiter–Saturn opposition: one of the more delicate stages of the business cycle. The planetary picture for this quarter is clear: that there will be a lurch toward the negative.

This argument is strengthened by the Sun–Saturn opposition (another sign of negative trading) just one week later and which coincides with Mercury and Mars aligning in Leo (Mercury then retrograde). While it is not unknown for a Mercury–Mars conjunction to bring uplift in indices and to prove a positive time for business generally, neither the Cancer conjunction a few weeks earlier nor this one in Leo, show this promise.

Deals could come unstuck though true, and depending on the charts involved, it may be possible for these to be reinstated in August. The period between the two eclipses (July 2–16) should not be considered good for business. Avoiding the launch of new products or services through this period would be wise.

The lunar eclipse which concludes this period has the Full Moon aligning with Pluto whilst opposing the Sun. This is yet another cosmic signature likely to coincide with hard and unpleasant facts coming to light. Around this lunation it should be clear that some financial situations are simply unsustainable. From July to September, an increase in the number of recorded bankruptcies is probable.

Also, Jupiter, Saturn, and Pluto are in parallel formation. Though Jupiter will be moving through Sagittarius, and Saturn and Pluto are in Capricorn, their shared position by declination could coincide with legal challenges within the banking industry and, especially around the lunar eclipse, see corporate bond collapse.

This could prove an excellent time for canny investors. Bargains are possible. Indeed, those unafraid to buck the trend may determine that if played for the long-term, there are some prices too good to miss—especially if utilities or essential services are involved. Blue chip companies whose fundamentals are sound, are worthy of particular attention, as these could see growth in the early 2020s.

At the next New Moon on July 31, Mercury arrives at its direct station: returning to the degree held at the solstice on June 21. This could bring a small uplift to the market place. However, with Saturn still conjoined with the South Node (both retrograde and

moving at similar pace), any uplift will surely be temporary: perhaps lasting only a few days. Simultaneously, gold and currency markets could see change of trend in the early days of August.

Two weeks later, at the Full Moon, the Sun meets with Venus in Leo. It might be assumed that this would be a period of promise—especially for luxury goods. Yet with Saturn still with the south node, this really could be a case of survival of the fittest with equities falling yet again. Yet talk of mergers and acquisitions within the luxury goods sector may be enough to tempt those with cash to make investments.

Mercury, Venus, and Mars all align with the Virgo New Moon on August 30: at the same time aspecting Uranus in Taurus. This will surely throw attention on the distribution services mentioned earlier. Though many will surely be crying out for those services, delivery could be difficult given prevailing solar conditions.

Virgo is the sign associated with essential services. Those businesses able to fulfil orders will surely thrive with Saturn's continuing association with the lunar south node; companies trying to get off the ground may find that conditions are such that they are hard pressed to deliver.

Sadly, and while not wishing to be a doom-monger, another factor to bear in mind through this period is the very real danger of pandemic: something else that could contribute to financial mayhem through this quarter of the year.

For those healthy enough and not too risk-averse might like to consider this strategy: buying stock in early September when Mars and Uranus are 120 degrees apart and selling later as they reach opposition (November 24). In the past, this timing has brought profit. This "crash-cycle," if supported by technical analysis, has proved useful to traders.

On this occasion I would be tempted to wait until the night before the Full Moon on September 14 to make that purchase. Neptune is with the Full Moon at this lunation: another signal for low prices. By waiting until this period to buy, even greater profit could be realized.

Once Mercury and Venus move into Libra the following week, the mood amongst traders should shift as investors slowly but surely return to the market place causing prices to rise.

## Fourth Quarter

Saturn's alignment with the Moon's south node is still apparent at the september equinox. Yet a change in the cosmic weather is indicated by Mercury's square to both the Moon and Saturn. It is as though the negative mood can no longer be tolerated: especially by those born under one of the Mutable signs of Gemini, Virgo, Sagittarius or Pisces—the latter arguably more than ready to get back into the trading waters. Note the square aspect between Jupiter and Neptune, the two planets ruling Pisces. This could prove a siren's call to those who feel they have lost enough.

With Jupiter at right angles to Mars' position in the chart for the New York Stock Exchange, it may be felt by some that a mood change MUST occur. Unless your personal chart suggests something to the contrary, however, it might be as well to resist this siren call until there is greater clarity. Jupiter is the ultimate host/hostess, always ready to provide another drink and hopelessly unaware of the effect this might have. Though obviously you should discuss matters with your financial advisor before taking action, this is not the time to trade as indices could fall further. Until Saturn parts company with the south node during October, improvement is unlikely.

Actually even then, few, barring those who are cash rich may be in a position to buy into stock markets. In the equinox chart, Jupiter, Saturn, and Pluto are all in parallel aspect with the Moon in contra-parallel to all three. That would seem to indicate that many will be running away from investments entirely.

With a large grouping of planets in cardinal signs at the New Moon on September 28, the potential for indices to rise increases—though, perhaps not at the pace some will recall from 2017. Research shows that with a bias toward cardinal signs, the markets tend to push forward.

Where money is concerned there is, of course, always a benefit somewhere: those who are invested in global brands providing essential services should find comfort in dividends payable at the end of 2019.

Though there does appear much to be excited about in the first few days of October, by the Full Moon on October 13th, a corporate bubble could burst. At this lunation, Pluto in Capricorn is in exact square to both the Sun and Moon. Pluto's presence in a planetary configuration can, at times, signal the potential for great wealth. On this occasion however, and with Saturn still close to the lunar south node, hidden facts could come to light bringing with them the collapse of a major corporate edifice. It is probable that clues as to which corporation will be most affected should be apparent from July.

A further possibility at this Full Moon is the exposure of yet more corruption—not necessarily within corporations but, more likely, within governments. The potential collapse of at least one political structure should be anticipated.

This possibility is further amplified by the New Moon on October 27. The chart for this event shows an exact opposition with Uranus: the planet often present when a political idea is given particular attention with, at times, violent opposition to ideas presented. As this same chart contains a square aspect between Mars and Saturn, it is not inconceivable that the word "dictatorship" will be used and that there might be trouble on the streets of various cities.

This has implications for investors and traders alike. Companies offering security and protection should see increased interest in their products and shares while insurance and reinsurance companies face having to make large pay-outs.

Political instability threatens currency markets too: as can be seen in the chart for the Full Moon on November 12. In this chart, Mercury lies in opposition to Vesta across the Scorpio–Taurus axis. These two signs are often noted for financial acumen. The opposition of planet a of commerce, Mercury, with the trader's asteroid, Vesta, suggests a busy time for Forex traders.

The currencies affected are likely to be hard currencies as opposed to crypto-currencies: with implications for both silver and gold prices. Should it be that the previously identified February 2019 key time for silver proves to have been correct (i.e., a key level was then reached), then this November Full Moon period should prove equally important. Again, it is essential to link this time frame with technical analysis so as to devise a suitable trading system to take advantage of any price move.

On November 19, and slightly ahead of the Sun's move into Sagittarius, Mars arrives in Scorpio. It is around this date when those who have been preparing to make investments show increased interest in returning to the market place. These investors may feel that the worst is past and that the last weeks of 2019 will see a stock market rally. They may not be wrong.

The New Moon charts of November 26 and December 26 both show promise. Indeed, at the former, Jupiter is close to the Galactic center. This should coincide with a power surge with global brands taking the lead.

Exhilarating as this period promises to be for some (especially those "trigger happy" and who think that markets have indeed bottomed), a word of caution: as of early December, Jupiter joins Saturn and Pluto in Capricorn. In fact, the planetary alignment in the last few days of 2019 has not been witnessed since the end of the thirteenth century!

Though Capricorn is the sign of the goat aiming for the mountain peak, and yes, true, there are times of risky jumps, it is more usual to see relentless plodding to the summit. This end of year period then is likely to mark the start of a long, slow, slog upward with blue chip companies the ones most likely to realize gain providing much needed dividend for jaded investors.

The year concludes with a south node solar eclipse on December 26. This eclipse, with the Sun, Moon, Jupiter, Saturn, and Pluto all in Capricorn should be viewed as a spotlight being shone on corporate structures and the banking industry in particular. It would not be surprising if, even over the holiday period, there were to be shocks and surprises: including, perhaps, as in 1933, the disclosure of how many banks have failed during what will have been a singular year.

## In Summary

To recap: exactly ninety years after the Great Crash, 2019 may well offer singular financial drama—especially from the solar eclipse in early July through to October. Those who are risk-averse might choose to leave the market place well ahead of this period, returning much later in the year—perhaps after the December solar eclipse.

Those determined to ride through these storms should go back to basics, studying carefully the balance sheets of the companies in which they have interest: only those with strong foundations will surely withstand the above forecast tough financial conditions.

It is worth reemphasizing that the combination of solar and lunar conditions in 2019 threaten extraordinarily difficult terrestrial weather conditions and the distribution systems on which we have all come to rely. It will surely be imperative to invest in good friends and community.

## About the Author

*Christeen Skinner is author of* The Financial Universe *(2004 and 2009), in which she forecast the banking crisis of 2008,* Exploring the Financial Universe *(2016), and* The Beginner's Guide to the Financial Universe *(2017). She works in London and has a broad clientele—city traders, entrepreneurs, and private investors. She taught for the Faculty of Astrological Studies for a decade, was Chair of the Astrological Association of Great Britain, and is now Director of Cityscopes London Ltd, Chair of the Advisory Board of the National Council for Geocosmic Research, and a Director of the Alexandria I-base Project.*

# New and Full Moon Forecasts for 2019

*by Sally Cragin*

Can you believe it's been a half-century since Apollo 11 landed in the Sea of Tranquility? I was a child watching this incredible broadcast in my grandmother's house in Massachusetts. Our family had a special connection to NASA, as my uncle, Dr. James Trainer, was a space physicist who worked on many space engineering projects. Uncle Jim was working during the moon landing, but he'd told us about the capsule that would bring the astronauts safely down—and then launch them Earthward again.

That night, I went outside and gazed—somewhat myopically—at the moon. I'd had glasses for a couple of years, but my prescription was such that the moon resembled a gauzy, gleaming gray gem. It was the Moon I'd seen all my life—but it was different now. It was occupied.

The dark Mariae were lined with sparkling white, and try as I might, there was no seeing Apollo 11. I went back and forth between the yard and the den (this was an era where an entire family had one TV in the house, and the broadcast clarity was dependent on the antenna and the weather).

I imagine more people looked at the Moon that night than had ever done so in human history. We found that it's made of basalt and lava (heavy rocks), that it's got a transcendent view of mother Earth. And once we stuck our flag in the sparkling lunar landscape, we checked that off our "to-do" list as a nation.

Nevertheless, the Moon looms large for we astrologers, and if you're a regular reader of this *Almanac*, it's because you find it helpful to know what's going on with the Moon as she shifts her gaze to us depending on what phase she's in.

## Before and During the New Moon

Initiate activities, start projects, try not to "pile on" too much, but pay close attention to what or who comes into your life. Friendships may begin tentatively during the New Moon, and then deepen in intensity as the Full Moon arrives. People in your life— or you!—may be afflicted with melancholy. That "what's the use" or "why bother" feeling, which is neither accurate nor helpful, may fill your heart. Wait it out!

## Before and During the Full Moon

Expect acceleration in all areas of your life. This can be a confusing time, particularly as far as communication is concerned. People may be inclined toward "oversharing," or making presumptions that cause confusion to all. Overlooked projects may suddenly be crucial, and folks you know (or you!) may be inclined toward a degree of drama or exaggeration that seems out of line with their personalities. A great time to attend a party—but avoid folks who like to make a scene.

## The New and Full Moons at a Glance for 2019

For each entry, you'll find that all signs are mentioned, as well as suggestions for best activities or actions to avoid. We are also including information about other planets, as they affect the Moon. Remember that the New Moon is always in the same sign as the Sun, and the Full Moon is in the opposite sign. So: Sun in Capricorn/Full Moon in Cancer, Sun in Aquarius/Full Moon in Leo, and so on.

### New Moon in Capricorn, January 5

An excellent lunar phase for a building project, or for settling up accounts. Capricorn rules the skin, knees, and other joints. New Moons are excellent for addressing physical ailments with skilled professionals. Capricorn helps us see situations with a practical eye, particularly Capricorn, Taurus, Virgo, Aquarius, Pisces, Scorpio, and Sagittarius. Leo, Gemini, Libra, Cancer, and Aries could be at cross-purposes with a loved one. Or feeling territorial over trifles. With Mars and Jupiter harmonizing in firesigns, this time is super for reviewing your ability to get your heart rate up in healthy exercise. Do: bake, work with clay or wood, begin projects that will need much time and attention to complete. Don't: rush people who need time to absorb, respond, or make decisions.

### Full Moon in Leo, January 21

The Lion rules the 5th house of children, merriment, and public relations and Leo Full Moons have one purpose: shake things up! And with the lunar eclipse, you may find that someone (or a group) previously held in high regard no longer has the charisma that held others spellbound. This is a weekend to party—or to behave like a kid. It's also a fine weekend for making dramatic changes in your hair-style. Find the fun if you're a Gemini, Cancer, Leo, Virgo, Libra, Sagittarius, or Aquarius. Be cautious—especially if you're the target of others' interest—if you're an Aquarius, Taurus, Capricorn, Pisces, or Scorpio. Do: take a chance on a new party place, or cocktail. Don't: act like a child when you don't get your way—no matter how invigorating throwing a tantrum is.

### New Moon in Aquarius, February 4

Innovation and eccentricity rules the sign of the water carrier. So if you turn up at work ready to do the same-old, same-old, someone in your circle will have a bushel-full of new notions they'd love for you to sign on for. Full speed ahead with that if you're an Aquarius, Pisces, Capricorn, Gemini, Libra, Aries, or Sagittarius. However, Taurus, Scorpio, Leo, Virgo, or Cancer: you'll find changing your pace a little painful. Do: Indulge in a trend that makes you smile (when's the last time you had fun with a yo-yo?) Don't: expect too many specifics from folks in your circle who are inclined to be vague, or fail at "follow-through."

### Full Moon in Virgo, February 19

The Virgin rules the 6th house, which is focused on health and work. So if you've been waiting for an opportunity to initiate a new system or program among your colleagues, now's the time. Innovations can be difficult to push forward—particularly in environments grounded in tradition, but this Full Moon could embolden even the shyest. Virgo, Libra, Leo, Cancer, Scorpio, Capricorn, and Taurus should be fearless about gambling. Sagittarius, Pisces, Gemini, Aries, and Aquarius: words meant kindly could be heard as hostile or peevish. Mind your tone. Venus is working closely with the moon, so relations with maternal figures in your life could be joyful. Do: explore other employment options, nutrition innovations, or communication devices. Don't: micromanage, no matter how tempting or justified!

### New Moon in Pisces, March 6

Spring is in the air, and the focus is on the feet (which are governed by Pisces). Whether it's buying new shoes for the gym or putting your best foot forward, this new moon brings a mid-week boost, particularly those who work with folks who are depressed, mentally challenged, or incarcerated. Pisces is excellent for art, so dig into your creative side, whether it's photographing a favorite scene or shopping for fresh pillows for the couch. Pisces, Scorpio, Cancer, Aquarius, Capricorn, Aries, and Taurus: your insights into others will bring a career boost. Virgo, Sagittarius, Gemini, Libra, and Leo: beware of feelings of paranoia—they will mislead you. With Mars making an easy angle to the moon, there may be affectionate moments with characters that play a paternal role in your life. Do: let yourself go in terms of rushing. Pisces moons bring a langorous pace. Don't: kick yourself!

### Full Moon in Libra, March 20

The Scales keep everything "even steven," and Libra's occupation of the 7th house governs partnerships and public relations. This may be the time to bring on a new member in a work environment, or a social scene. Or perhaps you're the new member! Libra, Aquarius, Gemini, Leo, Virgo, Scorpio, and Sagittarius—others want to hear your opinion, so if you're on the fence about an important matter, use friends as a sounding board. Capricorn, Cancer, Aries, Pisces, and Taurus: getting swept away by something that looks pretty good (but needs closer scrutiny) is a hazard. Do: remember Venus rules Libra, so fun times with friends or making yourself more attractive is an excellent use of resources. Don't: kick yourself if you're overcome with indecision. It happens to the best of us, and Libra Moons encourage!

### New Moon in Aries, April 5

The spring ram symbolizes Aries, and if you have been needing a boost, or feeling that inspiration is lacking, this lunar phase gets you going. Since Aries symbolizes the head, a spring hat, or sassy new haircut could ease you into the weekend. Aries, Leo, Sagittarius, Taurus, Gemini, Pisces, and Aquarius: take everything on—I mean everything. This is the time to say YES! Libra, Cancer, Capricorn, Virgo, and Scorpio: the word today is "impulse control." You may be tempted to sound off in righteous indignation, but discretion is the better part of valor, and all that. Saturn is at odds with the moon, so be very deferential with females who are in an authority position in your life. Do: look for projects that take very little time to complete. Don't: get yourself provoked by others who are blunt in their comments, particularly when it comes to appearance.

### Full Moon in Libra, April 19

This Full Moon brings urges to examine our relationships. Partnerships that had been motoring along may hit some potholes, particularly where missed communication is concerned. It may be easy to strike others as ambivalent about matters that do mean something to you, especially for those who are Capricorn, Cancer, Aries, Pisces, and Taurus. But for those who are Libra, Aquarius, Gemini, Leo, Virgo, Scorpio, and Sagittarius—this Full Moon may bring out the truth, the whole truth, and nothing but the truth. Which turns out to be a relief. Saturn, the planet of limits is making a difficult angle to the moon, so finding a solution that works for all may be difficult. Do: make yourself as attractive as you can, and make a point of drawing out the wallflowers. Don't: kick yourself for saying "not now," instead of "no." "Not now" can mean the same thing.

### New Moon in Taurus, May 4

Acquisition is the theme with this lunar phase, and if you are a shopaholic by nature, you may want to lock up your charge card. Taurus rules the throat, so singing (or enjoying vocal music) could bring joy and delight today. Even if you're not an opera fan—listen to some of the greats, and see if your perception and appreciation isn't sharpened! We'd suggest Taurii Maria Callas and Kiri Te Kanawa. Taurus, Virgo, Capricorn, Aries, Pisces, Gemini, and Cancer: you can speak soothingly to the most riled-up folks in your circle. Use that talent! Leo, Scorpio, Aquarius, Libra, and Sagittarius: others may perceive judgment or criticism in what comes out of your mouth. Cultivate your smile instead. Do: look for practical investments, particularly in items that make you feel good about yourself—Mars, Saturn, and the Moon are in harmony. Don't: unload on folks who try to provoke you. Taurus Moons bring out stubbornness in all.

### Full Moon in Scorpio, May 18

Mystery, sexuality, and borrowed funds oversee the 8th house, where Scorpio dwells. This Full Moon could find you attracted to someone with a dark side or some cause that has depths that aren't immediately visible. Scorpio Moons can also bring out a sharpness in others (the Scorpion rules knives, lawyers, and butchers), so if you're feelings are hurt, you are in tune with the Moon. Scorpio, Libra, Virgo, Sagittarius, Capricorn, Pisces, and Cancer: deep feelings need to be explored—now's the time. Taurus, Aries, Gemini, Leo, and Aquarius: foot in mouth is a danger. No one needs to know "everything" you think right now. Do: understand that Pluto's rulership of Scorpio could make you feel "what's the use," especially for half-completed projects. Now is the time for inward study, not outward exuberance. Don't: underestimate schemers. Scorpio Moons are their time to frolic.

### New Moon in Gemini, June 3

The "Twins" are staring in two directions, and if you are feeling torn about which way to turn, today is not the day to make that decision. Since Gemini rules the lungs, you may be surrounded by Chatty Cathys who want to analyze the smallest of details. However, a better strategy with this lunar energy is evaluating

both sides of a situation, particularly those dealing with communication, travel, and data. Analytical abilities should be in high gear for Gemini, Aquarius, Libra, Taurus, Aries, Cancer, and Leo. However, Sagittarius, Pisces, Virgo, Scorpio, and Capricorn could tie themselves in knots when looking for the clear path. Mars in Aquarius facilitates forceful words that are precise and inspiring. Do: look for electronic devices that make it easier—or faster—to get your message across. Don't: get forced into a decision if you are truly on the fence. Gemini lunar energy is about celebrating being on the fence!

### Full Moon in Sagittarius, June 17

Mythical beasts make us smile, and Sagittarius's centaur oversees deep belly laughs, higher education, and long-term justice. The 9th house is about forward momentum in terms of gathering knowledge, and though this season is traditionally all about "Dads and Grads," now is the time to think about your next step in terms of being a professional. Sagittarius, Leo, Aries,

Libra, Scorpio, Capricorn, and Aquarius: keep your sense of humor and you can go far. Stick with those who make you laugh. Virgo, Pisces, Gemini, Taurus, and Cancer: self-righteousness (in others) will rub you the wrong way. Yet you may be "full of your-self" (according to those near and dear) and unaware. Humility counts. Do: focus on exercise that uses your legs or tools that take you places quickly (new car, running shoes, train trip). Don't: move so quickly you're accident-prone—another hazard with Sag full moons!

### New Moon in Cancer, July 2

The year is halfway over, but it's never too late to renew your commitment to a romantic or familial partnership. Cancer rules the stomach, so baking or bringing food home that adds to a cozy environment is indicated. However, Cancer has a sensitive side, so Capricorn, Libra, Aries, Aquarius, and Sagittarius could have their feelings hurt. (Or realize belatedly, that some acquaintance has dissed you without you realizing it). Cancer, Scorpio, Pisces, Leo, Virgo, Gemini, and Taurus: your perceptions are spot-on, and if you have any interest in developing your psychic abilities, make time for meditation today. Do: celebrate being generous. Venus is in alignment with the Moon, and that planet is all about being big-hearted. Don't: grow a hard crab shell if you don't need to. The Cancer Moon is about self-protection, not always seclu-sion!

### Full Moon in Capricorn, July 16

Time has dissolved the glorious fish-tail that originally adorned "Capricornus," the half-goat/half-fish, but this practical-minded sign oversees 10th house matters, such as success in the work-place. If you've been building toward something, this interval could get you over the hump. Capricorn, Taurus, Virgo, Aquar-ius, Sagittarius, Scorpio, and Pisces should be in workaholic mode. This will pay off bigtime. Libra, Cancer, Aries, Leo, and

Gemini: seeming "too serious" may deflect others from what you want them to do. Go slow. Uranus is harmonizing with Capricorn, so alternative energy, power-sources, or structures deserve your attention. Mercury retrograde July 7 to August 1. Read the fine print twice. Do: take on projects that take a *long* time to complete. Don't: be mired in a depressed worldview if you can help it. Capricorn makes everything seem more serious.

### New Moon in Leo, July 31

This is a jolly New Moon, and one designed to bring out the kid in us all. Leo rules the heart, so romantic feelings could be riding high. And since Leo also rules hair—get thee to a salon, and see what cool new look will take you through the end of summer. Leo, Sagittarius, Aries, Virgo, Libra, Gemini, and Cancer: let the good times roll, and if others are in a mood to unload their vexations, you should redirect. Resentments that fester during Leo moons can go thermonuclear. Scorpio, Aquarius, Taurus, Gemini, and Pisces: your short attention span is normal! Do: plan to get together with people who make you laugh. Don't: overspend, exaggerate, or try to impress others if you can help it. Leo Moons bring out bravado.

### Full Moon in Aquarius, August 15

The sign of the Watercarrier rules the 11th house, which oversees everything we can't live without and makes us a better person: friends, hopes and dreams, and concerns for humanity. An excellent time to be beguiled by an eccentric charmer, or an idea so crazy that it might just work. Aquarius, Libra, Gemini, Capricorn, Sagittarius, Pisces, and Aries: nostalgia isn't what it used to be—look to future trends for happiness or gain. Taurus, Scorpio, Leo, Virgo, and Cancer: you may feel twitchy around others who don't take things seriously. Right now—they can't. Do: improve the lighting in your home. Aquarius rules electricity, and maybe it's time to ditch the fluorescents. Don't: lose track of what's most important, particularly when it comes to dear friends. Everyone has a short attention span now.

### New Moon in Virgo, August 30

If you've been waiting to get "back in the swing" of your work environment, this lunar phase will get you focused on business, improving how you work, and being more efficient. Virgo rules the lower-digestion, so take no chances on fancy food or fussy ingredients. Your focus should be on what others need (to help you along) and Virgo, Taurus, Capricorn, Leo, Libra, Cancer, and Scorpio have tremendous endurance. Sagittarius, Pisces, Gemini, Aries, and Aquarius: irritability comes easily and you may need to have some "alone time" to be sociable later. Do: look for ways to be healthier, even if this means avoiding folks who have a sweet-tooth (and doughnuts in the bottom drawer). Don't: get fussy about trifles. Yes, you can "catch" them all, but others don't need to know about these minute little details.

### Full Moon in Pisces, September 14

The fish swimming in opposite directions is Pisces' totemic creature. As the fish rules the 12th house (endings, hidden places, the intoxicating arts of music and dance), this full moon brings an urge to escape—or have memorable escapades. Those inclined towards mental-health challenges could have a breakdown (or a breakthrough—and "helping others" is a huge part of the Pisces personality). Pisces, Scorpio, Cancer, Aries, Taurus, Aquarius, and Capricorn: over-indulgence is a danger—can you have twice the fun with half the risk? Do: enjoy photography, films, music, and the visual arts. When is the last time you danced? (Pisces rules the feet) Don't: wear the wrong shoes, buy the wrong shoes, or underestimate the pain that the wrong shoes provide. Ditch 'em!

### New Moon in Libra, September 28

Make a list of all your partnerships: romantic, familial, and career-wise. This new moon sheds a light on those one-on-one relationships that make your life so fulfilling. Are there any folks you haven't seen in a long time? Pick up the phone and check in—Libra moons facilitate partnership. And on a more prosaic note, Libra rules the kidneys and urinary tract, so if you are subject to headaches, consider increasing your consumption of clear liquids. Libra, Gemini Aquarius, Scorpio, Virgo, Sagittarius, and Leo: look for an activity to do with a partnership to deepen a relationship. Capricorn, Aries, Cancer, Pisces, and Taurus: you could be impatient with those who can't make up their minds. Give them space! Do: look for opportunities to be in agreement with others, or to praise their judgment. Don't: force yourself into a decision if you don't want to. If you want both sweaters that look great on you, get them both!

### Full Moon in Aries, October 13

The nimble-footed ram goes fearlessly up the hill, full of the confidence of its 1st house rulership. This full moon could bring emotional impatience with those near and dear, and folks in your life who have a "childish" side (or who look younger than their years) may get up to some shenanigans and expect you to go crazy with them! Aries, Leo, Sagittarius, Taurus, Gemini, Aquarius, and Pisces: take a chance—take a risk—don't hesitate if it feels right. Aries, Libra, Cancer, Virgo, and Scorpio: tempers are flying—don't get caught in the cross-fire. Mar is opposing the moon right now, so male/female energy could be fizzy and fractious. Do: think about one last barbeque if the weather's good. Or a new hat that flatters your face. Don't: behave like a child unless you are a child.

### New Moon in Scorpio, October 27

Secrets and intrigue come with this New Moon, as well as schemes and dreams. Scorpio rules the sex organs, death, and other people's money, so there may be financial problems that need addressing this week. Scorpio, Cancer, Pisces, Sagittarius, Capricorn, Libra, and Virgo: your penetrating intellect will stagger others. And may put them off-balance. Share your brilliance selectively. Taurus, Leo, Aquarius, Gemini, and Aries: you could rush into some "romance" (could be platonic, not sexual) and get taken advantage of. You'll have a clear picture of what's going on in a few days. Do: be reticent about decisions from now through November 20, as Mercury will be retrograde. Don't: not make the first move on a romantic partner. Scorpio Moons are all about physical connection!

### Full Moon in Taurus, November 12

The bull is one of the easiest to underestimate of the signs. The second house rules security, banking, and fiduciary partnerships, and with Venus as it's ruler, the urge to accumulate beautiful items of value is strong. This is a great time for splurging for clothing or luxury items, particularly for Taurus, Virgo, Capricorn, Gemini, Cancer, Aries, and Pisces. Libra, Scorpio, Leo, Aquarius, and Sagittarius could be annoyed by others who are bullying or bull-headed. How to resolve? (wait it out—"bull-headed" = Taurus). Do: indulge in artistic or musical experiences or increase your collection of artists you love to listen to or to watch. Don't: stick to your guns unless they're worth sticking to. Taurus's lunar energy can slow down projects quickly.

### New Moon in Sagittarius, November 26

Making friends with folks from different cultures could make for an excellent Thanksgiving. Is there someone in your workplace who doesn't have plans? Sagittarius Moons facilitate comradeship among peers, and this New Moon is also nudging those of you

who've been out of school to explore improving your career prospects with extra education. And since Sagittarius rules the upper thighs, put on those sensible shoes and get some walking in. Sagittarius, Leo, Aries, Libra, Scorpio, Capricorn, and Aquarius: keep your sense of humor front and center. Do: enjoy comedy, a good joke, and a shared sense of humor. Jupiter is harmonizing with the Moon, bringing out the merriment. Don't: wear awkward shoes. Sagittarius is about taking missteps and being accident-prone.

### Full Moon in Gemini, December 12

The Twins rule the 3rd house, which governs short messages, short journeys, and quick lessons. This Full Moon is an excellent time for a conversation that has a solid impact. Group meetings, or colloquys can be highly productive since everyone's synapses are flashing away. Gemini, Aquarius, Libra, Taurus, Aries, Cancer, and Leo: this is the best time for networking. Sagittarius, Virgo, Pisces, Capricorn, and Scorpio: you may have difficulty getting the whole story. Ask folks to repeat themselves so you understand. Do: buy books and other reading matter for folks on your gift list. Don't: be impatient with those who fail to follow-through or who haven't shown up for something they committed to.

### *New Moon in Capricorn December 26*

This solar eclipse mirrors the July summer eclipse, so difficulties that arose then could be resolved. And if that was a low point for you, upward is the only direction. Christmas with a Capricorn Moon suggests that one's favorite presents (to give and receive) will be the most practical. For those who drive in snowy climates, a decent ice-scraper is beloved. And since Capricorn rules the joints and skin, a high-quality moisturizer makes a super present). Capricorn, Taurus, Virgo, Aquarius, Pisces, Sagittarius, and Scorpio: go slow and steady—your qualities of resilience and grit will be admired. Libra, Cancer, Aries, Leo, and Gemini: you may enjoy being the contrarian at the Yule table—especially if you can lighten up the "sad sacks" in your circle. Do: be steady in your course of action, and dependable. So many planets are in Capricorn right now, so responsibility is the theme. Don't: be impatient with those who take a *long* time to commit. See above about planets in Saturn!

**About the Author**

*Sally Cragin is the author of* The Astrological Elements *and* Astrology on the Cusp *(both Llewellyn Worldwide). These books have been translated and sold in a number of countries overseas. She does readings (astrological and tarot). Visit "Sally Cragin Astrology" on Facebook or email sallycragin@verizon.net*

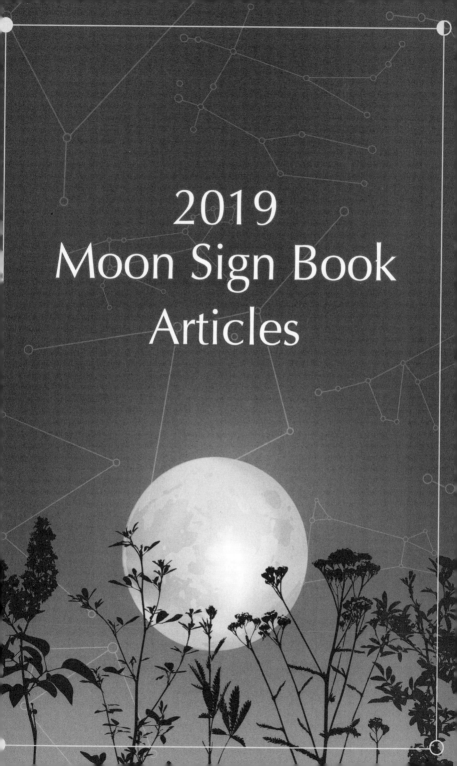

# 2019
# Moon Sign Book
# Articles

# Moon Herbs: Chickweed, Mugwort & Wild Lettuce

*by Calantirniel*

In astronomy, the Moon correlates with the shifting of the planet's ocean tides. In astrology, the Moon has dominion over our emotions, nurturing, and dreams. We can easily connect to lunar energies using plants that for millennia have been designated as possessing connections or qualities of the Moon. We can pay special attention during the New Moon for bringing us what we want; the Full Moon for psychic work and releasing; and on Mondays, the day of the week ruled by the Moon. While you can purchase these at a reliable herb store, it's easy and available to get your own, and it may further inspire you because you are creating a deeper relationship with the herb as well as self-reliance. A quick Google image–search for the Latin name of any of these plants will provide many photographs and drawings; you may wish to then reference the websites to learn more about these herbs. They quite likely grow by you—all three of these herbs are prevalent throughout the temperate regions around the world: North America, Europe, Asia and even Australia/New Zealand. Double-check to make sure you have the right plants by checking with your local botanist, herbalist, or agricultural resource center. Let's begin.

## Chickweed

One of the first weeds to break through frost, chickweed (*Stellaria media*) is an easy-to-identify, plentiful shade-loving ground-cover that has culinary use in salads and is often eaten by birds. Other names are adder's mouth, birdseed, Passerina, satin flower, starweed, starwort, *stellaire* (French), stitchwort, tongue grass, winterweed, and qoqobala. Herbalist Susun Weed calls this plant maidenwort. The flowers look like beautiful white stars (thus the Latin name), and the lightly-fuzzy leaves and stems have a moist, mild taste. While it is first and foremost a nutritive, it is cooling, lubricating, and amazing for nearly all skin problems. If you itch, this is your medicine! For those of you who wish to lose weight, this herb has a remarkable quality: it regulates water levels, lubricates dry conditions while driving off excess dampness and fats. It stimulates the metabolism, building where needed but breaking down what is not needed, then easily and gently eliminating it. This is not a short-term water-loss solution, but a long-term plan to dissolve fat deposits, including cellulite. Now, that is useful if you ask me!

### *History and Magical Lore*

As just noted, if weight loss in your goal, use this in your salads or as a tea or tincture by starting on a waning Moon to build momentum. Scott Cunningham says you can use chickweed to attract or maintain love and to increase fidelity by carrying it with intention. Since this herb has an early-bloom, maiden quality, this could be a good offering for lunar deities like Artemis and Diana, or possibly even Persephone. I will add that any health magic would certainly benefit because it is such an excellent nutrient-rich herb that is gentle in taste—even kids will usually eat it. Chickweed salve is great to have on-hand and can easily be applied externally for magical use as well in this form (think of your third-eye area), or to anoint a white or silver Moon-dedicated candle. As a flower essence, it helps those who have trouble letting go of the past. It addresses unresolved emotional issues that create tension or insecurity that can stop a person from entering the present in a joyful state. This especially applies if this builds a "layer" of weight around the person that may allow them to feel safe but also stuck, not moving forward with life.

### *Herbal Qualities and Medicinal Use*

Chickweed is cooling, moistening, nourishing (high in iron and copper), lubricating, balancing, and is effective against fever. It has saponins, which can have a cortisone-type of pain relief, but safer and over time more effective. It can be specifically used for dissolving fat deposits, clearing the lymph and kidneys while helping assimilate nourishment and building where needed. Helps in cases of hypothyroidism, ulcerated, inflamed throat and mouth, deafness, respiratory issues, excessive appetite, digestive tract inflammation, constipation, hemorrhoids, lactation, rheumatism, arthritis, any external skin application, especially itching, sore eyes (as poultice), blood poisoning, and can even draw out pus or infection in the skin (as salve).

## Mugwort

If you are looking for a Moon herb that will help you with psychic development, divination, and protection, look no further than mugwort (*Artemisia vulgaris, A. douglasiana*). Herbalist Susun Weed calls this herb cronewort, likely due to many women after raising families having more time to explore their inner selves and their spiritual needs, as well as for changing hormonal balancing needs. There are other *Artemisia* genus plants, like wormwood (*A. absinthium*), Sweet Annie (*A. annua*) and even a plant here in Southern California called coastal sage (*A. californica*), of which all could be used for offerings to the Greek Moon maiden Artemis and the Roman Moon maiden Diana. However, I hope to specifically cover these two species: the commerce herb, *A. vulgaris* and the stronger *A. douglasiana*, in this article. Other names: felon herb, muggons, naughty man, old man, old Uncle Henry, sailor's tobacco, and St. John's plant.

## History and Magical Lore

This tea is a fantastic wash for your scrying crystals, mirrors, or other tools used for seeing the other world. You can apply it to your eyelids and third eye as well before doing your divinatory work. Drinking it, or taking the tincture with spring water, can also help open up your psychic centers while keeping them protected from lesser energies. The dried herb can be stuffed into dream pillows for prophetic dreams, and the herb can aid in astral projection. Scott Cunningham says it was thought to keep you from being harmed by poison, wild beasts, or sunstroke, and it seems Chinese and Japanese lore use mugwort to keep evil spirits away. It apparently was thought to cure hysteria, madness, and disease. If it is placed in shoes, you can gain strength for long walks or runs (to use this way, say "*Tollam te artemesia, ne lassus sim in via*"). Indeed, Anne McIntyre shares lore of St. John wearing mugwort as a girdle for remaining strong and eliminating pain. So it's not a stretch to see that it can even be used to increase lust and fertility as well. As a flower essence, it allows better integration of the psyche and dream world with practical application in the real world. It brings deeper understanding and even significance into daily life; it is helpful for those who are bright, intelligent, but spend lots of time in the psychic realms or dream life and have a hard time with mindfulness and focus when awake in present, conscious earthly activities, or who have trouble shifting from night to day. It can provide balance to menstrual cycles too.

### Herbal Qualities and Medicinal Use

CAUTION: Do not use internally if you are pregnant unless you are in the care of a healthcare professional. Mugwort's taste: bitter, fragrant. Herbal properties: cholagogue, vermifuge, emmenagogue, hemostatic, antispasmodic, nervine, diaphoretic, bitter tonic, and mild narcotic. Mugwort is the herb that is processed and formed into sticks of "moxa," which a skilled acupuncturist first lights with flame then holds the lit stick close to the area of the body that needs warming, stimulation, and healing. Matthew Wood goes into over three pages of detail for a description of someone who would benefit from mugwort as herbal medicine, and it needs to be read to be appreciated fully, but the most striking notation that I believe will help many women is: If they have a diagnosis for high-androgenic (testosterone, DHEA) in polycystic ovarian syndrome (PCOS). Most advice on PCOS is on the high-estrogenic type, and there are a remarkable amount of women not being addressed.

## Wild Lettuce (or Prickly Lettuce)

Wild lettuce (*Lactuca virosa*) and other wild species, including prickly lettuce (*L. serriola* aka scariola) and Canada lettuce (*L. Canadensis*), are extremely plentiful "weeds" virtually identical to the cultivated garden lettuce (*L. sativa*) but are instead very salty-bitter and have a long history of safe medicinal use. Amongst other common names are bitter lettuce, horse thistle, compass plant, opium lettuce, and wild opium. The most tell-tale giveaway on how to determine prickly/wild Lettuce from other plants in the aster family—besides the smell/taste of the milky latex—is that on the underside of the leaves on the center vein is a row of

2018 © FotoLesnik image from BigStockPhoto.com

prickly hairs, and depending on the species, sometimes on the outside edges; the rest of the leaves are fairly smooth.

## History and Magical Lore

The Egyptians associated this plant with their god Min, the god of fertility, power, and agriculture, also associated with the Moon. He is often depicted with the *L. serriola* rosette, and offerings of lettuce were offered to him, associated with East. Ancient Greek manuscripts referred to this magical plant as "Titan's Blood," and the Romans, ranging from Augustus to Pliny the Elder also held this medicinal plant in high regard. Strangely, the dried latex was also used to adulterate (cut) opium, which originates from poppy flowers. Wild lettuce is Moon-ruled due to the milky substance, and, as a tea or tincture, is used as an excellent sleep or dream aid, bringing vivid detail and better recall upon waking. It is co-ruled by Saturn due to its chemistry being similar to henbanes (but much gentler). You can use dry leaves crushed as incense for working divination with darker deity energies, i.e., Hecate.

Garden lettuce is a little different: it can be used for love, chastity, protection, and sleep.

### Herbal Qualities and Medicinal Use

Wild lettuce is a very safe herb, described as a sedative nervine, hypnotic, analgesic, gentle laxative, expectorant, cough-suppressant, and diuretic. It is somewhat diaphoretic, and though it contains no opiates or opioid chemical constituents, it can act as a weak narcotic. The milky latex fluid in this plant (sometimes called lettuce opium) is an effective yet mild sleeping aid, and is also an amazing pain reliever. Other uses: soothes chapped or sunburned skin, helps nursing women with lactation, corrects nervousness and hyperactivity, respiratory issues, cough, acne, hysteria, dropsy, digestive issues (including colic), pain/stagnation with menses, infertility, and can even lessen, or enhance, sex drive (try different dosages to see what works). It also isolates, breaks down and moves out toxins from poisonous bites and stings. It even has psychological applications for helping those with negative thinking and lack of motivation that tend toward cold extremities and tension in neck, shoulders and lower back. It can also help those who are overactive (e.g., teenagers with high hormonal levels). Whether overaggressive or suffering a lack of motivation—the presence of frustration is the key.

## Resources

Cunningham, Scott. *Cunningham's Encyclopedia of Magical Herbs.* Woodbury, MN: Llewellyn Worldwide, 2005.

McIntyre, Anne. *Flower Power.* NY: Henry Holt and Company, Inc., 1996.

Tierra, Michael, LAc, OMD. *The Way of Herbs.* NY: Pocket Books, 1998.

Wood, Matthew. *The Earthwise Herbal, A Complete Guide to Old World Medicinal Plants.* Berkeley, CA: North Atlantic Books, 2008.

## About the Author

*Calantirniel (Southern California) is published in over two dozen annuals through Llewellyn Worldwide since 2007. She is also published through the small UK press, John Hunt Publishing/Moon Books with vignettes in Paganism 101, Pagan Planet, and the upcoming Everyday Magic Book. She has practiced many forms of nature-based spirituality for a quarter century and is currently exploring her Irish roots. Professionally as Lisa Allen MH, she is an astrologer, herbalist, tarot card reader, event timing expert, dowser, reiki master, energy healer, ULC reverend, and flower essence creator/practitioner. She is also a cofounder of Tië eldaliéva, meaning the Elven Path, a spiritual practice based upon the Elves' viewpoint in J. R. R Tolkien's Middle Earth stories, particularly The Silmarillion. Find her at IntuitiveTiming.com and ElvenSpirituality.com.*

# Moon: Protector of Life

*by Bruce Scofield*

In astrology the Moon (*Luna* in Latin and *Selene* in Greek) has always been interpreted as a nurturing influence and a symbol of concern, protection, preservation, care, and mothering. A person with the Moon strongly placed in their birth chart has those characteristics and may excel in care-giving work, in cooking, gardening, or other activities that require sensitivity to the needs of others. Obviously, maternal parenting is a classic expression of the Moon, but so is collecting things and preserving the past. But let's shift our focus from humans to the planet. Earth's Moon is very special, and in this article I want to explore how it really does protect and nurture life on our planet.

Not long after Earth was formed (4.55 billion years ago), the Moon became its satellite. There are several hypotheses for its formation. One is that the Moon formed on its own, a result of the accretion (accumulation and fusion) of dust and rock that was spread around the growing sun, and then, when it grew to its present size, it was drawn into orbit around the much larger Earth. This scenario is called the capture hypothesis. Another idea, called the fission hypothesis, proposes that when Earth was formed and was a rapidly spinning molten sphere, Earth budded off the Moon, which then circled it. Yet another explanation is the twin planet condensation hypothesis that has both Earth and Moon forming through accretion at the same time and in the same region of space.

The most widely accepted hypothesis of the Moon's origin is one that posits a collision between a Mars-sized object, which has been named Theia (the mother of the Moon goddess in Greek mythology) with Earth. This impact produced a cloud of debris that orbited Earth and then condensed into the Moon. The best evidence for this hypothesis is the fact that Moon rocks, of which many were collected during the age of lunar exploration, have isotopic ratios—that is, the relative abundance of different forms of the same elements—that are very similar to those of Earth. But regardless of how the Moon came to be, it is an extremely unusual situation for a planet the size of Earth to have a Moon as big as ours. Our Moon is the fifth largest Moon in the solar system, just behind three of Jupiter's moons and Saturn's Titan. It's large size stabilizes the Earth's axis, something that creates far steadier environmental conditions that might be the case without it. This is one way the Moon protects the Earth.

Four billion years ago, the Moon's orbit was not like it was today. The Moon was much closer to Earth and produced immense tides, which must have kept the oceans in a state of constant mixing—like a giant washing machine. Tides would flow well onto land, perhaps for miles, leaving behind tidal pools that would become increasingly saline as they evaporated. Not long afterward, about 3.8 billion years ago, life originated. The scientists who study the origin of life have a few hypotheses about what happened. One is that life formed in these tidal pools where repeated evaporation and refilling mixed the chemicals they contained. In such pools mixtures of naturally occurring amino acids, nucleic acids, and lipids were found, a mixture that origin of life scientists call the "primordial soup." This soup of pre-life was also stirred by the constant and powerful gravitational tides of the Moon. It was as if life's chemical ingredients were being shaken in a test tube. Other origin of life hypotheses focus on volcanic vents in the deep seas where heated minerals from the Earth's interior meet cold water and cause complex chemical reactions. So far, no one theory is proven by any means, but it is interesting to consider that the Moon may have played a major role in the origin of life if the primordial soup theory turns out to be right.

Another effect of the strong tides produced by the Moon has to do with ocean circulation. Moon tides mix the seas and, like a bath tub being filled with both hot and cold water, this evens out temperature differences in the water. If there were no tidal mixing, waters in the higher latitudes would be frigid and those near the equator very hot. But with the strong tides produced by our large Moon, these extremes are broken down and evened out. With more stable ocean temperatures, the temperature of the air is also regulated, and this means that climate conditions are more stable and predicable, and that is something life on our planet needs.

The fact that the first life on Earth took hold and evolved into more complex forms is obvious from our perspective, but it may not have been so easy if our very large Moon didn't exist. It has significant gravity and it could offer some protection from stray asteroids that may be deflected away from Earth by its gravity. But without any doubt, the strong gravitational effects of the Moon work constantly on the equatorial regions of Earth and keep its axis steady. Without such an effect, the poles would tilt wildly, creating cycles of climate extremes that make it far more difficult for life to find the stability and regularity it needs to thrive. It's possible that the lack of this kind of stability on Mars, which has only two tiny Moons, is a reason for the lack of life on that planet.

The tilt of Earth's axis is called its obliquity. This tilt, which is 23.45 degrees today, does vary, but not by much. Over a cycle of roughly 41,000 years, the tilt ranges from 22.1 to 24.5 degrees. This doesn't sound like much, but it does change the amount of solar radiation that reaches the higher latitudes during summer and winter. This is enough of a difference to cause ice build up when there is less sun in summer in northern areas where there is more land mass. When not all the snow melts during summer, what remains builds up, glaciers form and, like an ice pack in a cooler, cold periods are prolonged and may cause ice ages. In fact, there were times in Earth's history when ice ages (glaciations) were occurring in 41,000-year intervals.

Now contrast this with the situation on Mars. It's known that the tilt of Mars's axis oscillates widely over a cycle of about 124,000 years, from as much as 10 to 40 degrees or greater. This means that for part of this cycle the poles are more or less like those of Earth, but at other times they lie closer to the equator and then the equatorial regions freeze. This is a situation of climate extremes where subsurface ice can build up at higher latitudes but then migrate slowly toward the equator and back over the course of the cycle. The shifting of cold from poles to equator and back causes strange melting patterns like the runoff gullies that scientists are now studying. But one thing is clear, climate changes on Mars can be more extreme than those on Earth.

We known that the spin rate of Earth is slowing down and that this causes the length of day to increase over time, though this change is not at a constant rate. We also know that the Moon's tidal forces are the cause of this decrease. At the same time, the

Moon is moving farther away from Earth, at the rate of 1.5 inches per year, and its gravitational effect is slowly decreasing. About 500 million or more years from now the Moon will be far enough from Earth that solar eclipses will no longer occur. It's possible to make calculations based on today's measurements that can answer questions about spin rate and lunar distance in the very distant past, but there is also evidence in the fossil record.

## First Life on Earth

The earliest life on Earth was bacterial life. As far back as three billion years ago, colonies of bacteria built columns of sediment called stromatolites. These structures, which are very rare today, are composed of layers of bacteria with those on the top being photosynthetic and those underneath living off the byproducts of the photosynthesizers. Sediment in the water mixes with the bacterial secretions and builds up in layers that vary according to seasonal and tidal cycles. With microscopes, the depth of these layers can be measured and information about conditions long ago can be discovered. There are several natural processes that produce patterns in sedimentation found in stromatolites. There is the alternation of day and night that affects photosynthesis, and there are the twice daily tides and the twice monthly highest tides that occur at full and new Moons. So as pulses of water flow over the bacterial columns, more sediment will be deposited and glued down when the higher tides bring in nutrient and mineral rich water.

Scientists have studied the layers found in fossil stromatolites and have studied modern ones as well to get a baseline on what the sedimentation rates are like today. Their findings do suggest that Earth was rotating more rapidly and the Moon's orbit was closer and therefore the lunar month was shorter than it is today. Some results from two billion year old fossil stromatolites show that the year way back then may have been about 880 days long. That's 880 spins on Earth's axis as it made one trip around the Sun. Stromatolites that were formed about 850 million years ago have layering patterns that suggest at that time there were about 435 days per year. This is more evidence that the spin rate was slowing down as the Moon's orbit moved further away.

Circadian (daily) cycles of about 24 hours and lunar rhythms that are tidal and monthly are found in most organisms, from bacteria to humans. Being in sync with the alternation of day and night is crucial to survival, especially if you are a photosynthetic organism. Being in sync with the Moon is crucial for organisms that rely on the tides to bring them food particles. But have the lengths of these rhythms, which are found in all kinds of life, always been as they are now? One of the implications of changing year, month, and day lengths over deep time is that life, as it evolved, must have made constant internal adjustments.

As far back as 3 billion years ago, photosynthesizing bacteria developed biological clocks to keep them locked into daytime when they could harness solar energy. So if the day and month back then were different from today, i.e., the day was 15 hours and the month was 20 days long, life must have had to continuously adapt and not be locked into steady signals like 24 hours is today. This suggests that biological rhythms began as passive responses to the environment, which supports the idea that many different ways of setting internal rhythms that matched the environment arouse independently. The study of genes that regulate rhythms in photosynthesizing bacteria seems to confirm that circadian rhythms have indeed been "invented" many times. Some researchers have even found what might be vestiges of ancient and much faster rhythms in cells that they call ultradian and mutant rhythms. Life, it seems, has always followed the Sun and Moon.

The rhythms of life are many, and they match the rhythms of the day and the Moon, something that aids in survival. Marine organisms are particularly sensitive to the Moon. For example, fiddler crabs react strongly to the Moon's tidal effects. Their activity cycle is tidal: twice a lunar day, which is 24.8 hours.

They release their larvae at new or full Moons when the tides are highest. In one experiment, oysters entrained to the tides in the Atlantic were moved to Chicago where they retained that tidal rhythm—but after two weeks it changed to where the tides would be in their new location. This raises questions of what the organisms are responding to—it is just the tides, light levels, or the actual gravitational effect. Most researchers think that life registers external rhythmic signals (light, dark, pressure, motion, etc.) of all kinds and then sets up a routine in the cell machinery that functions like a clock that can be adjusted when needed. So there's an internal clock that can run on its own in case something happens in the environment.

Without our large Moon, there would be very dark nights and no variations of light over the course of the month—there would be no lunar cycles. Without lunar cycles life would probably survive, but it would be different in many ways. Without our Moon sea temperatures would be more extreme and climate more volatile. The Moon's stabalizing effect on Earth's axis keeps extreme climate changes in check and give life time to grow and evolve. With no Moon, the tides on the early Earth would not exist and there would be no mixing of the "primoridal soup." Without our Moon, our protector, life would have had a much harder time gaining a foothold on Earth—and humans might not even be here.

## About the Author

*Bruce Scofield, Ph.D., is an author of numerous books and articles and teaches evolution at the University of Massachusetts and astronomy and astrology for Kepler College. He has an international practice as a consulting astrologer. His interest in Mesoamerican astrology, mythology, and astronomy has a web presence at www .onereed.com.*

# Compost: The Living Magic of Soil

*by Penny Kelly*

Composting is as old as the Earth, for everything that grows here eventually returns to soil, giving back the unused minerals, vitamins, and materials that were taken from the soil to begin with. Although some people think that composting is the thing to do because it makes use of what would otherwise be wasted, the biggest reason for composting is because the soil needs constant renewal if it is going to produce fruits, vegetables, and grains that have the nutrients needed to maintain a healthy body.

You can look around at the population everywhere and see the results of dead soil…obesity, depression, disease, and dysfunction are everywhere and in every family. People are tired, irritable, impatient, and they lack clarity in their decisions, many of which are made in bouts of emotional drama and fearfulness. Much of this stems from poor food that does not contain the high-level nutritional elements needed for calm, joyous, creative existence, yet very few know this because of our disconnection from the soil. Most are tied to cell phones and computers, not Mother Nature. The result is an epidemic of problems from autism and Alzheimer's to diabetes, cancers, and a host of other physical, mental, emotional, and spiritual ailments. A well-made compost restores the soil so that it contains all of the elements needed by plants, animals, and people.

If you have a chance to grow anything, whether that's a one-acre garden or a pot of herbs on your window sill, compost will make it grow better, stronger, and with more disease resistance. So let's say you decide to try a little composting.

The first thing to know is that almost anything can be made into compost—fruit, vegetables, droppings from your birdcage or hamster cage, feathers, wood chips, leaves, weeds, sawdust, old cornstalks or other plants stems and roots, garbage, nut shells, manure from cows, horses, goats, sheep, and other vegetable or animal matter.

The second thing to know is that your ingredients will greatly affect the nature of your compost as well as what you may have to put up with until those ingredients have been completely broken down into soil.

When I was a girl growing up in the 1950s, my parents planted a one-acre garden every year and made us work in it every day. At the end of growing season, we collected the dead plants and threw them into a pit my father dug. Over the winter, we threw our daily kitchen scraps into the pit until it was full. After that, we just scattered the daily scraps around the garden. Since we had a family of eight with frequent borders and extra family members, there was always a lot of this daily stuff, which provided a bit of food for wild animals such as rabbits, raccoons, and deer, who grazed and also pooped in the garden over the winter. I didn't know it back then, but I was learning the basics of composting along with food self-sufficiency.

It was not until I moved to the city and tried to grow a couple tomato plants that I began to seriously look at and then draw on what I had experienced earlier in life in the family garden. Not until then did I try to figure out the hows and whys of soil.

It started when I bought some pots and some soil, put my tomato plants in them, and set them on the deck in the sun. One of the first things I noticed was that as the plants got larger, the soil began to dry out more and more quickly. Then it collapsed into something rather hard and compacted. Next I noticed that no matter how much water I gave them, the tomato plants were always yellowish and 'wilty-looking.' After a while I was fighting molds and mildews constantly. When the breezes blew, the plants would blow over easily, and if the wind was strong, they ended up broken and laid out on the deck. It was a while before I understood that all of these problems were related to the soil issue.

1. The pots were too small and did not hold enough soil to allow the roots to go deep or to expand. Roots below ground are often as expansive as the top-growth and help to stabilize the plants, but this can't happen when the base pots are too small.

2. The purchased soil did not have any minerals in it, nor was it alive, which was why the tomatoes always looked sickly. Minerals form the structure of a plant.

3. When soil overheats, the microorganisms in it die and

the soil collapses. Living soil is full of microorganisms and tiny tunnels that plant roots move through easily. When the microorganisms die, the tunnels collapse and the soil becomes hard-packed.

**4.** When the soil microorganisms die, no further humic acids are produced, which then creates a perfect climate for molds and mildews.

**5.** Using city water full of chemicals further stresses the plants and contributes mightily to molds and mildews.

**6.** I needed good, old-fashioned compost, but certainly couldn't make it the way we used to make it back home. Thus, I began experimenting.

As noted above, you can make compost out of almost anything. However, let me share some things that would have been helpful to me when I started experimenting.

For many kinds of compost, you have to start a year before you intend to use it. There are exceptions, but a year is a general rule of thumb. You'll probably need a shovel, a rake, and a wheelbarrow or some big buckets, but not much is needed in the way of tools because Mother Nature does most of the work.

Compost can be made in a pile, row, box, pit, barrel, or a countertop composter. Your compost pile, row, box, or pit can be any size, but you want to turn it over once or twice in order to get aerobic compost rather than anaerobic, so keep in mind that the bigger the pile the more work you will have to do.

Barrel composters are somewhat expensive, but they are made to turn easily and to produce finished compost in three to six weeks, while countertop units are almost carefree. Keep in mind that, as your ingredients break down, the size of your pile will shrink dramatically, eventually by one-half to two-thirds. So, what looks like a lot of compostable material is going to break down to very little finished compost.

You can make a compost pile, but a row is easier to turn and to manage than a pile. However, a row is more easily raided by critters and scattered about. You can build a box and put your compost ingredients in it and cover it up to keep animals out, but rats can get into anything, and eventually the bottom edges of the box will compost right along with your ingredients. Or you can dig a shallow 8-to 12-inch-deep pit about 4 feet square, put your ingredients in it, and put a plywood cover over it with something heavy like a cement block on it so it doesn't blow away. The pit doesn't have to be moved, is easily turned, you can put unsightly garbage in it and won't have to look at it, and once the ingredients have composted completely, you can plant your seeds and seedlings right in the pit where they will grow to magnificence.

What to do with the soil you dig out of the pit? Consider creating a raised bed for growing things in while you wait for your compost. I have even dug a pit, composted all sorts of things in it, then built a frame around the pit and continued making compost until it was 2 feet deep. When I planted my seeds and seedlings in it, I got 40 lb. cabbages, 5-foot-long cucumbers, tomato plants that were 8–10 feet tall, and 6 bean plants that produced a bushel of green beans!

If you're filling a 1-foot-deep pit with leaves, fill it with 2 feet of leaves, which will break down to be about the general level of the surrounding soil. If you want to put kitchen scraps in it over the winter, only fill it level with the surrounding area. Then, when the ingredients break down, you will have room to put your kitchen scraps. Keep in mind that you have to stop adding materials to the pile or pit about three months before you intend to use the compost, because the newly added scraps will not have broken down sufficiently to use. The composting process generates a considerable amount of heat, so if you have materials still

breaking down, you can fry your garden plants because compost temperatures can get up to 150 degrees!

If you live in the city, you can't really spread your garbage over a backyard garden since it looks bad and the neighbors will complain. If you live in the country but you're from the city and have a sort of inbred disgust for garbage to start with, you may want to start with leaves and twigs raked from your own yard. Leaves are loaded with minerals, and any pile of leaves is going to attract all sorts of worms and bugs that crawl around, leave their droppings, and make some of the richest, most mineralized compost you could ever want! Find a spot in a corner of your yard, designate it as your compost area, pile your leaves there, and water them down so they don't blow away. Then let it set. By late the following spring, you should have some wonderful compost.

If you live in the city and really want to compost your kitchen wastes, you might want to try worm composting in plastic bins, technically called vermicomposting. When I brought home my first worm bin, I was very uncertain whether or not it was a good idea. What if the worms crawled out of the bins and ended up all over my kitchen? They didn't, but I decided to keep the bin in my basement where the temperature did not go much below 60 degrees. Temperatures below 50 degrees and above 85 degrees are not conducive to good worm activity. It was clear after a couple weeks that one worm bin was not enough to handle all of the scraps from my kitchen. The scraps were not processed fast enough and I ended up with a million fruit flies. I went back and got two more. Surprisingly, the bins did not smell bad, although there was some smell when you opened them to put new scraps in. Worms require goodly amounts of moisture to stay healthy and active, and when my husband and I went away on a trip for two weeks, I failed to provide instructions to keep the worm bins moist and the worms died. I felt terrible when I returned and discovered they were all dead as they provided superb compost.

So let's talk about a few specific things regarding composting. If you get a serious amount of woodchips or sawdust, it can take up to five years to compost completely. Use a compost starter, either manure or purchased, to boost the rate of breakdown, and be aware that the finished compost will often be highly acidic. If you are composting all fruit, the finished compost will be highly alkaline.

You might have to invest in a pH meter to find out if your compost needs amending. You can get one on Amazon for anywhere from $12 to $300. The pH of a substance is actually a measure of the millivolts or electrical activity in that substance. If it is too acidic—let's say the pH is between 3.5 and 6.0—the voltage is too low to drive the necessary chemical reactions and you might have to spray lightly with ammonia and water (1:1 ratio). Soil that is too acidic does not promote flowering, and without flowering you won't have any fruit…farmers call everything fruit whether it's a fruit, vegetable, or grain. If your soil is too alkaline—say the pH is between 7.5 and 9.0—the voltage is so high that transactions are happening too fast for the plant to benefit from them. You would then spray it lightly with vinegar and water (1:1 ration). Whether the soil is too acid or too alkaline, test, spray, test, and if needed spray again, repeating until the pH measures between 6.5 and 6.9. A pH of 6.85 is ideal.

If your pile dries out, the composting process will drastically slow down, so if you don't have regular rain in your area, water your compost pile, bin, or pit when you water your yard. Try not to over-water though because the nutrients will run off, making your compost much less effective. In addition, if you drown the pile in water you will kill off or drive away the worms, bugs, mycelia, protozoa, fungi, and microorganisms that live and die in the compost and add to its humic qualities. Humus is not well understood, but it has an enormously powerful effect on plant metabolism and general constitution. It also helps produce more vitamins, amino acids, proteins, and resistance to infection in the fruit, vegetable, or grain. When humans or animals eat products raised in an environment rich in humus, everyone benefits.

Speaking of run-off, if you don't have room to do much composting in your yard, you can greatly expand the effectiveness of whatever compost you do have by making compost tea. Get a five gallon bucket and fill it two-thirds with water. Put one to two cups of compost in the water, stir vigorously for a few minutes, then allow to steep for forty-eight hours. Use the compost tea to water plants in the house or garden and you will see some beautiful growth and development.

In a world where change is continuous and security can sometimes depend on how self-sufficient you are, growing at least some of your own food is wise from so many angles. It keeps you in touch with nature, provides a kind of quality that is spectacular compared to store-bought foods, provides good exercise, and promotes excellent health. When it comes to growing anything, nothing provides a better guarantee of success than composting—an art that is unique to each farm and each individual.

### About the Author

*Penny Kelly is a writer, teacher, author, publisher, consultant, and naturopathic physician. After purchasing Lily Hill Farm in southwest Michigan in 1987, she raised grapes for Welch Foods for a dozen years and established Lily Hill Learning Center, where she teaches courses in Developing Intuition and the Gift of Consciousness, Getting Well Again Naturally, and Organic Gardening. She is the mother of four children, has cowritten or edited twenty-three books with others, and has written seven books of her own. Penny lives, gardens, and writes in Lawton, Michigan.*

# The Moon and Other Planets

*by Amy Herring*

The moon in astrology represents the instinct to fulfill our emotional needs. What we need to feel happy, what makes us feel sad, what comforts us and what makes us feel vulnerable can all be understood by the sign and house placement of the Moon in our own natal chart. Understanding our Moon sign provides a wealth of personal understanding and validation, both for our own selves and those we know and love.

Yet, a thorough understanding of our Moon in a sign and house is not complete without the context of its relationship to the rest of our natal chart and the other planets. This is especially true if one or more planets is directly involved with our Moon through a planetary aspect.

A planetary aspect is a relationship between two (or more) planets due to their specific locations in the sky at the same moment. One easy example is a conjunction—if two planets are in the same line of sight in the sky, they are said to be in conjunction with each other. Obviously they are not colliding with each other! But they appear to be almost on top of each other against the backdrop of the starry heavens.

## Aspects to the Moon

When a planet aspects the Moon in your natal chart, it will have something to say about the way you express your feelings and get your emotional needs fulfilled. An aspecting planet may feed and support your Moon in its efforts or it may seem to interfere or even compete for your attention as you try to understand and express your heart.

Planets in harmonious aspects such as the sextile (planets two signs apart) and the trine (planets four signs apart) are generally supportive of each other and have compatible agendas. Planets in

a challenging aspect such as the square (planets three signs apart) or the opposition (planets six signs apart) are generally awkward with each other and tend to have competing agendas. The conjunction (planets in the same sign) is sometimes thought to be an agent of either camp, depending on the planets involved and their individual placements and how difficult or easy it is to integrate the two planetary agendas in the context of the moon's sign and house as well as the rest of the chart.

Even though some aspects have an easier flow of energy between each other than some, there are no aspects that are all good or all bad; in fact, the most productive way to think of aspects is whether they are easy or difficult to work with and how you can get the best out of their partnership. Planets in aspect represent parts of you working together, and there is always potential for positive and negative outcomes from that union. But whether it's an instinctive harmony or a constant negotiation can determine how easy or difficult it is to bring out the best potential of that relationship.

An aspect between a planet and the Moon can have a pronounced effect. Even two people who have the same Moon sign and house will feel significant differences in their emotional needs and the way they fulfill them if the planet aspecting them is different. For example, one way a Gemini 11th house Moon person may fulfill their instinctual need to learn and communicate might be to engage with a lot of different people, seeking out dynamic discourse and debate to get lots of different viewpoints from the big, wide world. Add a dose of Jupiter to that and it can increase the tendency toward confident, spontaneous, and off-the-cuff expressions of one's opinions and feelings, right or wrong. However, add a dose of Saturn instead and you may get someone who is likely to engage in a more rational, conservative, and careful way, with a tendency to avoid expressing anything that may have them looking the fool if it hasn't been thoroughly researched or proven.

Here is some of what you'll see when a planet aligns with your moon in your natal chart:

## Sun and Moon

The Sun represents our central sense of self, not only as we are, but as we are developing. The sign and house in which the Sun resides in your natal chart can tell you the traits, pursuits, and values that you are likely to deeply identify with. When the Sun and Moon aspect each other, your identity is strongly influenced and informed by your emotional needs and nurturing instincts.

With these two powerhouses aligned, you may have a strong, singularity of focus and perspective, and your compassionate and intuitive instincts are apparent and present in everything you are. If the Sun and Moon are in a challenging aspect, you may constantly feel as though there is a negotiation or internal conflict going on inside of you, almost as if you are two people sometimes! The inner dialogue this generates can be powerful for growth and self-awareness.

## Mercury and the Moon

Mercury represents our mind and voice. How we take in and make sense of information, how we learn, and how we communicate as well as areas of interest and more are Mercury's domain. The way to your heart is through your brain! Whether your mode of choice is stimulating conversation, curling up with a good book, a romp through an internet research rabbit hole, or an impromptu game of truth or dare, your mind and heart are forever joined.

The benefits of a Moon–Mercury union can include the ability to put your feelings into words and intuitively knowing what to say to make a loved one laugh at just the right moment. A challenging Moon–Mercury alignment can make it difficult or frustrating for you to communicate what's in your heart, especially when strong emotions are involved, and impatience may sometimes get the better of you.

## Moon and Venus

Venus represents the desire for connection: to the world around us and most often to another person. It is how we relate to those around us and the things we do to enhance harmony and connection with others, as well as what we need from others to feel friendly toward them. The moon's influence on Venus increases your empathy and instinctual responses in your relationships and you have strong tendencies to protect and take care of everyone in your life.

You are always aware of others' needs and tend to anticipate them even before they've become obvious and may be a little too good at adapting to others in some situations. Depending on the signs in which they are placed in your natal chart, you may avoid conflict because your need for harmony is inherent to your emotional wellbeing; yet, you can excel in handling your own conflicts and mediate others' with grace and understanding because of your ability to navigate the emotional space between people.

## Moon and Mars

Mars symbolizes our will and from it stems our drive, desires, and passion. Aligned with the Moon, your heart, the red planet lends its heat, warming your heart but sometimes making your blood boil! At its best, you have a constant supply of passion that can be converted to motivation and to action to pursue what your heart longs for. One of your primary emotional needs is to be free to act, which could reveal itself in ambition, restlessness, or both.

The war planet is sometimes too good at protecting and coming to the defense of your heart and you may see or create conflict where none is intended if you feel vulnerable or threatened. When emotions run high, you can act impulsively, but you certainly have strong instincts to act when you see something you want!

## Moon and Jupiter

Jupiter's status as the biggest planet reveals itself in your big and generous heart when Jupiter and the Moon align in your natal chart. You thrive emotionally on loving and living large. A sense of optimism and possibility is a large part of the fuel you need for happiness and a sense of freedom of spirit is inherent to your emotional makeup. You tend to spontaneously throw your heart into whatever you love, even risking disappointment or exposing your vulnerable side.

You can feel low just like anyone when life deals you a blow but you instinctually bounce back as soon as you can. It's important for your emotional wellbeing for you to be able to see the bright side of a situation and keep a positive attitude, but you may instinctively avoid acknowledging or dealing with the difficult things in life for too long as a result, especially things that make you feel sad or heavy.

## Moon and Saturn

Saturn's rings rein in the heart when Saturn and the Moon are in aspect. You may prefer to express your feelings more subtly or even downplay them, tending toward emotional expression that is more restrained, dignified, and doesn't expose your vulnerability unnecessarily. You have a primary need for a sense of security which can come from self-reliance and stability. Your emotional resilience makes for a strong heart but can also create a sense of loneliness or isolation if you demand too much of yourself and are too rigid with your heart and don't allow yourself to have and fulfill emotional needs that seem too impractical or risky.

You don't commit yourself easily or quickly but when you do, you take those commitments seriously and are inclined to see them through with patience and continued effort, although they may feel like crushing burdens more than commitments and goals if they are undertaken against your heart's desires. It may be more difficult for you to act in a way that seems impulsive or reckless, even when the situation calls for such rapid response.

## Moon and Uranus

Like Uranus rolls to its own rhythm in space*, you have an independent heart (with a mind of its own!). It is important for you to feel like you are free to express yourself authentically, without catering to archaic or restrictive social norms or fake niceties. Depending on the rest of your chart, you may even get a little wicked glee from provoking others if it forces them to think outside of "autopilot" responses to everyday life.

Your moods tend to be quite mercurial (pun intended!) and you have a restless heart. You need a great deal of emotional freedom; while you enjoy relationships, you can feel boxed in quickly if there are too many "rules" to follow in the unspoken agreement between you and another person.

In challenging aspects between Uranus and the Moon, you may feel inner conflict between a desire for emotional security and a need for change which can disrupt that stability. You may sometimes sabotage otherwise stable situations or relationships if you feel too stagnant.

*Unlike the other planets in our solar system, Uranus is tilted so far on its side that it appears to roll, rather than spin, on its axis.

## Moon and Neptune

With Neptune and the Moon aligned in your natal chart, you've got a heart that's out of this world! You are drawn to things, people, and aspects of life that speak of the fantastical, the creative, the mystical, or even the metaphysical—things that take you out of the sometimes harsh or mundane realities of this world and into the larger view. Inspiration, creativity, and imagination fuel your happiness; negativity, discord, and worry can make you retreat and want to emotionally check out.

You are tender-hearted and react to life with exceptional sensitivity because your heart is always engaged. You are highly empathetic, both in the sense that you are compassionate to the plight of others but also intuitive. This doesn't mean you can read minds but you can sometimes read hearts, and even if you don't know the language, you are drawn in by what others are feeling. However, hearts are changeable and you may sometimes be taken in by what you want to be true or intend to be true, rather than seeing what is realistically happening.

### *Moon and Pluto*

You have the heart of a phoenix—you long to experience the depth and intensity of life and your own heart and this need takes you to your edges, sometimes burning you (and others) up in the process. Your emotional resilience and depth knows no bounds; you may struggle with deep fears or anxiety because there is something in you that always senses the frightening and precarious nature of life but you also have the heart of a survivor. When you summon courage to go through the fire you are stronger on the other side. "The only way out is through" is a good motto for Moon–Pluto people.

You tend to be impatient with insincerity, lies, or posturing—you long for the kind of authenticity that comes from boldness and bareness and sometimes can come across as emotionally harsh because you don't like to sacrifice truth even when it's hard to hear.

You don't reveal yourself easily and tend to keep your heart well-hidden but you delight in knowing the hearts and secrets of others. You pick up on the hidden emotional undercurrents of others and can sometimes sense their needs, fears, and the motivations behind their behaviors. You have an instinctual understanding of human nature which is why some people often feel they can share their most taboo secrets with you—which can make you a trusted confidante or a deadly enemy!

## No Aspects?

Although somewhat uncommon, it is possible to have no aspects to the Moon whatsoever. In cases like this, the Moon may be more free to act on her agenda without hindrance (or help) from the agendas of the other planets. Because planetary aspects are relationships, an unaspected planet doesn't have anyone to answer to immediately. This, like aspects, can produce positive or negative results! A runaway train can do some damage but a planet unrestrained can have an easier time fulfilling its potential.

### About the Author

*Amy Herring is a graduate of Steven Forrest's Evolutionary Astrology program and has been a professional astrologer for over 20 years. She has written two books on astrology:* Astrology of the Moon *and* Essential Astrology. *She especially enjoys teaching and writing about astrology. Visit HeavenlyTruth.com for readings, classes, and educational videos.*

# Talking Sh*t: Natural Fertilizers

*by Mireille Blacke, MA, RD, CD-N*

Let's face it: maintaining a successful and thriving home garden year after year is not easy. I know this from both having a Victorian garden of my own and from writing about common problems in gardening over the last few years. It's not surprising that as home gardeners invest significant time and effort into these landscapes, some feelings of competition may develop among gardeners in their neighborhoods. To be blunt, rational and friendly neighbors often become catty, gossipy saboteurs who talk sh*t about each other to each other, rivaling any episode ever aired of *Real Housewives* (or *Real husbands*) of any city. Yes, I'm including the reunion specials.

When the urge to outdo others hits, some home gardeners feel the temptation to outspend. But maintaining an impressive home landscape doesn't have to be a pricey undertaking. It can also be done naturally, without using synthetic or chemical products, which is better for you, your garden, and the environment. While I don't expect my neighbors to follow my advice, there is no reason you should spend extra money and time on your garden like they might. Keep it simple and save the effort and expense for better results. First things first: It all starts with your soil, and continues with appropriate fertilizer maintenance.

## Soil Conditions

Understanding your soil conditions, such as texture and structure, will allow you to choose flowering plants, trees, shrubs, and vines that are suitable and will thrive on your particular garden site. The relative amounts of three mineral components—sand grains, fine clay particles, and smaller silt particles—determine your soil's texture. Try it for yourself: Grab a moist handful of your own soil and squeeze it. Will the soil "clump" in your open hand? If not, it's sandy soil. As you might expect, sandy soil is light and contains a larger amount of sand grains. Sandy, light soils tend to be dry and infertile because they easily and quickly lose water and nutrients.

Perhaps your soil formed a gummy, moldable lump? This type of soil is heavy and high in clay, with a tendency to become waterlogged when wet, with poor drainage. Does the soil form a loose "clump" that falls apart with a light touch of your finger? If so, you should be pleased, as this loamy soil is a more balanced mixture of the three components that works best in most gardens. In this case, you may expect fertile soil that drains well while holding enough water and nutrients to stimulate plant growth.

While you can only do so much about the texture of your soil, you can certainly work with your soil's structure: the connections between the sand, clay, and silt particles in your soil. In loamy soil, numerous small clumps create ample space for oxygen and water that roots need for healthy growth. Adding organic matter will restructure sandy or clay soils, and improve drainage and fertility. Simply stated, organic matter consists of dead, natural material (such as fallen leaves, dead plants, grass clippings) that soil organisms breakdown and ingest. During this process, organic matter releases a steady supply of nutrients for plant growth and also forms humus, which loosely connects the soil particles and provides the soil with a desirable, crumbly structure.

## Nutrients in Soil

Organic matter imbues soil with richness because it provides significant supplies of three key nutrients vital to plant growth: nitrogen (N), phosphorus (P), and potassium (K). Nitrogen helps to regulate how nutrients are used and promotes healthy green leaf growth in plants. Phosphorus is critical to the formation of healthy roots and flowers, as well as increasing a plant's protection against pests. Potassium also fortifies root growth and general

resistance, but contributes to photosynthesis as well. Aside from "the big three," plants also need calcium and iron in smaller quantities to keep gardens thriving. Ample amounts of these nutrients are usually found in organic matter, which is another reason for its addition to your soil.

Even if your soil contains the right nutrients, your soil's pH must also be at the right level (near neutral: around 6.5 to 7) for roots to receive those nutrients. Very acidic (with a lower pH) or alkaline (with a higher pH) soils form chemical compounds that block nutrients from reaching your plants. A professional soil test or home soil test kit (available at garden centers or online) can tell you whether your soil is acidic or alkaline and whether the supply of different nutrients is adequate. For example, lime will balance acidic soils, and sulfur will treat alkaline soils. The results will also tell you exactly what and how much to add to correct any nutrient deficiencies. Alternatively, adding ample quantities of organic matter (as chopped leaves or similar materials) will help to improve just about any kind of soil without negatively impacting its pH balance.

## Fertilizer

Now it's time to talk sh*t in the literal sense: fertilizer. Just as your soil is your garden's foundation, its continued well-being depends on its fertilizer. My Real Gardeners of Connecticut neighbors can talk at each other for hours about the best types of fertilizers to use, and why their choices are the best. However, if you ask any of them how to tell if fertilizer is even needed, not one can. I know, because I did, and no one could. (I'm annoying like that.) Yes, dear reader, it is possible that you may not need any fertilizer at all. Most trees, shrubs, and vines don't need much, if any. But an indication that your garden's soil is in fact low in nutrients and could benefit from some fertilizer would be any of the following: slow-growing plants, few blooms or flowers per plant, or small and pale leaves.

In this case, adding organic matter to your garden ensures adequate nutrients and optimal soil conditions; creating compost and mulch from your own organic matter makes the most sense to me. This is a sustainable, DIY method to restructure your soil and provide nutrients your garden needs from waste you would discard anyway, allowing you to save time and money in the long run.

## Compost

Think of compost as a soil "conditioner" and fertilizer. Compost blends recycled garden and yard detritus with kitchen scraps (eggshells, cooked or uncooked pasta, nutshells) and household wastes (hair, shredded paper) to a balanced, dark, crumbly organic matter. Compost is made by a hot or cold method.

Making a hot compost pile has been compared to cooking: ingredients are mixed and stirred together, and allowed to cook. Blend one part soft, green plant trimmings (lawn clippings, lettuce scraps, dandelion leaves) with two parts tough, brown scraps (fallen leaves, coffee grinds, woody flower stalks). Vegetable scraps from the kitchen are appropriate. But unless you want to attract a fleet of scavengers to your compost pile, avoid meat scraps, discarded dairy, fats, and bones. While manure from rabbits, chickens, cows, and horses is fine to add, avoid the same from cats, dogs, and humans as it may carry diseased organisms. The moisture provides the decomposer organisms (bacteria and fungi) in the soil with nitrogen to consume as they break down dead plant and animal tissues, creating "heat."

As you add ingredients, chop the material and pile it roughly 3 feet high and wide. Keep the pile moist by adding water as needed, and provide oxygen by turning the pile weekly (via pitchfork or shovel). When the ingredients are unrecognizable, the compost is ready! The entire hot composting process usually provides quality compost in several weeks to several months. Visit www.the-compost-gardener.com/hot-composting.html for detailed information and instructions about hot composting.

In contrast, cold (passive) compost takes substantially longer (up to one year or more) to decompose but is much easier to make. This is an "add as you go" type of composting. As with the hot method, be sure to select a shady location with adequate drainage to grow your compost heap. Build the pile up to the same measurements as your hot compost pile (3 feet square) and basically…wait. Because there is no "heating" in cold composting, seeds and organisms carrying disease will not be killed, so take extra care not to toss diseased plant material or weeds into your cold compost pile. Visit http://homecompostingmadeeasy.com /addasyougopile.html for witty details and additional information on cold composting.

So once you have your compost, what do you do with it? For general use in planting, spread a generous layer (about 3 inches) of compost over the area you've chosen. (You may spread a layer of chopped leaves instead of compost if you prefer.) For best results, this layer should be worked into the top 12 inches of soil.

For perennials, it's ideal to spread 1 inch of compost over the bed in mid- to late spring to provide the nutrients these plants need to thrive. For perennials that benefit from extra nutrients (delphiniums, peonies, phlox), use compost for planting them, working it in as you dig a new bed. Timing matters: place compost in the spring so perennials will maximize nutrients for blooming instead of making new growth right before the frost.

Note: Avoid the roots of well-established trees and shrubs when adding compost (or any fertilizer) under or around them, as it could cause damage.

Prefer a liquid fertilizer? Brew "compost tea" by soaking one cup of finished compost in five gallons of water for seven days (recommendations vary widely); strain out the drenched compost.

You can adjust the amount to your preferences, of course. Use the tea to spray on leaves or water plants weekly or bimonthly.

Extra compost on your hands? To contain loose compost but keep it accessible, use a circular wood and wire bin with a door. Place a large stick in the pile's center to collect water. Remember to situate the bin in a shady spot near your garden, allowing for adequate drainage.

## Mulch

While compost benefits your soil's texture and structure, and has the snowball effect of impacting the overall health of your garden and landscape, organic mulch protects your plants, retains moisture in the soil, controls weeds, and in the long-run will save you time, labor, and maintenance in the yard. I don't know about you, but weeding and watering my garden does not rate highly on my bucket list!

In the most basic sense, mulch acts as a layer of protection for your soil, shielding it from hard rains and frost heaving. A thick layer (2 inches or more) of organic mulch results in less watering duties for you because mulch keeps plant roots cool and moist. However, avoid too much mulch around plant stems, as the moisture-holding mulch around stems could encourage disease. Your weeding decreases as you add more inches of mulch; mulch is very effective with hindering weed growth.

If you know weeds will be a problem or your organic mulch supply is limited, newspaper is your answer. To smother weeds, lay down several pages of newspaper, in sections. Covering the newspaper with mulch holds the paper in place and also hides it from view. As a bonus, the newspaper becomes additional organic matter for the soil as it decomposes over time.

Unsurprisingly, mulch and compost are often used together in gardening. It is important to replace old mulch after adding compost as fertilizer. Hot or cold compost can serve as mulch,

alone or beneath another mulch. For an old, established garden bed, consider compost as a mulch substitute. The most appealing concept to me was the idea of "living mulch," consisting of low-growing annuals and/or perennials, both functional and aesthetically pleasing.

Don't search in vain for an "ideal" mulch. Consider your location and go from there for the best prices, if you're shopping for organic mulch materials (pine needles, herbicide-free grass clippings, bark chips, small wood chips, shredded bark, etc.). As with compost, use fallen, shredded leaves as an excellent foundational material. Being from New England, where fallen leaves and acorns are limitless for a good chunk of the year, making my own mulch is not much different than regular autumn clean-up!

Following the first hard frost, add a generous layer of mulch for protection from frost heaving and drastic temperature changes. Specifically, spread either 1 inch of heavy material (bark chips) or 3 inches of lighter material (pine needles, chopped leaves). An extra layer of pine or fir branches will provide additional coverage in areas where snow is not guaranteed. When spring rolls around, be sure to remove the mulch from plant bases so the soil will warm up.

Most annuals don't need help, but it's smart to add mulch in early summer when the soil has warmed up, and plants have grown to at least 4 inches in height. Most organic mulchers (or at least my neighbors) recommend maintaining the winter layer's depth—they couldn't agree, so let's meet in the middle with a 2-inch layer—taking care to keep the mulch 1 inch or more from the plant stems. (The organic mulchers also increase this amount to please water-craving perennials or attempt weed annihilation.) For perennials, try aged bark chips in your mulch. Replenish the mulch once or twice as needed over the course of the summer, because organic mulch (like compost) continues to break down. Some gardeners decide to turn over mulch into the soil at season's end. Others, to maintain soil fertility, covered beds with 2 inches of mulch annually and maintain that layer throughout the year (snowfall covers the mulch over the garden area).

## Garden Bedlam

Using natural fertilizers helps to restructure your soil and provide nutrients your garden needs from yard waste and kitchen scraps you would discard anyway. The time and effort you invest making and applying compost and mulch to your garden will be rewarded tremendously with heartier soil and healthier plants. Or maybe you have something better to do with all of those raked leaves and used coffee grounds?

As for the Real Gardeners of Connecticut around here, human nature continues to emerge in its truest form. As I write this, Halloween is just around the corner, and the urge to outdo each other with excessive demonic decorations, cornfield mazes, pumpkin wonderlands, and houses of hellish horrors has possessed my neighbors. I am at once disappointed, bemused, and mesmerized from a safe distance, because the coveted gardens they so meticulously tended (and obsessed over) a few weeks earlier have been dug up, torn apart, and worst of all, discarded and forgotten, in current efforts to surpass each other with outlandish Halloween displays.

## About the Author

*Mireille Blacke, MA, RD, CD-N, is a registered dietitian, certified dietitian-nutritionist, and addiction specialist residing in Connecticut. Mireille worked in rock radio for over two decades before shifting her career focus to psychology, nutrition, and addiction counseling. She has been published in* Llewellyn's Moon Sign Book, Today's Dietitian, *and* OKRA Magazine. *Follow Mireille on Twitter @RockGumboRD and read her irreverent blog posts at rockgumbo.blogspot.com and radiowitch.com.*

# Moon Garden Mega Guide

*by Michelle Perrin, Astrology Detective*

While basking under bright sunshine, day gardens burst forth in a vibrant painterly manner worthy of Van Gogh, but the moon creates a much more evocative landscape that is at once peaceful and mysterious, where the senses are heightened as the harsh edges of the world melt into darkness.

Hectic schedules and intense daytime heat can prohibit the full enjoyment of one's garden; a moon garden offers the perfect place to unwind after a busy day, as well as experience nature and the universe in an enchantingly new way. Whether you enjoy the metamorphic experience of watching the landscape as the day transitions into night, or the poetic tranquility of a post-sunset panorama, a moon garden is a magical realm for peaceful, solitary contemplation, long dinners al fresco, romantic nights with your sweetie, or charming get-togethers with friends.

The basis to creating a moon garden is choosing plants that make an impact after dark due to their color, scent, texture, or the sound they make as their leaves rustle in the breeze. A moonlight garden is, above all else, a sensual experience. As nighttime falls, the picture changes from Technicolor to a monochromatic, black-and-white world, where we see everything by means of contrast. It is, therefore, important to choose flowers that are white or silver to reflect the moonlight. When placed against a backdrop of dark green foliage or an evergreen hedge, these light-colored flowers almost seem to float and dance in the blackened air. Meanwhile as our vision becomes less acute, fragrances become more intense, enveloping us in a bewitching, perfumed world.

People born under the sign of Cancer will be particularly drawn to moon gardens, as it is ruled by the moon and associated with white flowers, particularly white roses.

## How to Enjoy a Moon Garden

One way to best experience a moon garden is to sit and watch it as the sun goes down and the day transitions into night. A full symphony of colors emerges as the final golden rays of the sun warm the earth, which will settle down slowly into a calm, silent and mystical darkness.

If you enter your moon garden at night, wait for approximately ten minutes for your eyes to adjust to the dark. As they do, faint white shimmers will emerge from the black, and light colors will take on a new brightness. Flowers will seem to float in the sky, as their dark leaves blend into the night. The leaves of variegated plants will dance like skeletons throughout the garden.

Plants that grow under a Full Moon are thought to contain powerful lunar energy that can help the subconscious mind, heighten intuition, bring protection, or aid in dream therapy.

Harvest plants at the Full Moon and dry them. They can be used in sachets, talismans, charms, baths, and dream pillows. Set out a large jug filled with water and let it sit outside overnight to absorb the rays of the Full Moon. This healing and empowering liquid can be used in teas or on its own, to be sipped while taking in the splendors of your moon garden.

## Moon Gardens throughout history

Moon gardens were especially popular in the Art Nouveau period of the 1920s and 30s, with the love for the white-on-white color palette, as well as during the Victoria Era, when women prized porcelain complexions and tried to stay out of the sun as much as possible. Victorians also enjoyed heavy scents, and most strongly fragrant flowers were white blooms from far-off tropic locations. As these flowers were hard-to-get, expensive, and needed to be kept in hothouses, they became status symbols associated with the aristocracy and cultural refinement.

Out of all moon gardens, three in particular stand out.

### *The Taj Mahal, Agra, India*

The moon garden of the Taj Mahal was founded upon a walled Moonlight Garden originally built circa 1526 by the first Mughal emperor of Hindustan, Babur, as a way to assert political domination through artistic and cultural means. It evoked his homeland of central Asia, where pleasure gardens served as important stopping points on the journeys of the nomadic Mughal people. This started a trend, and local nobles built similar palace gardens all along the banks of the Yamuna River. These gardens offered a cooling refuge of waterways, flowers and foliage, where families and friends could relax in the evening far from the heat and dust outside. When Emperor Shah Jahan built the Taj Mahal in 1631 on the opposite shore, he recognized Babur's gardens as the perfect spot to view his magnificent new structure and incorporated this land into the Taj complex. This moonlit pleasure garden was called the Mehtab Bagh, and featured white plaster walkways, airy pavilions, pools, and fountains amid the fruit and broadleaf trees, narcissus, and fragrant night-blooming white flowers. It was much more sumptuous and less formal than the garden on the Taj side of the river. The Moonlight Garden was built on a flood plain and was eventually covered with silt, but it was excavated by archeologists in the 1990s.

### Indian Hill Farm, West Newbury, Massachusetts

The most famous moon garden in the United States was that of Benjamin Perley Poore, built in 1833. His farm featured two massive tracts of white flowers, including almond trees, candytuft, honeysuckle, jonquils, and spireas. Poore was a standout character in his day; even in the mid-1800s, he was an avid antiques collector and preservationist of colonial American crafts and furnishings. After losing a bet with an associate, he fulfilled it by personally bringing him a wheelbarrow of apples. The journey took two and a half days by foot, and he was greeted by 30,000 people as he entered Boston, securing his reputation as a man of his word. A popular song commemorating the event was published in 1856, The Wheelbarrow Polka. Keeping in step with his unique individuality, Poore was so obsessed with white that his entire farm featured the motif in its vast herds of snow-white cows, as well as white dogs, pigeons, poultry, oxen, peacocks and sheep.

### Sissinghurst Castle, Kent, England

Many consider Vita Sackville-West's moon garden at Sissinghurst Castle as the most famous of its type in the world. While originally conceived as a rose garden in 1931, it soon transformed into a white garden in 1949. She not only used white flowers, but also silver-foliaged plants, such as wormwood, that reflected the moonlight and glistened in its glow. This garden is currently open to the public for daytime visits.

# Designing a Moon Garden

A moon garden does not need to be big; it can be just a small corner of your overall garden, as well as a more elaborate layout, or even a terraced garden if your land is on a slope. The most important thing is to make sure it is in an area with open access to the sky where the moonlight will not be impeded by branches or other structures, as well as far away from streetlights and other artificial sources of illumination. You will also want to have a place to sit in your moon garden so that you can allow your eyes, ears, and nose to slowly adjust to the nighttime ambiance. Try white seating, such as a stone bench, stained deck chairs, or a swing or hammock. This seating could be in the center of the garden, off to the side, at the end of a meandering path, or from a vantage point, such as a deck or bedroom window. Make sure to have tables for eating or placing a drink.

Get creative with your moon garden, perhaps by planting it in a crescent shape or by making it a maze with a surprise waiting for you at its center, such as a candlelit seating area or fountain. You could also form an enclosed outdoor private relaxation chamber formed from hedges, with archway openings covered with vines and flowers. If you do not have a green thumb, a Zen garden filled with raked white pebbles that reflect the moonlight, surrounded by paper lanterns and aromatic incense, can create a midnight oasis of serenity and contemplation. Apartment dwellers can create a moon garden on a balcony or in a window area filled with white flowers and silver foliage in hanging baskets or individual pots in staggered height displays.

Jazz up your moon garden with gazebos, a hot tub, birdbaths, an orb-shaped gazing ball, reflective mirrors, marble or stone statuary, fountains, and large Medici planting vases. You could also have a pond filled with white fish and aim a spotlight to reflect off its surface, mimicking the reflection of the moon.

Adding accents of low, natural lighting will help you enjoy

your garden even on cloudy or moonless nights. Try to avoid harsh artificial light. Tiki torches, battery-powered hanging paper lanterns, white string lights, candle lanterns, oil lamps, and hidden soft spotlights will all add sparkle and flair. Solar powered lamps will illuminate pathways long after sunset.

It is important that pathways are wide and level to avoid tripping or falling in the dimly lit conditions. Use light colored tiles or steppingstones to reflect the moonlight and help guide your way. Likewise, bleached pebbles or marble chips will not only feel soft under the feet but also emit an evocative sound when walked upon.

Sound is an important aspect of a moon garden. Not only will you hear the delightful sounds of insects and nocturnal animals surrounding you, but you could add a gurgling fountain for added audial texture. Wind chimes made from bamboo or aluminum will tinkle delightfully in the breeze.

# Choosing Plants For Your Moon Garden

You can plant your moon garden in containers or directly in the ground, but it is important to clump mass plantings together so that they make a visual impact, as one white flower here or there will not show up in the darkness. Choose plants of differing lengths, with shorter plants in the front gradually moving up to taller species and windswept ornamental grasses, to create a wall of various textures, sounds, movements and shades. The same goes for the size of the bloom, while a large blossomed flower makes a dramatic impact, a spray of tiny buds can look like shimmering bits of glitter within the garden. Choose vertical and climbing plants to adorn a trellis or archway. If you live in a northern climate, you may want to choose plants you can enjoy throughout the year, not just in summer.

When it comes to color, white and silver plants will glow under the moonlight, as does gold. Silver plants also add dimensionality and texture to the overall garden and last longer than flowering plants. Add some pastel shades to offer ghostly chromatic distinctions in unlit conditions, and be sure to include some vibrant reds, pinks, and oranges that will make a dramatic impact at sunset. Blossoms that contain white with another color will also reflect light in a stunning way, as does two-toned variegated foliage. Make sure to include plants with dark green leaves, so that the flowers seem to float above them as specters. You will soon discover there are many shades of white to paint with, from snowflake white to eggshell, ivory, pearl, and cream.

Throughout history, the moon has been linked to the subconscious mind and dreams, and herbs were used as a means to connect with these inner forces. For this reason, no moon garden is really complete without some of these magical herbal plants.

For inspiration, many public gardens are open for visits at night.

# A List Of Plants for Your Moon Garden

It is important that your moon garden is a sensual experience that plays to all five senses.

For sound, plant ornamental grasses and bamboo that swish in the nighttime breeze. For taste and touch, herbs that release their gentle aromas when crushed by hand often also have silvery foliage that shimmers in the moon glow. Berries with white flowers, such as alpine strawberries and white vegetables are also scrumptious additions to a moon garden; just make sure they are planted far from any toxic species. Be sure to add plants in a variety of textures so you can reach out and enjoy their tactile surfaces. Finally, for sight and smell, many flowers bloom after sunset, releasing their fragrance in order to attract nighttime pollinators. Night fragrant flowers are a particular treat on moonless nights.

Many night-blooming plants can be poisonous, so pay careful attention to what you plant.

## Night Bloomers/Night Fragrant

Evening primroses (*Oenothera*): Soft white, pink and yellow sweetly scented perennials that spread quickly. Its roots are edible and seeds can be used for bird feed. Place their buds in a shallow bowl of water with floating candles; over time, the scent will perfume the room.

Moonflower (*Ipomoea alba*): This nighttime relative of the morning glory has large white flowers known for its intoxicating scent. It grows best with the support of a trellis, arbor or fence.

Angel's trumpet (*Brugmansia*) and its cousin devil's trumpet (*Datura innoxia*): Fragrant, very large, white, trumpet-shaped flowers that appear from midsummer until the first frost. It can be moved indoors in the winter if planted in a container. Toxic.

Night pPhlox (*Zaluzianskya capensis*): Its pinwheel-shaped blooms have a honey-almond-vanilla fragrance reminiscent of baked goods, garnering its name "night candy."

Evening stock (*Matthiola incana*): Its small mauve flowers cast off an intoxicating fragrance at night, described as a blend of vanilla, rose, and cloves.

Four o'clock (*Mirabilis jalapa*): Native to Peru, these trumpet-shaped flowers bloom in the late afternoon to release their jasmine-like scent. They come in red, magenta, pink, white, violet, and yellow, with different colored flowers sometimes appearing on the same plant.

Nottingham catchfly (*Silene nutans*): Its scent is similar to hyacinths, and features flowers that open three successive nights before fading.

Night blooming cereus (*Selenicereus*): This cactus has large, fragrant, night-blooming white flowers. It does not survive in temperatures below 55 degrees F, but can be planted in a container and brought indoors.

Queen of the night (*Epiphyllum oxypetalum*): This cactus' white flowers resemble a water lily.

Night blooming jasmine (*Cestrum nocturnum*): Its tiny star-

2018 © StellaL Image from BigStockPhoto.com

shaped blossoms have a powerfully sweet scent. Toxic.

Lilac (*Syringia vulgaris*): Its reflective white flowers emit a decadent scent that is stronger at night.

Flowering tobacco (*Nicotiana*): The stalks of this plant can grow as high as 5 feet tall, and their long, bell-shaped blooms, which open in the late afternoon, have an intense jasmine scent that is strongest at night. Beware that some modern cultivators do not have a scent, so ask when you buy. Toxic.

Night gladiolus (*Gladiolus tristis*): Almond-scented, butter-cream yellow blooms on a twisted stalk.

Fragrant columbine (*Aquilegia fragrans*): These dairy white flowers have an aroma reminiscent of honeysuckle.

Cottage pink (*Dianthus plumarius*): Clove-scented pale pink flowers.

Fairy lily (*Chlidanths fragrans*): Stalks of yellow, fragrant flowers that grow in midsummer.

Mock orange (*Philadelphus coronaries*): This fast-growing shrub can grow as high as 10 feet tall. In early summer, its white, orange-scented blossoms perfume the air.

Daylilies (*Hemerocallis*): This flower has a cleaner, lighter scent than many night bloomers.

Other night bloomers/night fragrant: sand verbena; plantain lily; evening campion; yucca; night-flowering catchfly; thornapple; scarlet gaura; lemon lily; evening iris; evening star: gumbo lily; soapwort; vesper iris; tropical waterlilies; desert lily; white guara; climbing hydrangea; honeysuckle; petunias; sweet autumn clema.

### White Flowers

Mandevilla: This vine grows to 5 feet tall on a trellis and has large, white, funnel-shaped flowers.

*New Guinea impatiens*: Available in a rainbow of shades, including white, this flower grows even in shady areas. Its dark, shiny leaves meld into the darkness, making the blossoms seem like they are floating.

Baby's breath (*Gysophila*): Puffs of these tiny white flowers will add romantic softness to the garden.

Chamomile (*Asteraceae*): This daisy look-alike can be used to make a calming tea, which you can enjoy as you contemplate your moon garden.

White horehound (*Marrubium vulgare*): This plant has the perfect combo of silvery green foliage and white flowers.

Iceberg Rose (*Rosa spp.*): This stunning white blossom is one of the most easy-to-grow roses.

Summer snapdragon (*Angelonia angustifolia*): The Serena white variety of this flower has apple-scented foliage.

Matilija poppy (*Romneya coulteri*): These large flowers feature white petals around an egg-yolk yellow center, meriting it the nickname, the fried-egg poppy.

Climbing hydrangea (*Hydrangea petiolaris*): This plant climbs along trees, walls and rocks, and has white blooms in late spring and early summer.

Alba plena camellia (*Camellia japonica alba piena*): This plant is often called the rose of winter as its snowy petals bloom from fall to early spring.

White Trillium (*Trillium grandiflorum*): This three-petaled romantic flower is easy to grow in the shade.

Yarrow (*Achillea millefolium*) and moonshine yarrow (*Achillea taygetea*): The Latin names for these plants were named after Achilles, who is said to have used them to heal soldiers in the Trojan War. Their white and yellow buds can grow to three feet tall and are extremely reflective, looking magical under the moonlight. As a plus, they are resistant to deer.

## Gold and Colored

Moonbeam coreopsis (*Coreopsis verticillata*): Butter-colored blooms.

Gillyflower: The Elizabethans used the sweet scent of these colored blooms to ward off bouts of melancholy.

Other gold plants: golden tulips; waldsteinia ternata; stella de oro daylily; black-eyed susans.

Other colored plants: passionflower; lilac; lavender; pinks (*Dianthus*); plumeria; sweet William.

### The Bright Foliage Plants: Variegated

*Carex* 'ice dance': Thin, grass-like leaves with white margins.

Hosta (*Hosta* 'Fortunei albomarginata): White margins around large silvery leaves glow in the moonlight.

Brunnera: The varieties of Jack Frost and Looking Glass have silvery-white leaves that work well in a moon garden. Jack Frost's silver leaves are heart-shaped with light green veins.

Caladium: Also known as elephant's ear, this plant has large, heart-shaped leaves. Excellent varieties for a moon garden include: white christmas; white queen; candidum; and moonlight.

Fountain Grass (*Pennisetum setaceum*): Growing up to 2 feet tall, these thin blades of grass have white margins.

Other variegated plants: *Plectranthus forsteri,* variegated dogwood bushes, variegated euonymus, gold mops, cannas, lamium; *Cornus sericea* silver and gold.

### The Bright Foliage Plants: Silver

Lavender cotton (*Santolina chamaecyparissus*): This aromatic plant, also known as Santolina, is not a member of the lavender family, but, in truth, is a daisy that boasts fluffy yellow buds in the summer. It was a popular choice in the formal knot gardens of sixteenth century England. When dried, you can use it in anti-moth sachets.

Lamb's Ear (*Stachys byzantine*): The soft, velvety leaves of this plant make a wonderfully tactile addition to a moon garden. This wooly plant with antibacterial properties was even used for centuries as bandages on battlefields.

Japanese painted fern (*Athyrium Niponicum pictum*): The elongated willowy leaves of this fern add sophistication and softness.

Mullein: This gentle giant features large, wooly leaves and a hearty stalk of yellow flowers that reach up vertically to the sky; it can grow up to six feet tall.

## Herbs

Tarragon: This member of the Artemisia family is delicious in salads or when used in cooking fish and poultry. It can also be used to infuse vinegar.

Sage: Their fuzzy tactile leaves emit a heavenly aroma when crushed with the fingers. The standard version of sage can be used fresh or dried in cooking. The name salvia comes from the Latin, salvere, which means to heal or save, referring to its medicinal properties. Taken as a tea, sage can be used as a balm for sore throats. *Salvia arborescens* is a night-blooming variety, with fragrant white blossoms.

Lavender: The gray-green leaves of this plant are highly effective at reflecting moonlight. When crushed in the hand, they emit a powerfully romantic scent. Add to bath water for a relaxing experience. The dried flowers can be used to create scented anti-moth sachets. Anouk silver, with its almost white foliage, is a good choice for a moon garden.

Curry plant (*Helichrysum Italicum*): While this silver-leaved plant is widely used in Indian cooking and smells like curry, especially after a rainfall, it doesn't taste like curry and is not used in curry powder.

Other herbs and plants/trees with magical qualities: anise seed, camphor tree, fennel, white sandalwood, eucalyptus, moonwort, sleepwort, sweet cicely.

## *Bioluminescent Mushrooms*

Across the globe, there are more than seventy varieties of bioluminescent mushrooms. You can buy spores, such as those for foxfire or faerie fire, and place them on a log to watch them glow in the dark for dramatic, mesmerizing effect. Foxfire and faerie fires are not only the brightest bioluminescent mushrooms, but they also release air-purifying enzymes.

## *White Vegetables and White Flowering Fruits*

NOTE: *To avoid accidental ingestion, do not place these plants near toxic varieties.*

Eggplant: white alba, white egg, or white lightning.

Pumpkin: white baby boo or lumina.

Other white vegetables and fruits: white okra, white bell pepper, white chili pepper, white tomatoes, alpine strawberries with white flowers.

### About the Author

*For more than ten years, Michelle Perrin, aka Astrology Detective, has built a reputation as one of the world's most trusted and sought-after astrologers. Her work has appeared in some of the most influential titles online and in print, making her one of the few astrologers who has garnered respect from both a mass audience as well as the astrological community. Her horoscopes have appeared on the website for Canada's W Dish Network, Tarot.com, and Dell Horoscope Magazine, among others. Her writings have also been featured in The Mountain Astrologer, the leading trade journal for the astrological community.*

# Weekly Tips Provided by:

Penny Kelly is a writer, teacher, author, publisher, consultant, and naturopathic physician. After purchasing Lily Hill Farm in southwest Michigan in 1987, she raised grapes for Welch Foods for a dozen years and established Lily Hill Learning Center, where she teaches courses in Developing Intuition and the Gift of Consciousness, Getting Well Again Naturally, and Organic Gardening. She is the mother of four children, has cowritten or edited twenty-three books with others, and has written seven books of her own. Penny lives, gardens, and writes in Lawton, Michigan.

Charlie Rainbow Wolf is happiest when she is creating something, especially if it can be made from items that others have cast aside. Pottery, writing, knitting, astrology, and tarot are her deepest interests, but she happily confesses that she's easily distracted, because life offers so many wonderful things to explore. She is an advocate of organic gardening and cooking, and she lives in the Midwest with her husband and special-needs Great Danes. Follow her at www.charlierainbow.com.

Mireille Blacke, MA, RD, CD-N, is a registered dietitian, certified dietitian-nutritionist, and addiction specialist residing in Connecticut. Mireille worked in rock radio for over two decades before shifting her career focus to psychology, nutrition, and addiction counseling. She has been published in Llewellyn's Moon Sign Book, Today's Dietitian, and OKRA Magazine. Follow Mireille on Twitter @RockGumboRD and read her irreverent blog posts at rockgumbo.blogspot.com and radiowitch.com.

## GET MORE AT LLEWELLYN.COM

Visit us online to browse hundreds of our books and decks, plus sign up to receive our e-newsletters and exclusive online offers.

- • Free tarot readings • Spell-a-Day • Moon phases
- • Recipes, spells, and tips • Blogs • Encyclopedia
- • Author interviews, articles, and upcoming events

## GET SOCIAL WITH LLEWELLYN

Find us on **f**   🐦 @LlewellynBooks

www.Facebook.com/LlewellynBooks

## GET BOOKS AT LLEWELLYN

### LLEWELLYN ORDERING INFORMATION

**Order online:** Visit our website at www.llewellyn.com to select your books and place an order on our secure server.

**Order by phone:**
- • Call toll free within the US at 1-877-NEW-WRLD (1-877-639-9753)
- • We accept VISA, MasterCard, American Express, and Discover.
- • Canadian customers must use credit cards.

**Order by mail:**
Send the full price of your order (MN residents add 6.875% sales tax) in US funds plus postage and handling to: Llewellyn Worldwide, 2143 Wooddale Drive, Woodbury, MN 55125-2989

**POSTAGE AND HANDLING**
STANDARD (US):
(Please allow 12 business days)
$30.00 and under, add $6.00.
$30.01 and over, FREE SHIPPING.

INTERNATIONAL ORDERS,
INCLUDING CANADA:
$16.00 for one book, plus $3.00 for each additional book.

Visit us online for more shipping options. Prices subject to change.

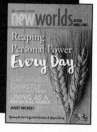

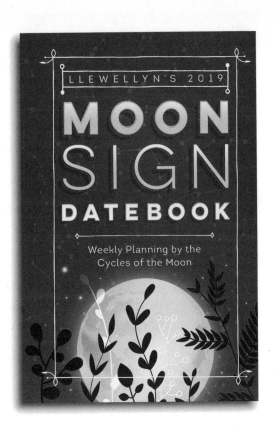

# Llewellyn's 2019 Moon Sign Datebook

*Weekly Planning by the Cycles of the Moon*

Now in its second year, *Llewellyn's 2019 Moon Sign Datebook* is a perfect companion to the bestselling *Moon Sign Book*. This weekly planner features Full Moon lore, tips for gardening by the Moon, Mercury retrogrades, void-of-course dates, equinoxes, and solstices—everything you need to plan a successful future.

The *Datebook* has been designed to be used in conjunction with *Llewellyn's Moon Sign Book*, so combining the strengths of these books increases the practical effectiveness of each. With this planner, you will be able to determine the best day for an appointment or special event, and you will be able to make a note of it in the book. Plan your important gardening, career, and personal milestones far in advance or even within days or weeks for optimal outcomes using the power of the Moon.

**978-0-7387-5259-4, 192 pp., 5¼ x 8**     **$12.99**

# Notes